EVERYTHING

YOU NEED TO KNOW

ABOUT MONEY

AND INVESTING

A Financial Expert Answers the 1,001 Most Frequently Asked Questions

SARAH YOUNG FISHER, C.F.P. AND CAROL A. TURKINGTON

PRENTICE HALL PRESS

Library of Congress Cataloging-in-Publication Data

Fisher, Sarah Young.
    Everything you need to know about money and investing / Sarah Young
  Fisher, Carol Turkington.
      p.. cm.
    Includes index.
    ISBN 0-7352-0041-6 (pbk.)
    1. Finance, Personal. 2. Investments. 3. Estate planning.
  I. Turkington, Carol. II. title.
HG179.F5343   1998
332.024—dc21   98-26309
                                                   CIP

© 1999 by Prentice Hall

Printed in the United States of America

10 9 8 7 6 5 4 3 2 1

ISBN 0-7352-0041-6

ATTENTION: CORPORATIONS AND SCHOOLS

Prentice Hall books are available at quantity discounts with bulk purchase for educational, business, or sales promotional use. For information, please write to: Prentice Hall Special Sales, 240 Frisch Court, Paramus, NJ 07652. Please supply: title of book, ISBN, quantity, how the book will be used, date needed.

 PRENTICE HALL PRESS
Paramus, NJ 07652

A Simon & Schuster Company

On the World Wide Web at http://www.phdirect.com

Prentice Hall International (UK) Limited, *London*
Prentice Hall of Australia Pty. Limited, *Sydney*
Prentice Hall Canada, Inc., *Toronto*
Prentice Hall Hispanoamericana, S.A., *Mexico*
Prentice Hall of India Private Limited, *New Delhi*
Prentice Hall of Japan, Inc., *Tokyo*
Simon & Schuster Asia Pte. Ltd., *Singapore*
Editora Prentice Hall do Brasil, Ltda., *Rio de Janeiro*

DEDICATION

I dedicate this book to my mother, Lois. She has spent her life as an example of one who is ethical, hardworking, and dedicated to learning, yet successful in her career. I pray I can pass these qualities to my children.

S.Y.F.

FOREWORD

My career in the financial world began twenty years ago when I started a job as a paralegal in a law firm. Next came sixteen years as a banking trust officer and then nine months as a broker with an insurance license—what an interesting time! This, along with being an enrolled agent, has prepared me well to be a registered investment adviser and financial adviser, the owner of Fisher Advisers in Lancaster, Pennsylvania. Over the years, I've found that it's imperative to keep learning because the financial world keeps changing. Twenty years ago there was very little material about managing your money available for the general public.

Products change daily—as quickly as people's imagination conceives of new ideas. It's a challenge to understand all that financial planning entails and to stay abreast of the changes.

As a consumer, it's imperative to understand what you're buying, whether that's car insurance or a limited partnership, whether you're planning your future or how to pay for your children's education.

A lack of knowledge can end up costing you in errors, duplication, and unnecessary coverage. As an adviser, it's frustrating to review financial plans with people who have lost considerable money investing in products they did not understand. All too often, they were never told about the risks and problems in these investments, and they were often too afraid to ask.

People who question the cost of their children's clothing never consider asking about the cost of a $100,000 annuity, never think to ask the internal rate of return or the fee paid to the seller. If it sounds too good to be true, it probably is.

Everything You Need to Know about Money and Investing is an overview of the most common questions asked of financial advisers every day. Many of us think about how to reach our goals in very different ways, yet our goal of security is so similar. I hope you enjoy this book, that you learn a great deal, and use the general information provided as stepping stones to a future of understanding and financial security.

Sarah Young Fisher

ACKNOWLEDGMENTS

Because *Everything You Need to Know about Money and Investing* covers so much material in so many areas, there are a great many people to thank. The professionals who reviewed the manuscript and gave suggestions and guidance were many of my dear friends from Fulton Bank, particularly David Hostetter, executive vice president; Jim Wagner; Patricia Eichmann; Jeff Keeports; Lisa Neil; Vince Lattansio; and John Garry. I'm especially appreciative of Robert D. Welsh, CPA (and, of course, Kelly) and Karen Ambacher, who were so willing to give of their time and energy to review the manuscript. James P. Wohlsen demonstrated his expertise in so many ways, as did the wonderful James D. Wolman, Esq.; Lois A. Young, CLU, ChFC; Carl Reigle; and Thomas R. Hoober.

A special thank you to Donald Gross, Jr., CFA, my dear, dear friend. He always listens and guides with patience and kindness.

Thank you to Arthur K. Mann, Sr.; David Ashworth, Esq.; Frank Dogger, Nancy Hughes, Esq.; the staff at Land Transfer; Sara Thibault; Jeff Barnes;and the guidance department of Hempfield High School for their help and support. Everyone was most supportive and informative. I was impressed with everyone's kindness and generosity.

A special thank you to Carol Turkington. I appreciate our friendship and look forward to years and years of working together. You're a talented lady. I'm in awe of your many gifts.

And finally my family (Chuck, Rob, and Catie) who prepared their own meals, waited patiently while I was researching on the phone, and planned Christmas vacation around the completion of this book—thank you for your patience and love. It warms my heart. You are very, very special people.

Sarah Young Fisher

INTRODUCTION

As the baby boom generation approaches retirement, more and more people are becoming interested in investments and money. People who haven't saved much of anything in 45 years are suddenly realizing that unless they start investing soon, they may not be able to maintain their comfortable lifestyle in the future. The good news is that while sooner is better than later, it's never too late to start saving and learning more about managing your money.

Our goal is to answer your most common questions about money management, investments, college, retirement and estate planning. We've added lots of charts, forms, and planning tools to help you organize your financial life, and we've also included lots of news you can use, together with phone numbers, addresses and Internet websites so you can get information tailored to your needs.

Who is this book for? Everyone. Men, women, young or old, rich or just-getting-by, all of us need to understand where we stand financially, and how we can do better with the money we have. But you may be surprised to find out that many people don't know enough about even the most basic financial areas—especially women. For example, in a recent Bank of America survey of 1600 women, 91% said they had little investment experience. More than half of these women had college degrees, and

26 percent had graduate degrees—yet when it came to money, they just didn't have any experience.

These days, being a woman should not be an excuse to abdicate your financial responsibility. Sound money management is the same whether you are a man or a woman: Start early, save often, use 401(k)s, make certain you have wills. Yet so many people who seem so confidant in other areas of their lives feel uncomfortable when it comes to money.

You'd be surprised how many people come to me with many of the same questions:

- How do I find a realtor?
- Should I invest in a Roth IRA or a regular IRA?
- How do I figure out how much mortgage I can afford?

Answering one question leads to another, and then to another. Unfortunately, many people are afraid to ask questions for fear they will look foolish. As far as I'm concerned, there is no "stupid" question. If you need information or want to have a particular question answered, it's imperative to ask it.

If you're just starting out, this book will give you a financial overview so that you can develop your own savings and investment plan to meet your short-term and long-term goals. Many investment products are difficult to interpret, but it's important to understand the fees you're paying and the product you're buying, whether it's insurance, an annuity, or a mutual fund. It's important for you to feel comfortable with your savings, and how these funds are invested. If you're in over your head, you need to understand how to get back out of debt. With the increasing popularity of 401(k)s, more and more employees are faced with the responsibility of choosing investment options for the funds within their retirement plans. You should know what options are available and what each option means. You should know the risks when you invest, although all too often you don't know the right questions to ask your adviser or broker.

We designed this book to help you, whether you're just starting out or you're a sophisticated money manager. For those new to the financial world, this book should answer all your questions about money management. If you're using a financial planner to help plot your financial course, you'll find helpful tips to evaluate your adviser's recommendations or suggest what questions to ask. If you're a professional adviser, you'll find helpful information that can help affirm your advice to clients, or provide more details in an area outside your realm of expertise.

My clients often ask me for a book that will provide information on many different topics written in a clear, simple way. That's exactly what this book is designed to do. In my opinion, many money management books can be intimidating and dry; we've tried to make this book readable and accessible so that everybody can find simple answers to their money questions. It's organized in a clear question-and-answer format so that you can either read only a few sections at a time if you wish, or chapter by chapter as necessary.

Remember: Knowledge is power—the power to take control of your future security.

Sarah Young Fisher

CONTENTS

PART I

MANANGING YOUR MONEY

CHAPTER 1

MONEY MANAGEMENT BASICS

Managing your money sensibly starts with understanding some fundamental principles. Proper budgeting requires you to have a firm grasp on how much money you are making and how much you are spending. Then you can start to systematically save a little bit extra from each month's money. By learning about the key aspects of banking, you can get better service from your bank at the lowest possible cost to you. If you want to invest your hard-earned money to earn more money, you need to know about basic investment concepts. There are various ways you can gain control of how much you are spending. Should you buy or lease? The right answer depends on many factors and it can be different in different circumstances. Are you getting the most for your money? Sensible money management is not penny-pinching. It's the first step toward financial independence. This opening chapter covers all these topics and more.

BUDGETING AND SAVINGS

1. How do I prepare a budget?

List all your household income. These figures are compiled from pay stubs, brokerage statements, child support, alimony, social security benefits, and so on.

Then list all your expenses. Use your checking account register for the past year, categorizing payments into various areas, such as taxes, mortgage, and entertainment.

2. Where is the easiest way to control expenses?

Pay off your credit card debt and watch the fees you are paying (i.e., ATM fees, checking account fees, and brokerage account fees). Then begin the process of cutting the discretionary expenses in your budget.

3. Our family makes $40,000 and we haven't been able to save anything. What can we do?

It *is* possible to save by simply making up your mind to live on less. It can be done, I guarantee it. There are people living comfortably on $35,000, $30,000, and less. If they can do it, so can you. The key is not to think you have to save a large amount of money or it isn't "worth" it. Even saving $5 or $10 a week is better than nothing.

4. Isn't saving a waste if I can only invest small amounts?

Remember that you'll triple your money if you only invest $50 a month at 8 percent interest for twenty-five years. The sooner you start, the more you

Compounding Interest

		You would have this much at these ages:			
		35	45	55	65
If you save $10 a week at these ages at a 12% rate of return:	25	$10,057	$43,041	$153,957	$520,506
	35		$10,057	$43,041	$153,957
	45			$10,057	$43,041
	55				$10,057
	60				$3,565

make. Most of us have an "all or nothing" attitude—we think if we don't have $500 to invest each month, we won't bother to invest anything. Remember investing *any* amount of money is better than nothing.

5. I'm having trouble saving money. What are some ways to get started?

First of all, it's just not true that you need a lot of money in order to invest. This is one of the biggest myths that people believe. You can start small—the point is, you have to start. When you realize how important it is, you can usually find the money to invest. There are several ways you can start investing *now*. Even a small amount put aside every month can grow.

- Pay off the balance of your credit cards. Once that's done, try putting the amount equal to the interest you were paying into an investment each month.
- The next time you get a gift, bonus, or some other unexpected windfall, invest it instead of spending it.
- If you have a retirement investment plan at your job, start putting money into it as soon as you can.

How Savings Can Grow

	Amount Saved per Month					
Years	$5 4%	$5 8%	$10 4%	$10 8%	$20 4%	$30 4%
1	$ 61	$ 63	$ 123	$ 125	$ 245	$ 429
2	125	131	250	261	501	876
3	192	204	383	408	766	1,341
4	261	284	521	567	1,043	1,825
5	333	370	665	740	1,330	2,328
6	407	463	815	926	1,630	2,852
7	485	564	971	1,129	1,942	3,398
8	566	674	1,133	1,348	2,266	3,965
9	651	792	1,302	1,585	2,603	4,556
10	739	921	1,477	1,842	2,955	5,171
15	1,235	1,742	2,469	3,483	4,938	8,642
20	1,840	2,965	3,680	5,929	7,360	12,880
25	2,579	4,787	5,158	9,574	10,317	18,055
30	3,482	7,501	6,964	15,003	13,927	24,373

- Got your heart set on an expensive new suit? Don't buy it if you planned on putting it on your credit cards. Instead put that amount of money into your investment account.

6. Investing is fine for people with dispensable income, but my husband and I both work and we have three kids. By the time we pay our bills, there's just nothing left. Isn't it true that investing just doesn't make sense for someone in our position?

The tighter your budget, the more imperative it is for you to have the extra income that an investment will produce. Nobody said it was easy. Rather than cutting out one budget category, such as "entertainment," or "other," why not try trimming from several categories? This way you avoid the psychological burdens of feeling deprived.

7. It seems like money just slips through my fingers. How will I ever end up with enough to invest?

The key is first to figure out where the money is going. You need to be as specific as possible.

8. I just don't have any extra money! What can I do?

I think you'd be surprised how quickly your money could accumulate. Let's say you spend $1.80 a day on incidentals (a bagel or coffee at work, for example). If you took that $1.80 a day, five days a week, for ten years, and invested it in your 401(k) at a 12 percent return, you would have $8,300. If you just put that money in a piggy bank, you'd still have $4,300 after ten years.

9. Do you have any good tips for saving money? We just can't get started.

Each day take a $1 bill out of your wallet and put in into a bank deposit envelope. At the end of a month, deposit the money into your savings account. Cut down on ATM withdrawals; visit the cash machine for spending money just once a week, and make that money last for seven days. Throw all of your coins in a jar, and then once a month count the change and deposit it in your account. Put all your loose change in a piggy bank. You may feel too guilty to raid the bank once it's in there.

Where Your Money Goes

Item	Estimated	Amount/Month
Housing		
Mortgage/rent		$
Utilities		
Phone		
Cable		
Furniture		
Appliances		
Maintenance		
Total:		
Transportation		
Gas		
Maintenance		
Tolls		
License/taxes		
Public transportation		
Insurance		
Total:		
Taxes		
Federal		
State		
Local		
Social Security		
Luxury		
Total:		

Item	Estimated	Amount/Month
Debt		
Credit card		
Car loans		
Student loans		
Personal loans		
Line of credit		
Total:		
Entertainment		
Movies, concerts, and theater		
Vacation		
Hobbies		
Pets		
Magazines and books		
Videos and music tapes		
Restaurants		
Total:		
Personal		
Food		
Gifts		
Clothes		
Shoes		
Jewelry		
Dry cleaning		
Hair/makeup		
Health club		

(continued)

Item	Estimated	Amount/Month

Personal

Other

Total:

Health Care

Co-payments

Drugs

Total:

Insurance

Car

Home

Disability

Life

Health

Total:

Children

Day care

Babysitters

Toys

Clothes

Other

Total:

Charity

Donations

Grand Total:

10. I'm a real shopaholic. Any suggestions for saving money at the store?

Limit gift spending to a sum that can be paid off in three months if you have to charge some of your gifts. Shop the wrong season, so that at the end of summer you're buying summer stuff for the next year. The day after Christmas, stock up on Christmas cards, wrapping paper and bows. The day after Halloween, shop for discount costumes for your kids or grand-children. There are also some good sites online to get the most for your money:

- FirstAuction: http://www.Firstauction.com
- CompareNet: http://www.compare.net.com
- Amazon: http://www.Amazon.com

Shop from mail order catalogs; if you get lots of catalogs, you can often comparison shop and find the same item much cheaper in one catalog over another.

11. But shipping costs can be so expensive when shopping from a catalog.

That's true. Shipping can be expensive in mail order. You may want to shop from catalogs with a set amount for one order, and then combine your order with friends. If you're mailing gifts to out-of-town friends or family, save time and money by ordering from a mail order catalog and having the gift wrapped and sent directly to the recipient.

12. I'm renting a house. How can I save money in housing costs?

To cut costs, consider getting a roommate. If you don't want to share your place, try negotiating your rental increases as they come up each year. If your landlord hasn't done much around your apartment to fix problems, you have more leverage. If you're a good tenant, your landlord won't want to lose you.

13. I'm just starting out, and I don't have a lot of money to spend on our first home. What can I do?

You can buy many things for your home wholesale, including furniture and appliances, through the mail. Order the "Wholesale By Mail Catalog" by calling 800-242-7737. Frame a poster; change artwork regularly. Switch to washable fabrics and save about $200 a year in dry cleaning bills. Shop at yard sales and flea markets and discount stores.

14. Are there any ways to save on utility bills?

Yes. Eliminate one premium cable TV channel and save about $95 a year. In winter, lower the thermostat (each degree cuts the heating bill by 3 percent). In the summer, save on air conditioning by raising the thermostat.

15. My clothing allotment in our family budget is out of sight, and my husband says I have to cut back. I'm having a hard time doing that.

When you buy clothing, check to make sure it's machine washable; dry cleaning costs add up after a few years. Buy coordinating classic clothes that will last a long time so you get your money's worth, and consolidate your accessories (shoes, purses, jewelry). Buy only what you need, and if you buy high quality items, they should last for years.

16. My wife and I disagree about how much to spend on a vacation. I say that it's important to recharge our batteries. She says I spend too much.

Here's a good rule: If you can't take a vacation without charging it, then you can't afford it. A vacation isn't an investment—don't put it on your credit card. Getting away can be important, but you don't have to spend a great deal of money to relax. Try camping at a national park in your state. Stay home and tour all the sites within 50 miles that you've always wanted to visit but never had the time. If you do travel, consider off-season vacations. I use a vacation club account, saving a little from each pay, to finance next year's vacation.

17. Can we find the best rates for our vacation by using a travel agent?

A good travel agent may be helpful, but agents work on commission. They may not work hard to find you the best prices, so you'll have to do your own homework, too. Read "bought but can't use" ads for tickets in your local paper, and sign up with online travel services that keep you apprised of the latest cheapest fares. Let your travel agent know if you're flexible about dates. You might be able to save big by traveling a week earlier or later. If you can travel midweek, you often can save big on airfare.

18. How can I save on hotel reservations?

When making hotel reservations, remember that the reservation desk doesn't usually quote you a cheaper rate unless you ask. Ask: "What's the best you can do for me?" Stay over a weekend; you'll usually find much cheaper hotel rates if you stay over a Saturday. When you call, ask if they have a "weekend package." For example, in Washington D.C., the Grand Hyatt slashes its mid-week rate of $265 per night to just $119 over the weekend.

For the easiest, fastest way to get the best hotel rates (up to 65% off), check out a hotel consolidator for great rates in certain city hotels at no charge:

- Quikbook (800-789-9887), at http://www.quikbook.com
- Accommodation Express (800-444-7666) at http://www.accommodationexpress.com
- Hotel Reservation Network (800-964-6835) at http://www.80096hotel.com.

19. Are there other ways to save on accommodations when we go on vacation?

Consider a house swap; exchange your home with somebody who lives in an area where you'd like to vacation. Contact Vacation Exchange Club (800) 638-3841; Intervac U.S. at 800-756-HOME or Trading Homes International at (800) 877-8723.

20. What are the best ways to save money when flying?

You can find cheaper airline seats on the Internet. A variety of specialty travel sites can regularly send you notice of cheapest seats to destinations that you preselect. If you have the flexibility of last-minute travel, you can save big. Cash in on fare wars. If the ticket price drops after you've bought your ticket, you may be able to trade it in on a cheaper seat.

21. I really love to take cruises for my vacation. Are there any good ways to save with this type of holiday?

Of course. Cruise during the less-expensive season (that's mid-August to mid-December). When booking a cruise, ask for a run-of-the-ship rate. You pay a minimum rate and you may be able to upgrade a week before you leave. Choose an interior room on a lower deck, since new ships have standard rooms throughout.

22. I like to look my best, but my stylist charges more than $70 for a cut. Is it possible to save money on personal items such as this?

As you've discovered, getting a good "look" can cost a lot of money. If you really like that cut, you can visit the stylist for the cut but go to a discount place in between, for maintenance. On the other hand, you can really save by getting your hair cut at a local beauty school.

23. My husband wants to cut out our expensive exercise club, but I think exercise is important.

Exercise is important, but it doesn't have to be expensive. Visit your local community center (many offer fitness programs), or see if you can use a local school's running tracks, tennis courts, swimming pools, and so on. Or simply start a running program around your neighborhood, set up a badminton net in your back yard, or get some basic gym equipment for your home. You can often find good equipment at yard sales.

24. The "health care" line in our budget is really big. Are there ways to save on medical care today?

There are many ways to save. Always get a second opinion for any major surgery. Buy health insurance with high deductibles. If you have to take medicine for an ongoing health problem, get your prescription filled through a mail-order company. To find less expensive drugs, try calling Family Pharmaceuticals of America (800-922-3444); Pharmail Corp. (800-237-8927); or the Retired Persons Services, Inc. (AARP) (800-456-2277).

25. Food seems to eat up a large part of our disposable income. What's the solution?

When it comes to saving money around the house, it's easier to spend less than it is to earn more. One of the biggest parts of your budget will probably go for food—but there are lots of easy ways to save without spending lots of time doing it.

- Avoid buying bulk foods; they may seem cheaper, but the shelf life is usually shorter and the food may be contaminated. If you have to throw it out, it's no bargain.

- Try store brands of some items. Will you really notice the difference in store brand vs. premium rice?
- Cut down on meat in your recipes; try using half the amount the recipe calls for. Make vegetables, pasta or rice the main course and use meat as a side dish.
- If you do buy meat, buy it on loss-leader sales which are advertised on front and back pages of the store's weekly flyer. These are items that the store sells for a loss in the hope that you'll buy other more expensive items as well.
- Make a list and stick to it. Ignore the end-of-aisle displays. Shop as quickly as you can; for every minute you're in the store, you spend an average of $1.70
- Buy large bags of rice; cook more than you need and refrigerate the rest. Reheating rice takes just a few moments in a microwave—so you've saved money and time, too.
- In summer, buy extra vegetables and freeze the leftovers.
- Carry a brown bag lunch just two days a week instead of spending $5 each day on a meal will save you $300 a year. It's fast, it's easy and it saves money; packing a lunch five days as week will save $750 a year.

BANKING

26. Do you have any advice on picking a bank?

Look for a small, community bank or credit union. They usually will charge less for loans, pay more on savings, and set lower minimum deposits on checking accounts than bigger banks will. You will be able to get to know the staff, which can help a lot when it's time to ask for a loan. If you don't have any small banks where you live, look for a small branch of a big bank.

27. Which is better: an interest-bearing account or a low-cost, no-interest checking account?

Pick the checking account without interest. At the present, most interest-bearing checking accounts offer about 1.35 percent interest. You usually need to maintain a balance of between $1,000 and $5,000 to earn this interest; if you fall below their minimum, you'll pay a fee (often $7 or more per month). If your balance falls below the minimum just a few times, you've canceled out all the interest you could earn.

If you don't write many checks per month, you're best off using a no-frills checking account with low (or no) fees that require a low minimum balance and charges nothing for the first ten or fifteen checks you write.

28. What's a money market deposit account?

Most banks offer this type of interest-bearing account that allows you to write checks. It usually pays a higher rate of interest than a checking or savings account, but it often requires a higher minimum balance to start earning interest.

Withdrawing your money from a money market account may not be as convenient as a checking account, since you are limited to six transfers per month, and only three of these can be by check. Most banks impose fees on money market accounts.

29. What's the difference between a passbook savings account and a statement savings account?

A passbook savings account provides you with a record book in which your deposits and withdrawals are entered so you can keep track of your account. This record book must be presented when you make deposits and withdrawals.

With a statement savings account, your bank simply mails you a monthly statement that shows withdrawals and deposits for the account. Both accounts may have minimum balance requirements and various banking fees.

30. I want to close out my savings account. Does it matter what time of the month I do so?

Find out when the interest is credited. Your bank may compound interest daily, but it probably won't pay you until the end of the month or the end of the quarter. If you close your account before that time, you'll lose money.

31. I have $1,000 I'd like to keep in some sort of interest-bearing account. Where should I put it?

With that amount, you should qualify for a money market deposit account. These accounts pay a variable interest rate (typically a bit more than you'd get in a regular savings account). You can withdraw the money anytime.

Usually you can write three checks every month, plus arrange for three automatic withdrawals (to pay for expenses like your mortgage). You'll pay a fee if your deposit falls below the minimum.

32. What is a certificate of deposit (CD)?

If you have some money you'd like to save that you won't be needing for a short period of time, look into a CD. They mature anywhere from three months to ten years and the longer the term, the more money you can earn in interest. If you have to withdraw the money before the term is up, you will usually pay a penalty of one to six months worth of interest. Odds are, however, that you'll be able to leave the money in place and you'll be earning more money. If you have $2,000 you'd like to put into CDs but you're a bit worried about needing to take some out, don't put all the money into one CD; split up the money into several smaller value CDs or stagger them so they don't all come due at the same time. You may accumulate the interest earned or have it paid to you incrementally. The bank will notify you before the maturity date for most CDs. Often, they renew automatically, so if you don't notify the bank at maturity, the CD will continue for another term.

Not all banks pay the same interest rates for CDs. Some federally insured banks with top safety ratings pay 1 or 2 percent more than others. To find such banks, check out this website: http://www.bankrate.com

33. What about these "virtual" banks on the Internet?

You may get high yields from these banks. Their low overhead means they can have low costs and high interest rates. Check out Security First Network Bank at http://www.sfnb.com

34. Will FDIC insurance cover my checking account, CDs, and money market fund?

Yes, all types of bank deposits are insured up to $100,000 (including accrued interest). However, remember that if you have several accounts at one bank, the insurance will only cover the $100,000 total.

For example, if you have $25,000 in a savings account, $100,000 in a CD, and $25,000 in a money market account with your local bank, you are not entirely covered by FDIC insurance. If all the accounts are in your name, your deposits total $150,000. Since the limit of the insurance is $100,000, $50,000 is not insured.

35. I'm frustrated with ATM (bank machine) fees. How do I control them?

There are several ways to control the ATM fees, which can accumulate to a significant amount each month if you're not careful. First, plan ahead. Use your bank's ATM machine when you need money rather than a "foreign" machine. If this isn't possible, use a bank that doesn't charge a fee (this is harder and harder every day), or use the machine at a convenience store (or grocery) to access cash.

Another way to save is to use your ATM card as a debit card. If you don't have enough money at the grocery store, use your debit card to pay the bill rather than tapping into a "foreign" ATM machine. You'll save the fee.

36. How can I save on banking fees?

If you have enough funds within the bank, you may be able to obtain fee discounts, fee waivers, and/or interest discounts. The bank is regarding you as a valuable client. The fee waiver can save you ATM machine fees, check fees and so on. Check around to see how much money you need in a money market fund, checking account, or savings account to save on fees. By having a minimum in a money market fund, for example, you may be saving a significant sum of fees each year.

CASH ACCOUNTS

BANK

Type of account _____ # _____

Joint account name _____

Address _____

_____

E-mail address _____

Contact _____ Work phone (   ) _____

ATM card # _____

Location of checkbooks/records _____

_____

BANK

Type of account _____ # _____

Joint account name _____

Address _____

_____

E-mail address _____

Contact _____ Work phone (   ) _____

ATM card # _____

Location of checkbooks/records _____

_____

BANK

Type of account _____ # _____

Joint account name _____

Address _____

_____

(continued)

E-mail address

Contact   Work phone (   )

ATM card #

Location of checkbooks/records

BANK

Type of account   #

Joint account name

Address

E-mail address

Contact   Work phone (   )

ATM card #

Location of checkbooks/records

BANK

Type of account   #

Joint account name

Address

E-mail address

Contact   Work phone (   )

ATM card #

Location of checkbooks/records

CERTIFICATES OF DEPOSIT

BANK

Type of account   #
_____

Name(s) on account
_____

Address
_____

_____

E-mail address
_____

Contact   Work phone (   )
_____

Principal $
_____

Location of certificate
_____

Date purchased   Maturity date
_____

BANK

Type of account   #
_____

Name(s) on account
_____

Address
_____

_____

E-mail address
_____

Contact   Work phone (   )
_____

Principal $
_____

Location of certificate
_____

Date purchased   Maturity date
_____

BANK

Type of account   #
_____

Name(s) on account
_____

Address
_____

_____

(continued)

E-mail address _____

Contact _____ Work phone (   ) _____

Principal $ _____

Location of certificate _____

Date purchased _____ Maturity date _____

BANK

Type of account _____ # _____

Name(s) on account _____

Address _____

_____

E-mail address _____

Contact _____ Work phone (   ) _____

Principal $ _____

Location of certificate _____

Date purchased _____ Maturity date _____

INVESTING

37. What is the difference between saving and investing?

Saving is holding money, usually in bank accounts or money market funds, specified for short-term or emergency needs. Investing is buying things of value that provide income or increase in value over the long term. Savings usually shrink in value over time due to inflation.

38. How do I begin to feel comfortable with investing?

Build your expertise gradually. Find one or two mutual funds that have an excellent track record and invest. Read the information provided by the mutual fund company, read the financial section of your local newspaper, read a financial magazine each month (there are many, so look for one that is on a level which answers your questions and concerns), and talk with family and friends. As you become more knowledgeable, you can diversify and expand your horizons.

39. How do you invest to keep up with or beat inflation?

Over time, you should have 40 percent of your portfolio in growth investments to keep up with inflation. Since 1926, inflation has averaged 3.1 percent a year (although there was one year with 14 percent inflation and one year with 1 percent inflation). Investing a portion of your portfolio for growth should help beat inflation even after expenses and taxes.

40. I'm concerned about tying up all my cash in investments. What if I should suddenly need some of my money? How can I invest but still have money to use if I need it in an emergency?

Liquidity is certainly important, but you don't have to stash all your money in a savings account to be able to sleep at night. In fact, there's as much liquidity with mutual funds or most stocks as there are with CDs, because if you need your money you can always sell the investments. (The risk here, of course, is that they may have temporarily decreased in value.) You could put some money in "cash equivalents," like a money market mutual fund, which usually pays more than a savings account and lets you get to your money simply by writing a check. You could buy some U.S. Treasury bills (T-bills) which usually pay more interest than savings accounts and can be easily sold. Even better, you can buy short-term T-bills that are timed to come due when you need the money, such as in thirteen or twenty-six weeks.

You also can invest in mutual funds and stocks, which provide significantly better returns. In addition, you can sell them at their current value if necessary. Of course, all your investments don't have to be liquid, especially if you plan major purchases or postpone expected bills for the time when one of your investments is coming due. If you're looking to buy a new van, wait until the next CD comes due.

41. What's the first step after I decide I want to invest?

Make certain you have an emergency fund. It's not a question of if you'll ever need the fund, but when. Your emergency funds should be easily accessible, in an interest bearing checking or money market account, short-term CD, or U.S. Treasury bills. Different people suggest different reserve amounts: It is generally felt that an investor should have 3–6 months salary held in funds to cover a job loss, illness, and so on.

Once this fund is set aside, use the funds previously allocated to building the emergency fund to begin investing. There are numerous methods of starting to save; find one that is comfortable for you and begin. You can use a tax refund, direct deposit from your paycheck, or withdrawal from your checking account.

42. How does this compare to cash flow?

Cash flow is the difference between the money you have coming in and what you are spending. Controlling your cash flow is an important step in the financial planning process. If your total income is more than your expenses, you can afford to build your investment portfolio.

43. How does investing differ from speculation?

Investing is the process of purchasing stable securities or property and a fairly predictable rate of expected return. Speculation is when you "invest" funds in an asset in which the future value and level of expected earnings are highly uncertain. Speculation is the "high risk" end of investing.

44. Can I have too many investments?

While you can never have too much invested, you can have too many investments. If you can't keep track of what you own, know how it's performing, what it does, and why you own it, then you own too many. A generalization followed by institutional investors (banks, mutual fund managers, and money managers) is that you should own no more than 10 percent of your portfolio in any one fund or any one investment.

45. How much should I invest every year?

How much you invest depends on your disposable income, retirement needs, college costs, and so on. It's terrific if you can save 10 percent of your annual income. However, too many people don't save anything because they can't save 10 percent. Start small and increase the amount when you receive raises, gifts, or bonuses.

46. How does inflation affect my investment dollar?

Inflation is a problem for everyone. Keeping your funds in savings accounts means that your money is actually worth less in future years because inflation has eaten away at its purchase ability. Cash in your pocket, a regular checking account, or most savings accounts doesn't grow. The clearest example of inflation is seen by monitoring the cost of a first-class stamp. What cost five cents to mail a letter in 1965 now costs thirty-two cents in 1998.

47. I have five $1,000 certificates of deposit (CDs). Is this the best place to keep this money?

If that is all you have and this represents your "emergency money," it may be the best place. However, over time inflation will eat away the value of this money, too. Think about beginning to invest in a mutual fund to outpace inflation.

48. Where should I place the funds for investment accumulation?

Everyone needs a checking account for daily expenditures. Emergency funds should be set aside in a money market fund. The money market account can be opened with your local bank, mutual fund company, or brokerage house. Wherever you open the money market fund, the interest earned should be more than what you could earn on a savings account. Once you have saved enough to reach the minimum you need to open a mutual fund account, all investment funds should go directly to this account.

49. Should I reinvest the earnings (in dividends or interest) from the investments?

Unless you are retired or you need the funds for daily living, reinvestment of the account earnings is an easy way to save additional funds for investment. Dividend reinvestment is easily accomplished with mutual fund investments and many stocks.

50. Should I pay the income tax due on the earnings from the investments or my salary?

Paying income tax on the earnings and growth is another way to save/invest. If you have reinvested the earnings, you have a choice: You could take out some of the investment to pay the tax or pay the taxes from your current income. Paying your income tax liability from your income is another form of savings.

51. How much money do I need to build a portfolio?

A portfolio is a collection of investments. The moment you open your first mutual fund or buy a stock or bond, you have begun a portfolio. As you continue to add to your funds, the value of the portfolio increases.

52. How often should I review my investments?

An important part of the financial planning process is weighing the risks you're taking against the rewards anticipated. You need to monitor your investments, individually and as a total portfolio, so you can review how well you're actually doing, and compare this to the general market performances, called benchmarks. Although you may calculate the return of your portfolio quarterly, portfolio changes should be made annually, when your investment objectives change, or there is a reason the asset needs changes (international markets are crashing), company management has changed, and so on.

53. What investment mistakes should I try to avoid?

- Putting all your money in one investment
- Investing in products you don't understand
- Investing in assets/products that sound too good to be true
- Focusing on quick profit
- Investing money you cannot afford to lose in riskier investments
- Putting money into newer, untried funds or companies

FINANCIAL GOAL

One Year

Goal   Total cost   Monthly savings

Three Years

Goal   Total cost   Monthly savings

Five Years

Goal   Total cost   Monthly savings

LEASING VS. BUYING

54. Does it make more economic sense to lease or buy a phone?

The same phone that you can buy in a store for $20 may cost you $77 a year to lease. Fancier models cost even more. While ten million Americans are still leasing their phones, it's *not* a good way to save money. The companies will tell you that leasing protects you against phone damage; you get a free phone if your leased phone breaks. But phones are one of those products that rarely break down and you can easily buy two phones for less than the cost of a year's lease. You could buy a new phone and still be paying less than you would if you leased for a year.

55. Are there other ways to save money with my phone?

If you call home a lot when you're out of town, consider getting a personal 800 or 888 number. It's usually cheaper (14 to 19 cents per minute) than a calling card (27 to 38 cents per minute). And for short long-distance calls, a prepaid phone card is almost always better than a calling card. The per-minute rate is higher, but you won't pay any surcharge. If you make mostly short calls, use a provider who offers billing in six-second increments. Instead of a second phone line for a home business, opt for a second ring service on the same line.

In addition, if you have a computer, there's an easy way to compare long distance plans now. Visit Webpricer at http://www.trac.org, which allows you to take the last three months' worth of your phone bill and compare prices of major long-distance carriers to find the best deal. This also works for cell phones.

56. How about leasing versus buying a car?

It's no easier to lease a car than it is to buy one, so think carefully about which option is best for you.

Pros:

- Many leases don't require a down payment.
- You may be able to lease a more expensive car than you could afford to buy.
- You don't have to worry about reselling the car when the lease expires.

Cons:

- When your lease expires, you may have to pay "disposition charges" (the dealer's cost of auctioning your car).
- The total cost of leasing is almost always more than buying a car with cash and usually more expensive than borrowing the money to buy a car.
- When the lease expires, you're left with nothing.
- Almost every lease comes with mileage limits; if you go over the limit, you pay a penalty (as much as fifteen cents a mile).
- You still have to pay for insurance and maintenance.

57. What kind of person benefits from leasing a car?

If you tend to get a new car every couple of years, you'll do better with a lease. Of course, if your employer subsidizes your lease, this makes it more attractive for you. Unless you have very good credit, you're better off buying a used car, since you need a higher credit rating in order to lease.

58. Who shouldn't lease a car?

Anyone with marginal credit or who usually keeps a car longer than three years shouldn't lease a car. Remember that the longer you keep a leased car, the greater the chance that you may interfere with the car's residual value. The residual value is the agreed-on value of the car after you've leased it; if the dealer feels poor maintenance or too many miles have eroded that value, you could be in trouble. If you tend to put a lot of miles on a car, leasing may not be for you; most leases limit your mileage to 12,000 miles per year.

59. What's an open-end car lease?

In this type of contract, you guarantee the value of the car at the end of the lease; if the car has less value by that time, either from wear and tear or excess miles, you pay.

60. Are there other ways to save on my car expenses?

Yes. Carpools save on tolls, gas and parking. In medium-large cities, carpoolers can save about $1500 a year. Try buying tires through mail order and save. Venders can ship the tires directly to your garage if you wish. For good rates, try Tire Rack (800) 428-8355. You can also take your car for free repairs to your local vocational technology center, where students will work on your car as part of their training.

DOES IT PAY?

61. Are extended warranties worth the price?

No. According to *Consumer Reports,* more than 95 percent of people who buy extended warranties on appliances and electronics never use them. Most breakdowns are caused by defects which are covered under the standard manufacturer's warranty. The rest of the problems are usually the result of wear or damage, which isn't covered by most extended warranties anyway. Avoid extended warranties and save as much as 30 percent of the sticker price.

62. Is premium gas worth the extra cost?

Premium-grade gas doesn't make your car run better since both domestic and foreign cars are now designed to operate efficiently with 87-octane gas. Many also are equipped with sensors that automatically adjust your engine to eliminate knocks. Only if you drive a high-performance car (like a Porsche, Mercedes, or Corvette) do you still need premium gas. Experts say that a higher grade gas may improve your car's fuel economy or performance, but the change would be so slight you wouldn't be able to tell the difference.

NET WORTH WORKSHEET

ASSETS

Bonds	$
Cash accounts	$
Certificates of deposits	$
Limited partnerships	$
Mutual funds	$
Savings bonds	$
Stocks	$
Tax refunds	$
Treasury bills	$
Cash value life insurance	$
Subtotal	$

Personal property

Businesses	$
Cars	$
Personal property	$
Subtotal	$

Real estate

Mortages owned	$
Residence	$
Income property	$
Vacation home	$
Subtotal	$

Retirement

Annuities	$
IRAs	$

(continued)

Keogh accounts	$
Pensions	$
Subtotal	$
TOTAL	$

LIABILITIES

Current liabilities

Alimony	$
Child support	$
Personal loans	$
Subtotal	$

Installment liabilities

Bank loans	$
Car loans	$
College loans	$
Credit-card bills	$
Furniture loans	$
Home improvement	$
Life insurance loans	$
Pension plan loans	$
Subtotal	$

Real estate liabilities

Residence (include second mortgage/ line of credit)	$
Income property	$
Vacation home	$
Subtotal	$

Taxes

Capital gains tax	$
Income tax	$
Property tax	$
Subtotal	$

Other liabilities

_____

_____

_____

TOTAL ASSETS $

                                    —

TOTAL LIABILITIES $ _____

TOTAL NET WORTH $

CHAPTER 2

CREDIT

It's hard to imagine the world today without credit. Used wisely, credit is a valuable tool for the modern consumer. By spreading your payments over time, credit enables you to buy things you are not able to pay for in cash—a home, car, major appliance, expensive piece of jewelry, or vacation that you've always dreamed of taking. However, the flip side to credit can be a nightmare. Because it's so easy to buy on credit, all too many people spend way over their ability to pay. As the bills mount up, these people find themselves overwhelmed by excessively high interest rates and backbreaking payments. The record number of bankruptcies these days is proof of the dangers of out-of-control credit. This chapter will examine the intelligent use of credit, lending and borrowing, how to check up on and improve your credit record, and what to do if you find yourself with too much debt.

CREDIT CARDS

63. I feel like I owe my life to the credit card companies. Is there a way out?

Yes, as a matter of fact, there is. If you add just a few dollars extra to the checks you write to those credit card companies, you can save in a big way. You can pay off your credit card debt faster and save thousands of dollars in charges.

The average American carries about $3,900 worth of credit-card debt every year. At 18 percent interest, if you pay the minimum due every month (usually 2 percent of the balance), it will take you almost 36 *years* to repay and cost you more than $10,000 in interest. (That's if you never charge another thing on that card!) However, if you add just $10 a month to your payment, your debt will be paid off within seven years.

Look at it in another way. If you owe $6,000 at 19 percent interest and you pay $100 a month until the card is paid off and never charge another item, it will take you twenty-one years to pay off the debt. If you add just $10 a month to the $100, you can pay off the debt in less than twelve years. If you pay $200 a month, the debt will be gone in less than four years. Paying off the debt at $500 a month erases the problem in just over one year.

64. How can I reduce my credit card fees?

Get rid of most cards, use cards without annual fees, and avoid fees for late payment exceeding your credit limit.

65. I'd like to switch to a credit card with a low annual percentage rate. How can I find those cards?

For a small fee, you can get a list of low-rate cards from the RAM Research Corp. (800) 344-7714.

66. How can I avoid interest charges on my card?

Don't charge on a card with an outstanding balance. Interest starts building up right away if you carry a balance. You may have a few weeks to pay your balance in full without incurring interest charges, but this is only if you don't carry a balance.

67. I was offered credit card protection for my credit card. Should I get this?

Credit card protection is an annual fee that covers any losses if your credit card is lost, stolen, or used by someone else. It doesn't make much sense since you are only liable for a maximum loss of only $50 per card anyway.

68. If I have a payment dispute with a company because the merchandise was flawed, what can my credit card company do?

If you have a payment dispute because of poor merchandise, you must file an official claim with your credit card company explaining the dispute. Your credit card company will list the disputed amount on your bill; however, payment will be suspended until the dispute is settled. It's your responsibility to rectify the matter and then inform the credit card company of the outcome of the dispute.

69. With all the credit cards that come to the house in the mail, does it makes sense to acquire all of them as a way of building up my credit?

Acquiring many cards doesn't build a good credit history. Using a few cards and paying on them on time each month builds good credit. A large number of credit lines available to you can be detrimental when applying for a loan. In fact, being able to get a great deal of money, due to numerous credit cards with large limits, can hurt you when you apply for a loan. Therefore, decide on the number of cards you want and close out the cards you don't use.

70. Should my sixteen-year-old son have a credit card to build credit?

A sixteen-year-old child can't have a credit card in his name alone because he is a minor and can't incur debt. However, your son can have a credit card in his name if you have the card on your account. If your son takes care of paying the monthly charges on the card, his name will also be included in the credit history on the card, and good credit information will be forwarded to the credit reporting services. Giving a minor a credit card in this way is a wise move if he is responsible.

71. If my husband just died, do I get his credit card in my name alone?

A creditor is never obligated to give you credit. If your spouse has died, and the account was in his name alone, you have the opportunity to apply for credit in your name. If you don't have a credit history, getting a card in your name will be up to the bank where you apply.

72. My husband and I are separating. What do I do with our joint credit card account?

Tell all your creditors immediately that you are separating. Your creditors will close your joint accounts and have you apply for an account in your name alone. This is a good idea if your spouse has had credit problems in the past. Any debts that occur after you separate are his debts, and thus are not considered part of the property settlement.

73. I want to acquire credit in my own name. Can I do this?

If you never acquired credit in your own name, it is imperative that you do so. Contact the companies in which you and your spouse have a joint account and ask for an account in your name alone. The Equal Credit Opportunity Act requires that if you are married, you must be allowed to apply for credit in your own name and you shouldn't be denied credit if your credit history is satisfactory. The credit card companies may start you with a small limit; however, you should use your card to build up your credit limits.

74. I have no one to be a guarantor, but I want to acquire credit. Can this be done?

Yes. There are what are known as secured credit cards/credit accounts. The creditor requires a deposit as collateral equal to the credit limit on the card. Then you are approved for a credit card with the secured limit. There are often fees charged to open such an account, and you don't usually receive competitive money market interest rates on the funds held in the secured account; however, it's a way to begin a credit history. When you open the secured account, ask if and when the account can be converted to a standard account. Put that date on your calendar so you can make the conversion as soon as possible.

CREDIT CARD INDEX

Credit card _____ # _____

Name(s) on card _____ Expiration date _____

Phone number _____ If lost, call _____

Limit _____ Interest rate _____

Credit card _____ # _____

Name(s) on card _____ Expiration date _____

Phone number _____ If lost, call _____

Limit _____ Interest rate _____

Credit card _____ # _____

Name(s) on card _____ Expiration date _____

Phone number _____ If lost, call _____

Limit _____ Interest rate _____

Credit card _____ # _____

Name(s) on card _____ Expiration date _____

Phone number _____ If lost, call _____

Limit _____ Interest rate _____

Credit card _____ # _____

Name(s) on card _____ Expiration date _____

Phone number _____ If lost, call _____

Limit _____ Interest rate _____

Credit card _____ # _____

Name(s) on card _____ Expiration date _____

Phone number _____ If lost, call _____

Limit _____ Interest rate _____

Credit card _____ # _____

Name(s) on card _____ Expiration date _____

Phone number _____ If lost, call _____

Limit _____ Interest rate _____

Credit card _____ # _____

Name(s) on card _____ Expiration date _____

Phone number _____ If lost, call _____

Limit _____ Interest rate _____

Credit card _____ # _____

Name(s) on card _____ Expiration date _____

Phone number _____ If lost, call _____

Limit _____ Interest rate _____

Credit card _____ # _____

Name(s) on card _____ Expiration date _____

Phone number _____ If lost, call _____

Limit _____ Interest rate _____

Credit card _____ # _____

Name(s) on card _____ Expiration date _____

Phone number _____ If lost, call _____

Limit _____ Interest rate _____

Credit card _____ # _____

Name(s) on card _____ Expiration date _____

Phone number _____ If lost, call _____

Limit _____ Interest rate _____

75. My husband purchased a computer for the family's Christmas gift on a credit card and I was surprised to receive a call from the credit card company verifying that we had made the purchase. Is this normal?

Because of credit card fraud, credit card companies frequently verify transactions made on your account for your protection as well as theirs. If you make a large purchase, a large number of purchases, or buy something out of town, you may receive a call verifying the transaction. Although you may have been surprised by the call, such calls can stop problems at inception rather than thirty days later when you receive your bill with a transaction that was not initiated by you.

LENDING AND BORROWING

76. My brother asked me to cosign a loan for his business. What exactly does that mean?

Cosigning on a loan means that you will guarantee to repay if your brother defaults. Cosigning is often needed when a borrower has a poor or nonexistent credit history or doesn't have enough collateral. Many young people are required to have parents cosign for their first credit card or first car loan.

Remember that co-signing means you must repay the loan if the borrower defaults on payment. If you cosign, find out the type of repayment options. (If the payments are late, can monthly payments continue if you bring the loan up to date or are you obligated to repay the loan in full immediately?) Also find out when you can be removed as cosigner. For example, if the borrower pays on time for three years, can you be removed from the loan? You don't want to be a cosigner on a line of credit that can be maintained forever. Limit your liability.

77. Will co-signing a loan help my daughter get a credit history?

In this case, you don't want to be named as a cosigner, you want to be named as a guarantor. If you are your daughter's guarantor, she will get a credit history. A cosignature situation may not provide her with credit.

78. If I use my attorney to collect a business debt, does he take a percentage of the debt?

Attorneys collect delinquent payments by charging on an hourly basis. It's a good idea to have an attorney make your collection if the debt is more than $20,000. The stronger your case for collection, the wiser it is to use an attorney. The tougher the debt is to collect, the more inclined you should be to hire a collection agency. You'll have to pay a percentage of the debt to the agency.

79. I have several customer delinquent accounts. What's the first step in collecting?

Work with the delinquent customers. Call them yourself and try to arrange a payment schedule. If this doesn't work, take them to small claims court. Small claims court is available for claims of less than $5,000.

80. Companies advertise purchasing appliances and furniture with no interest for six months. Does it make sense to buy items this way?

Buying items without interest for six months is a great way to pay for the items gradually. Most retailers who offer this plan ask you to finance through a credit company, although large firms like Sears have their own plans. Each plan is different. Some require monthly payments; others require no payments until the final due date. However, if you don't pay for the entire purchase by the end of the period, you will owe very high interest for the entire period. Therefore, if you take retailers up on this plan, be sure you can pay in full by the final due date.

YOUR CREDIT RECORD

81. Who keeps credit reports?

There are three main companies that collect data and maintain information on a person's credit for use by people or companies who subscribe to their service. Debtors report tardiness of payments to the following three companies.

Experian
PO Box 949
Allen, TX 75013
Telephone #: 888-397-3742
http://www.experian.com

Equifax Credit Services
PO Box 740241
Atlanta, GA 30374
Telephone #: 1-800-685-1111
http://www.equifax.com

Trans Union Credit Information Services
1561 E. Orangethorpe Avenue
Fullerton, CA 92631
Telephone #: 1-800-916-8800
http:www.transunion.com

Information regarding late payments, credit history, nonpayment, and past foreclosures is very important and its accuracy imperative.

82. How private is my credit report? Who else can see it?

The Fair Credit Reporting Act limits who can see your credit report. A reporting agency may furnish your credit report under the following circumstances:

- in response to a court order or a federal grand jury subpoena
- to anyone to whom you give your written permission
- to anyone considering you for credit
- to anyone who will use the report for insurance purposes
- to anyone for determining your eligibility for a government license or benefits
- to anyone with a legitimate business need for the report in connection with a business transaction involving you.

83. How can I get a copy of my credit report if I haven't been turned down for credit?

Each of the three largest credit agencies (Experian, Equifax and Trans Union) allows you to order a copy of your report by mail, with an enclosed check or money order. Equifax and Experian allow you to call in an order if you can charge the report to a major credit card. (Equifax and Trans Union offer a report-ordering service online). In most states, the cost is $8.

84. I was turned down for a car loan. Do I have a right to ask why?

By law, when you are turned down for a loan due to a bad credit report, the lender has to provide the reasons for the denial and the credit reporting agency has to provide a free copy of the report to you. You can then review your report and verify if the data in the report is accurate. If it isn't, you should work to have the incorrect information removed from the report.

85. I was denied credit from a credit card company because I don't have a checking or savings account. Why does that matter?

As a prerequisite to having good credit, you must demonstrate to the credit card companies that you have the ability to pay your bills. You can't pay the bill without a checking account, unless you obtain a money order every month. The first step on the road to good credit is to open a checking account.

86. How often should I check my credit information?

Experts advise that you get a copy of your credit report at least once a year. Before you buy a home or take out a loan, ask for a copy of your report to prevent problems due to an error. Also, request a copy of any credit report that a creditor has obtained for you.

87. How do I correct information on my credit report?

With a poor credit record, it is difficult to get any future credit. Thus, it is important to rectify all incorrect information on your report. While there are services that promise to correct your credit report for a fee, I recommend you try to work through the process yourself. These services cannot fix an account that accurately states past tardiness. Here's how to do it:

1. Contact all three credit reporting services and request a copy of your credit report in writing. Send the letter via certified mail. Within sixty days, you should receive a copy of the report. Another way to receive your current report is to call your local Credit Bureau and request a re-

port. You can even pick up the information if you pay for the report at that time. Review the report for inaccuracies.

2. Contact the three reporting companies by certified mail, stating the incorrect information and request they investigate.

3. If you haven't heard anything within sixty days, send another letter with a reminder that credit reporting companies are required by law to investigate incorrect information or provide an updated credit report with the inaccurate information removed from your report.

88. How long does a negative mark on my credit history remain on my record?

In general, two years for negative inquiries, seven years for general negative remarks, and ten years for bankruptcy. If you have information on your record that is longer than these time limits, you should be able to have such information removed.

89. How long does it take to get a good credit record into your credit report?

If you show a change in spending and that you are repaying your bills, your credit report should begin to change in approximately twenty-four to thirty-six months. Credit card companies rate you with a risk score. Each company is different; however, the ratings are produced based on your credit history. The better your repayment history, the higher your score, and the better chance that you will receive a favorable report.

90. Is there any way to erase a credit history and start fresh?

Yes and no. Your history is your history. There are services that for an exorbitant fee show you how to illegally repair your credit record. Remember that changing federal identification numbers for a credit report is illegal, and it is illegal to provide false information to a creditor. You can't erase your history, but you can start today in building a better credit report.

91. How can I do that?

1. Cut up your credit cards.
2. Pay in cash and don't overspend.
3. Establish a realistic budget and stick to it.
4. Establish a plan to get out of debt.

5. Negotiate a repayment plan with creditors.
6. Establish a cushion for emergencies.
7. Create stability in your credit history—don't job-hop, for example.

92. My attorney advised me to use credit to repair credit. What does he mean?

Use one credit card and pay off the balance at the end of the month. Keep your purchases minimal and repay them monthly. This places a good payment history on your credit report. It's the first step in repairing your credit.

GETTING OUT OF DEBT

93. What is the first thing I should do when I can't pay even my minimum balance on a credit card?

Notify your creditor in writing that you can't make a payment. Close the account so there are no further charges and before the creditor closes the account due to delinquency. Work out a plan to repay the loan as you can; don't ignore your creditors.

94. I'm worried that my husband may have problems with finances. How can I convince him that he may have a problem?

You don't have to have bill collectors pounding at your door to be in a financial mess. Ask yourself these questions:

- Do you often spend more than you earn?
- Are you forced to make day-to-day purchases on credit?
- Can you make only the minimum payments on monthly credit cards?
- If you lost your job, would you have trouble paying next month's bills?

95. What are the steps to proceed when I have too many debts?

1. Find out your account balances. Call the credit card company and ask for your balance to date.
2. Prepare a list of all your outstanding balances. Most people are surprised to learn that their debts are not quite as bad as they thought.
3. Do something. Doing nothing defers current action but you incur greater expenses down the road. The trouble won't just disappear.

4. Sell a major asset that really isn't necessary. If you have two cars, sell one. Sell stock, your vacation cottage, or something else to bring your debts in line with your expenses.
5. Cut expenses. This is difficult, but often the first important move to a plan of recovery.
6. Plan a repayment plan. To get the situation in hand, any of the following can be done to accomplish the goal of consolidation and/or repayment of debt.
   • Withdraw money from an Investment Retirement Account (IRA). Although you are withdrawing future security, it's important not to ruin your credit today at the expense of tomorrow. Remember to withdraw the tax due as well as the 10 percent penalty.
   • Get an equity line of credit.
   • Refinance your mortgage, consolidating the outstanding loans.
   • Borrow from family.
   • Borrow from a bank.
   • Borrow from a finance company.
   • File for bankruptcy.
   • Borrow against the cash value of your life insurance policies.

96. At what point does a credit card company put a stop on your account—when you have hit your limit or higher?

Every financial institution has its own rules; however, the general rule seems to be that when you have exceeded your limit by 10 percent, you will either have the card frozen from further use until payment is made to lower your outstanding limit to an amount below your limit, or you request an increase in your limit. It's better to increase your limit before you charge over your limit rather than make the request afterwards.

97. I've gotten myself in a terrible financial situation because I can't stop spending. How do I get help?

There is a support group, similar to Alcoholics Anonymous, that is available for support and guidance. Contact Debtors Anonymous at General Services Building, PO Box #888, Needham, MA 02492-0009 or call (781) 453-2743. Call or write to find the group closest to your home.

98. My banker mentioned when I refinanced my mortgage that I have almost too much credit. What did he mean?

Most of us receive a myriad of credit cards in the mail promising low interest rates, high credit limits, and easy availability. If we take all the cards that we receive we really have too much credit. The high limits can hurt you when you apply for a loan, since lenders only want borrowers to have 36 percent of their gross income as debt. All you need are one or two gasoline cards, a few department store credit cards, one or two major credit cards, and a debit card.

99. My husband and I are really in a bind. Do we have any choice besides bankruptcy?

Before you file for bankruptcy, which often looks like an easy way to rectify a horrible situation, try working with the Consumer Credit Counseling Service (CCCS) to prepare a repayment plan. The CCCS is a national non-profit organization which guides you into preparing a repayment plan. A trained counselor will help you come up with a budget to maintain your basic living expenses and outline options for addressing your total financial situation. If creditors are hassling you, a counselor can negotiate with them to repay your debts through a financial management plan. Under this plan, creditors may agree to reduce payments or drop fees. After starting the plan, you deposit money with CCCS each month to cover these new negotiated payment amounts. Then CCCS will distribute this money to your creditors to repay your debts. The service charges approximately $9 a month; be wary of companies with similar names and promises who have considerably larger fees.

100. Where do I locate CCCS?

There are more than 1,100 locations nationwide, supported mainly by contributions from community organizations, financial institutions, and merchants. Contact the Consumer Credit Counseling Service at 8611 2nd Avenue, Suite 100, Silver Spring, MD 20910 or call (888) 288-3184 24 hours a day.

101. Should I file for bankruptcy?

If you have few assets, a lot of debt, and income that barely covers a limited lifestyle after covering monthly debt payments, bankruptcy may be a choice for you. Here is what you should know before you take the plunge:

1. Bankruptcy does not apply to everyone nor does it discharge all debts. Examine your situation before you file to find out if you qualify.
2. Bankruptcy destroys your credit history for ten years. If you are ready for bankruptcy, your credit history is probably already horrid.
3. Bankruptcy won't change your spending habits. It will relieve you of your debts, but you must change your compulsions or you will be in the same situation down the road.
4. Filing for bankruptcy is a public affair.
5. There may be other means to get creditors off your back without bankruptcy.
6. You will be required to give up everything but your exempt property.
7. Negotiate with creditors. If you use the threat of bankruptcy, they may be willing to work with you.
8. If you had cosigners, bankruptcy doesn't let them off the hook.

102. My attorney recommended bankruptcy. Should I take his advice?

Be careful about where the advice to file for bankruptcy originates. An attorney who earns a legal fee from doing bankruptcy filings may have a conflict of interest since filing for bankruptcy generates fees. On the other hand, the Consumer Credit Counseling Service, a nonprofit educational service, is funded by credit card companies. CCCS counselors may therefore not be anxious to recommend bankruptcy.

103. What types of bankruptcy are there?

There are two kinds of bankruptcy: Chapter 7 or Chapter 13.

- Chapter 7 lets you cancel your debts. You label exempt property; the trustee seizes all nonexempt property, sells the assets, and pays the debtors.
- Chapter 13 involves a repayment schedule requiring you to repay your debts over several years. Like Chapter 7, Chapter 13 stays on your credit record but it doesn't erase the debt. For this reason, it's a good idea for handling back taxes as these can't be erased through Chapter 7.

104. I must decide about filing for bankruptcy. What is a Chapter 13 reorganization?

Chapter 13 reorganizes your debts and reviews your future earnings rather than the property you own as the means of satisfying your creditors' claims. Chapter 13 is more like a forced payment plan than canceling debts through liquidation of assets.

105. Are there restrictions as to who can file for a Chapter 13 reorganization?

As with Chapter 7 reorganizations, you must have regular income that is stable enough to make the Chapter 13 payments. Like Chapter 7 debt, the filing creates an automatic stay against your property.

106. When would you undergo a Chapter 13 reorganization?

When you have property that exceeds the exemption limits which you want to keep, you should consider a Chapter 13 reorganization. Also, a person who is somewhat behind but who could make it if the payments were extended should consider this type of procedure.

107. What debts aren't canceled by bankruptcy?

Alimony, child support, taxes, court-ordered damages, and student loans aren't canceled by bankruptcy. You also will still have debts after bankruptcy incurred as a result of death or personal injury caused while drunk driving. Debts created as a result of a breach of trust (embezzlement), theft, and breach of fiduciary trust; debts incurred as a result of a willful or malicious act; fines and penalties owed to a government agency for violation of the law; and debts that couldn't be discharged in a prior bankruptcy because of fraud or wrongdoing are all still due.

108. Should I report debts on my bankruptcy list of creditors even if I know the debts won't be relieved?

Yes, you are required to list all property and a list of all creditors whether the debt is dischargeable or not. By filing bankruptcy you automatically receive a stay for any actions planned or taken by the Internal Revenue Service (IRS) while the bankruptcy process is underway. This can give you time to get your act together.

109. Do I have to list a creditor in the bankruptcy proceeding even if I want to keep the credit card afterwards? If the credit card company finds out, it may risk my account.

All creditors must receive notice of the filing of a bankruptcy proceeding; however, you don't have to inform a credit card company if you have an open account with a zero balance. Therefore, it's a good idea to pay off the account you want to keep before you file for bankruptcy. That way the credit card company won't need to be notified that you are filing for bankruptcy.

110. Can I take out a loan prior to bankruptcy and use it to pay off debts that aren't discharged by bankruptcy?

There are certain debts that bankruptcy doesn't discharge, and if you could take out a loan to pay off these debts, you would be free and clear of all liabilities after the bankruptcy. The question is who is going to give you a loan when your credit is so poor and you don't have collateral to cover such a loan?

111. Are wages exempt from bankruptcy?

Wages earned after you filed for bankruptcy are considered exempt; however, payment of wages earned prior to the filing, paid after the filing are not considered exempt.

112. What property is exempted?

Every state lets you keep certain items even if you file for bankruptcy. In some states (Iowa, Kansas, Florida, Minnesota, and Oklahoma) you can keep your home no matter how expensive it is. Other states provide no exemption for homeowners. Most states allow you to protect a certain amount of equity. For example, if you owe $50,000 on your $100,000 home, the exemption protects the $50,000 equity in your house, but it doesn't relieve you of the $50,000 mortgage obligation. That obligation will continue once the bankruptcy process is completed. Depending on your state, you may be allowed to keep other personal property. Most states will let you keep clothing, pensions, household furniture, and money in retirement accounts.

113. Should I hire an attorney to help me file for bankruptcy?

If you've already made up your mind to file for bankruptcy and have major assets to protect, you may want to hire an attorney. Realize that an attorney's fees may approach $1,000 or more for complicated cases.

114. How long will the bankruptcy process take?

Every situation is different. If the bankruptcy is challenged by a spouse or creditor, there is a business to run, or property to sell, it can take longer. The average length of time is approximately four months.

115. When should I file?

There are factors that you need to be aware of before you file for bankruptcy so you do not appear to be fraudulent.

- Level of creditor activity. You can wait until the creditors are ready to seize your property so you have time to try to remedy the situation besides declaring bankruptcy,
- When were purchases made? Luxury personal items purchased immediately prior to your filing may seem to be fraudulent transactions. You may want to delay bankruptcy if these types of transactions occurred.
- How recently was property transferred to family or friends, particularly for less than market value?

116. Will the creditors stop harassing me after I file for bankruptcy?

Yes. Bankruptcy prohibits a creditor from going after your assets as soon as you file. The creditor usually receives notice from the trustee; however, you may wish to advise your creditors of the filing in writing, with the filing date, name of location of the court, and the bankruptcy case number.

117. I went bankrupt several years ago and I am in a financial bind again. Can I file for bankruptcy again?

If you filed for bankruptcy under Chapter 7, you can't file again for six years. However, you can file for Chapter 13 relief regardless of how long it has been since you filed Chapter 7.

118. Must I list all creditors on my bankruptcy papers?

If you want to be discharged from the debt, you must file their claim. If you miss a claim, you will need to amend your bankruptcy papers to include the missed claim.

119. Will bankruptcy remove the liens on my property?

Real estate mortgages, car liens, and tax liens are not removed by the blanket of bankruptcy. To remove any liens, you must petition the court to have them removed. If you don't file to remove the lien within the proper time, you may not receive bankruptcy relief from the lien.

120. I was approached by a creditor to reaffirm his loan after bankruptcy. Is this wise?

When you file for bankruptcy, you ruin your credit history for many years and in exchange your debts are removed. Reaffirming your debt means that you agree to pay off a debt following the bankruptcy process. Why would you do this? You may want to negotiate for an agreement with a lender outside of bankruptcy that allows you to catch up with delinquent payments or even refinance the loan. You could file for Chapter 13 relief rather than Chapter 7. Try to negotiate the amount of the loan, the interest rate, and term of the loan. It can't hurt to request some considerations in exchange for the reaffirmation.

121. Can the court refuse to discharge my debts?

Beyond the basic statutory requirements for eligibility (you must live or have property in the United States and you can't have filed for bankruptcy in the preceding six years), a bankruptcy court can deny a discharge if it feels there has been fraud or a failure to cooperate in the process. It is important to be honest and not destroy financial information, make false statements, and so on.

122. What are the elements of fraud?

1. You lied about something that was important (a material misstatement of fact).
2. You knew it was a lie.
3. You intended to lie.

4. The creditor relied upon your lie as truth.
5. The creditor was injured as a result.

123. I received a delinquent notice from a collection agency. Why didn't the creditor deal with me directly?

There are several ways for businesspeople to deal with delinquent accounts: their billing department, via an attorney, or from an outside collection agency. Retailers like collection agencies because they have expertise in collection. The agencies usually charge by taking a percentage (20–50 percent) of what they collect.

124. My father-in-law died and we appealed nonpayment of part of the bill by Medicare. After several delinquent notices from the hospital, our account was sent to a collection agency. What do I do?

First, talk with the hospital. They had to help with the appeal, so they know that you are in the process of the appeal. Send a letter to the hospital notifying them of the appeal and explain that you will pay when the process is completed.

125. I'm behind on my mortgage payments. The collection agency threatened to put an ad in the paper about my delinquency. Can they do this?

The Federal Fair Debt Collection Practices Act of 1977 prohibits a debt collector from advertising in the paper on any nonpayment of personal debts. Advise them that you know about this and work out a payment plan.

126. What are some of the other limitations of the creditors?

Debt collectors must disclose that they are collecting a debt, which debt it is, and how much the debt is for. The agency is limited from asking about your employment and your family. They are not permitted to harass you or call you at work.

127. I'm receiving calls all hours of the day and night about the bills I'm behind on. How do I stop the calls?

Send a written notice to the collection agency and demand that they stop calling. Remember that the only way the agency can really get satisfaction is to file a lawsuit. Everything else they do is designed to get you to pay so they don't have to go to court.

128. What happens if they don't stop calling?

If the collection agency doesn't stop after your letter, send a letter to the Federal Trade Commission with documentation of the times and dates of the agency's calls with a copy also sent to the collection agency. You should be able to acquire the name of the state agency that polices collection agencies from your local representative's office.

129. What are the real methods of the collection agencies?

Threats are the easiest method. They will threaten to sue you and then garnish your wages. This is a legitimate claim. Within five days of their first call, the agency must send a letter of notice. They can't harass, publish names, or call you at work. After attempts to collect via threats, they probably will proceed with a lawsuit, but only after the original creditor has okayed the move. If possible, you should negotiate a settlement with the agency to settle the matter.

CHAPTER 3

TAXES

Whether or not you prepare your own taxes, you should understand your personal tax situation and have a basic knowledge of taxes in general. Recent legislation may provide for a kinder, gentler IRS, but you should still fully understand your own taxes. There's no reason to pay more taxes than you have to, so you should know how to take advantage of all the deductions to which you are entitled. On the other hand, you don't want to wind up with legal problems down the road, so you should be aware of all the income you are required to report. This chapter provides a broad overview of what you should know about taxes, including ways to defer taxes and how to handle special tax situations.

FILING BASICS

130. How do I get IRS tax guides?

It's imperative that you understand your tax situation so you can take advantage of all the deductions and include all your income on your returns. The IRS has more than 500 free publications that can help you. Publication 17 (*Your Federal Income Tax*) is designed for individual tax return preparation; publication 334 (*Tax Guide for Small Businesses*) is for small business owners. You can obtain a list of all current tax guides by calling (800) 829-3676 or by contacting the IRS at its website (http://www.irs.ustreas.gov).

131. Can I do my taxes myself?

Yes and no. It's imperative that you understand your tax returns. However, when your returns become complicated or cumbersome—when you no longer use the short form, perhaps—you should seek help to prepare your return. You'll be surprised how often a tax preparer knows of new deductions that you haven't heard about, and you can save on your tax bill. It's a good idea to have your taxes prepared by an experienced preparer if you:

- are self-employed;
- have bought or sold a home this year;
- have business expenses, car expenses, or depreciation; or
- have rental property.

132. Is tax preparation software any good? What programs do you recommend?

My favorite tax preparation software includes Kiplinger TaxCut, TurboTax, or MacInTax. Remember that when you buy the software, you can deduct the expense of the program. Another benefit of this software is that you can use it all year to check on your ongoing tax liability, plan your taxes, and so on. If you feel uncertain about accuracy after you prepare your return with a computer program, hire a tax preparer to check it over. You should expect to pay for this service.

133. I filed my income tax return early. How can I make sure my check is coming and when it's coming?

To find out the status of your tax refund, you can call the IRS refund hotline at 1-800-829-4477. Touch-Tone service is available 24 hours a day,

7 days a week; rotary service is available Monday through Friday from 7:30 A.M. to 5:30 P.M. Make sure you have a copy of your return handy so you can answer the recorded questions.

134. It's hard for me to get to the bank. Can the IRS direct deposit my refund?

Yes. At your request, the IRS will direct deposit the money into any checking or savings bank account (within specified guidelines)—for free! You'll get your refund faster and there's no chance your check will get lost in the mail. If you're interested, fill in lines 62 b, c, and d on Form 1040.

135. What are other ways to make sure my refund comes quickly?

Mail your return early, sign and date it properly, and use the address label that comes with your tax form, if possible. Don't forget to attach your W-2 form.

136. Can I use other forms of mail service to mail my income tax return?

Yes. The IRS used to accept only a receipt from the U.S. Postal Service as proof that you mailed your return on time. Today the IRS will accept a receipt from approved private delivery services, such as Federal Express and United Parcel Service.

137. I've heard that it's possible to file a return by phone. Is this true?

Yes, for some people. If you qualify, the government will send you a special tax package explaining how the system works. If you're single and have a Touch-Tone phone, you can take advantage of the TeleFile system available 24 hours a day provided you:

- have no dependents;
- made less than $50,000; and
- file your return from the same address as you did last year.

138. I can't pay all the money I owe in taxes. What should I do?

Mail in your return on time, pay what you can, and attach Form 9465 to the return that outlines a monthly repayment plan. The IRS will contact you within thirty days to let you know if your plan has been approved. You'll be charged a processing fee and perhaps a late-payment penalty. Once you start repaying, you can't miss *any* payments or the government will nullify your repayment plan and demand the rest of the money immediately.

139. What happens if I can't get my tax report completed by April 15?

You can file Form 4868 and get an automatic four-month extension. The form must show the full amount of tax due, estimated as closely as you can. You don't have to send the money along with the return, but the IRS will begin to charge you interest as of April 15.

140. I don't want my $3 to go to the Presidential Election Campaign Fund because I don't want the government to get any more of my money.

The $3 Presidential Election Campaign Fund is not extra money over and above your final tax liability. It simply takes $3 of whatever money you owe the government and earmarks it for the Presidential Election Campaign Fund. This means that $3 of the income taxes you pay goes to the campaign fund and the rest ends up in the government's general fund.

141. How long should I keep my income tax returns and corresponding records?

I keep my returns for five years; but I'm extra cautious. Most banks want to see your last three years' returns for loan considerations. The law says you must keep your returns for three years from the date you filed your return. This is also important because you have up to three years to amend your return if you find you've made a mistake and you want to file for a credit or refund. Returns filed before the due date are treated as if filed on the due date. However, if you don't report income that should have been reported on your return and the unreported income is more than 25 percent of the income shown on the return, the statute of limitations doesn't run out until six years after you file the return. Some experts recommend keeping your returns forever if you depreciate, or have dividend reinvestments. It's up to you. One final warning: If your return is false or fraudulent, there is no statute of limitations. The IRS can come after you at any time.

142. What is a marginal tax bracket and how does it affect me?

The federal income tax is a graduated tax meaning that the more money you make, the higher percentage of tax you have to pay. The lowest income tax bracket is a 15 percent tax; this applies to a single taxpayer who makes no more than $24,650 in taxable income. The next brackets rise to 28 percent, 31 percent, 36 percent, and the top bracket is 39.6 percent.

143. Does this mean that if I make $25,000 in taxable income, I have to pay 28 percent on the entire amount?

No. If your taxable income is $25,000 and you are single, you pay 15 percent of the first $24,650 and then 28 percent on the rest ($350).

144. Does everyone who files pay the same?

No. That single filer is in the 15 percent bracket up to $24,650. A head of household filer is in the 15 percent bracket until earning $33,050. A married person who files separately is in the 15 percent bracket until earning $20,600. Married people filing jointly are in the 15 percent bracket until their income reaches $41,200.

145. What is the so-called marriage penalty?

The marriage penalty refers to the extra tax that a married couple pays by having to file as married filing jointly rather than two single taxpayers living in the same home. Two single persons sharing a household earning $40,000 each would pay $7,996 in tax with a total of $15,992. A married couple earning $40,000 each would pay a total of $17,044. This extra $1,052 is considered the marriage penalty.

146. If I owe $700 in tax at the end of the year, am I penalized for underpayment?

The psychology of refund versus paying taxes differs from person to person. Many people would rather have more taxes withheld from their paychecks than they really owe so that they receive a refund in April. Others want to pay the least possible amount because they want to use their money throughout the year. The choice is yours.

1998 Tax Rate Schedules

ESTATE AND GIFT TAX

Unified Estate and Gift Tax Rates

Amount	Tax	plus	of the excess over
$0-10,000	$0	18%	$0
$10,001-20,000	$1,800	20%	$10,000
$20,001-40,000	$3,800	22%	$20,000
$40,001-60,000	$8,200	24%	$40,000
$60,001-80,000	$13,000	26%	$60,000
$80,001-100,000	$18,200	28%	$80,000
$100,001-150,000	$23,800	30%	$100,000
$150,001-250,000	$38,800	32%	$150,000
$250,001-500,000	$70,800	34%	$250,000
$500,001-750,000	$155,800	37%	$500,000
$750,001-$1,000,000	$248,300	39%	$750,000
$1,000,001-$1,250,000	$345,800	41%	$1,000,000
$1,250,001-1,500,000	$448,300	43%	$1,250,000
$1,500,001-$2,000,000	$555,800	45%	$1,500,000
$2,000,001-$2,500,000	$780,800	49%	$2,000,000
$2,500,001-$3,000,000	$1,025,800	53%	$2,500,000
$3,000,001-$10,000,000	$1,290,800	55%	$3,000,000

Phaseout: The tentative tax is increased by an amount equal to 5 percent of so much of the amount as exceeds $10,000,000 but does not exceed $21,255,000.

Estate and Gift Tax Unified Credit

Year	Unified Credit	Exemption Equivalent
1998	$202,050	$625,000
1999	$211,300	$650,000
2000 & 2001	$220,550	$675,000
2002 & 2003	$229,800	$700,000
2004	$287,300	$850,000
2005	$326,300	$950,000
2006 & later	$345,800	$1,000,000

Qualified Family-Owned Business Exclusion

Year	Exemption Equivalent	IRC 2033A Excludable Amount
1998	$625,000	$675,000
1999	$650,000	$650,000
2000 & 2001	$675,000	$625,000
2002 & 2003	$700,000	$600,000
2004	$850,000	$450,000
2005	$950,000	$350,000
2006 & later	$1,000,000	$300,000

INCOME TAX — 1998 Income Tax Rates

(For Returns Due in April 1999)

Single Taxpayer Rates

Over	But Not Over	Flat Amount	+%	Of Excess Over
0	$25,350	0	15%	0
$25,350	$61,400	$3,803	28%	$25,350
$61,400	$128,100	$13,897	31%	$61,400
$128,100	$278,450	$34,574	36%	$128,100
$278,450	—	$88,700	39.6%	$278,450

Married Filing Jointly Rates & Surviving Spouse

Over	But Not Over	Flat Amount	+%	Of Excess Over
0	$42,350	0	15%	0
$42,350	$102,300	$6,353	28%	$42,350
$102,300	$155,950	$23,139	31%	$102,300
$155,950	$278,450	$39,770	36%	$155,950
$278,450	—	$83,870	39.6%	$278,450

Head of Household Rates

Over	But Not Over	Flat Amount	+%	Of Excess Over
0	$33,950	0	15%	0
$33,950	$87,700	$5,093	28%	$33,950
$87,700	$142,000	$20,143	31%	$85,350
$142,000	$278,450	$36,976	36%	$142,000
$278,450	—	$86,098	39.6%	$278,450

Married Filing Separately Rates

Over	But Not Over	Flat Amount	+%	Of Excess Over
0	$21,175	0	15%	0
$21,175	$51,150	$3,176	28%	$21,175
$51,150	$77,975	$11,569	31%	$51,150
$77,975	$139,225	$19,885	36%	$77,975
$139,225	—	$41,935	39.6%	$139,225

1998 Standard Deduction Amounts

	1998 Standard Deduction
Single	$4,250
Married, filing jointly	$7,100
Married, filing separately	$3,550
Head of household	$6,250
Surviving spouse	$7,100

1998 Phaseout of Personal Exemption
Personal Exemption in 1998—$2,700

Filing Status	Threshold Phaseout Amount	Completed Phaseout After
Single	$124,500	$247,000
Married, filing jointly	$186,800	$309,300
Married, filing separately	$93,400	$154,650
Head of household	$155,650	$278,150

The rule is: If you owe more than $1,000 in taxes on your return, you will pay a penalty. However, there are exceptions. You won't have to pay a penalty if you pay 100 percent of last year's tax or 90 percent of this year's tax either by withholding money in your paycheck or by making estimated tax payments for the self-employed or persons who have investment income. If your income is more than $150,000, the rules are different, however. If you have income over and above your wages, you need to calculate how much you think the additional income will be, what the taxes will be on this amount, and whether or not you want to increase your withholding or pay estimated tax payments.

147. How do I fill out my W-4 if I want extra tax withheld?

Many times a company's human resources department wants to use the W-4 to calculate your withholding and simply indicates that someone is single or married with dependents. However, the entire purpose of the W-4 form is to help you calculate the amount of withholding you need and want on your return. Therefore, figure out the amount of your tax liability and have your employer work backwards to complete the form.

TURNING TO THE EXPERTS

148. What's the difference between a tax preparer and a tax planner?

A tax preparer's job is to prepare your tax return according to the law and to the best of that person's ability. Tax preparers generally do not give advice. A tax planner or tax adviser prepares your return and helps analyze and advise how you can save on your taxes. I have often worked with clients in the 36 percent or 39.6 percent bracket who have invested all their money in certificates of deposit instead of more lucrative tax-exempt investments, only because no one ever told them they had any other options. A tax adviser should guide you to find the best investments for your tax situation.

149. What's an enrolled agent?

An enrolled agent is a tax preparer who specializes in tax preparation. Enrolled agents must pass a four-part, twelve-hour test showing they have the knowledge required to prepare returns. Continuing education is required to maintain the "enrolled agent" designation.

150. Is a CPA the best person to prepare taxes?

A certified public accountant (CPA) is a professional who meets certain educational requirements and has passed the Uniform CPA Exam administered by the American Institute of Certified Public Accountants. CPAs must complete a certain number of continuing education courses to maintain their certification.

151. What is a tax attorney?

A tax attorney is a lawyer who has also earned a master's degree in taxation (LLM). I recommend going to a tax attorney if you are doing extensive, comprehensive estate planning or if you need advice on a complicated tax matter.

FILING STATUS

152. What is the "best" status—the one that costs me the least money—when filing a return?

The highest standard deduction (see question 160) is reserved for people who are married filing jointly; however, that standard deduction amount is for two people. The highest standard deduction for an unmarried person is for a "qualifying widow(er)," but this means your spouse must have died and you must also have a minor child. The "best" status besides qualifying widow(er) is for an individual to file as head of household because the standard deduction amount is higher than the "single" designation and the tax rates are lower.

153. How do I qualify as head of household?

To qualify to file using the head of household status, you must be single with a qualified dependent (see question 158). As usual, there is an exception to the requirement that you must be single to qualify as head of household. You may also qualify if you are legally separated, you file a separate return from your spouse, have paid at least half the cost of keeping up your home for the tax year, your spouse did not live with you *during the last six months of the tax year,* and the home was the main home for your child or stepchild for more than half the year.

154. Does it really matter whether I file as a married person or a single person? How does my filing status affect my return?

Your filing status is important in determining whether you are required to file a return, the amount of your standard deduction, and the amount of your tax liability. You usually do not have a choice of choosing among several filing statuses. If you do have a choice, choose the status that is most advantageous to your situation.

155. If my husband and I are separated, must we file as married filing separately?

No. If you have signed a formal separation agreement, you can file as a single taxpayer. If you are married but you have been *living apart for more than six months,* haven't signed a formal separation agreement and have a dependent, you may be able to file as head of household. Filing as a head of household will increase your standard deduction.

156. My husband and I are living apart but we don't have a formal separation agreement and I don't qualify as head of household. What can we do?

In this case, you would have to file as married filing separately—the most disadvantageous way to file your federal income tax return. If one spouse itemizes, the other spouse must also. You lose your child care credit. In this case, I would suggest that you both figure your tax return to see whether filing jointly or separately is more advantageous to everyone. If you can agree to file jointly and you'll save money, that's wonderful.

EXEMPTIONS

157. What is a personal exemption?

A personal exemption is the amount the IRS gives you for being alive at some time during the tax year. You even get a personal exemption on your final tax return (the year you die). You earn the exemption for yourself (unless you are claimed as a dependent on someone else's return) and you get an exemption for each dependent you claim on your return.

I receive an exemption for each of my children, since they are my dependents. To qualify as a dependent, the person must meet all five of the dependency tests. My children file their own tax returns since they have investment income over $650; however, they don't take a personal exemption on their returns since they are my dependents. You only receive one personal exemption.

158. What are the rules about being claimed as a dependent?

To be claimed as a dependent, the person must meet each of the following tests:

1. The dependent must be a relative who lives with you the entire year or an aged parent whom you care for. (If you pay more than half the costs of a parent in a nursing home, then your parent also qualifies as a dependent.)
2. Dependent must be a citizen or resident of the United States, Canada, or Mexico.
3. The dependent's gross income must be less than $2,650 per year. This doesn't apply if the dependent is a child under age nineteen or a student under age twenty-four.
4. You must provide more than 50 percent of the dependent's total support during the year.
5. Dependents may not be claimed as your dependents if they file a joint return with their spouse.

159. My ex-husband provides significant child support payments for our children. Who gets the exemptions on the tax return?

If both parents provide support, the custodial parent is considered to have provided more than half of the support, even if that person really doesn't actually provide more financial support. Thus, the custodial parent receives the dependent's personal exemption unless there is some other agreement.

If the noncustodial parent is going to claim an exemption, the custodial parent needs to sign Form 8332, Release of Claim of Exemption for Child of Divorced or Separated Parents.

DEDUCTIONS

160. What's the standard deduction?

The standard deduction is a dollar amount the IRS gives every taxpayer that reduces taxable income. Basically, the IRS is assuming that every taxpayer has about $4,000 in deductible expenses each year.

There are now limits on the standard deduction if your income is too high; however, most taxpayers can take the standard deduction. Once you have figured out your adjusted gross income, you subtract your standard deduction from this figure. This standard deduction enables many people to avoid itemizing deductions. The standard deduction is higher for people over 65, blind people, or both.

161. What are itemized deductions?

People itemize their deductions if they amount to more than their standard deduction. They list the deductions and then deduct that total from their adjusted gross income (using Schedule A).

The items that can be itemized are:

- Taxes: state and local income taxes, real estate taxes, foreign taxes, and personal property taxes
- Medical and dental expenses paid for yourself or a dependent, over 7.5 percent of one's adjusted gross income
- Interest expenses for home mortgages and home equity loan interest (there are limitations); points on purchasing a home
- Charitable contributions to tax-exempt organizations, both cash and property (within guidelines)
- Nonbusiness casualty and theft losses, such as storm damage to your home and theft of stereo equipment (amount must be more than ten percent of adjusted gross income)
- Federal estate tax on IRD income, gambling losses up to gambling winnings, impairment-related work expenses of person with disabilities.

You can deduct these expenses if they total more than 2 percent of your adjusted gross income:

- Unreimbursed car and other job-related business expenses (such as travel and entertaining)

- Educational expenses required by your employer to maintain or improve skills needed in your present job
- Professional dues, tools, uniforms, legal expenses used to collect income, tax preparation fees, and investment fees
- Cellular phone used for business
- Passport fee if the passport is for business travel
- Fees paid to your bank for a safe deposit box in which you keep taxable bonds or stock certificates
- Subscriptions to job-related magazines and newspapers and services that provide investment information or advice
- The cost of a home computer, if you can prove that the computer is required for your job

You ***can't*** deduct:

- Political contributions
- Trash collection fees
- Homeowners association charges
- Water bills (unless they are part of a business)
- Estate, inheritance, legacy, or succession taxes
- Credit card interest (except for a business)
- Car loan interest
- Interest on loans where proceeds are used to purchase tax-exempt investments
- Points if you are the seller of the property
- Interest on a loan to buy open land (without a house)

162. Is it better to take the standard mileage deduction for my business miles or should I deduct the actual expenses?

As a general rule, it is usually better to use the standard mileage rate ($.325 per mile) for business miles than to take the actual expense, including depreciation.

163. What items are included in actual car expenses for IRS purposes?

Actual vehicle expenses include the cost of insurance, gas, oil, maintenance, repairs, car registration and licensing, and so on. If you lease the car, you need to keep track of the lease payments; there is a table for depreciation allowable for each year. Actual expenses are prorated for the amount of business miles compared to total miles driven for the year. Thus, you need to read the mileage for the car on January 1 and then again on December 31.

You should figure your car expenses both ways and see which is more advantageous for your return. Remember that if you deduct actual car expenses in one year, you must continue to use this method as long as you own the car. As with all deductions for mileage, use an odometer and keep meticulous records with dates and destinations.

164. What about medical expenses?

You can deduct nonreimbursed medical expenses for yourself, your spouse, and dependents if the total is more than 7.5 percent of your adjusted gross income. This means that if your adjusted gross income is $50,000, you can start deducting medical expenses once you have spent more than $3,750. Deductible expenses would include:

- Premiums on health care insurance policies (including those for Medicare B and Medigap).
- Contact lenses and supplies.
- Health insurance premiums paid for students if the premiums are part of the tuition bill. Insurance costs must be included separately on the bill.
- Driving devices for the handicapped.
- Cost of cosmetic surgery *only* if required to correct a disfigurement caused by an accident or disfigurement that was present at birth.
- Childbirth classes.
- Weight-loss and stop-smoking programs, if recommended by your doctor.
- Remedial reading classes for a dyslexic child.
- Travel to AA meetings, if the meetings are recommended by your doctor.
- Cost of senior citizen facilities if the patient is there specifically for medical treatment.

165. I've had to modify my home because of a medical condition. Can I qualify for a tax write-off?

Yes, provided the costs (plus other unreimbursed medical expenses) exceed 7.5 percent of your adjusted gross income. This means if you built a wheelchair ramp, put in a pool to help with your severe arthritis, lowered your countertops because you're in a wheelchair, or installed an air filtration system for your allergies, you can use these as itemized medical de-

HEALTH CARE PAYMENT RECORD

YEAR _____

Patient	Date	Dr. name	Deductible satisfied?	Amount insurance paid	Date Insurance paid	Amount we paid

ductions. You can also deduct the electricity to run the air filtration system or the paint to refurbish the pool.

Remember that if the work was done in December 1998 but you don't pay for the work until January 1999, you can't deduct the expenses until you file your 1999 taxes because it's when you actually *pay* for the work that counts.

166. My adviser told me that if the improvement adds value to my home, I have to subtract that additional value from my deduction. Is this true?

Yes. You need an appraisal of your home before and after the improvement. If the modification boosts the value of your home, you can only deduct the amount the cost exceeded the increase in value. In other words, if a $5,000 air filtration system added $2,000 to the worth of your home, you can only deduct the $3,000 difference between the two. However, some improvements needed for a medical condition may actually interfere with the value of your home. In that case, you can deduct the modification but *not* the decrease in the value of the home.

167. How can I prove that I needed the improvements?

You will need to verify your condition by having your doctor write a letter saying the modification is medically necessary.

168. Can you give me an idea of what kinds of home improvements for medical disabilities are deductible?

Consult your tax adviser before making improvements, but here's an idea of possible modifications:

- Entrance/exit ramps for wheelchairs
- Door hardware
- Areas in front of entrances and exits
- Fire alarms and warning systems to accommodate deaf or hard-of-hearing
- Electrical outlets
- Doorways/hallways
- Bathrooms
- Stairways

FIGURE YOUR MEDICAL DEDUCTIONS

Cost of improvement   _____

Minus

Increase in home value   _____

Equals

Medical improvement expense   _____

Plus

Other unreimbursed medical expenses   _____

Minus

7.5% of your adjusted gross income   _____

Equals

Medical expense deduction   _____

Also, you may:

- Add handrails or grab bars
- Lower kitchen cabinets
- Install wheelchair lifts (but not usually elevators)
- Use doctor-prescribed air filtration or air conditioners

169. I was advised to "bunch" my deductions. What does that mean?

Bunching is the process of moving deductions from one tax year into another. This is a good idea if your income is higher in one year than another, if you are expecting a large bonus and you need the deductions to lower your tax liability, or you are close to the next tax bracket. Bunching your deductions is a method of tax planning.

170. Can I deduct educational expenses?

Education expenses are deductible if you spent them to maintain or improve skills required by your job or the requirements of law. For example, to maintain my licenses I need to take continuing education courses and these expenses are deductible. However, if I decide to attend law school, these expenses are not deductible.

171. Can I deduct job search expenses?

You can deduct them if you're looking for work in the same trade or business in which you're currently employed, whether or not you actually get the new job. Also deductible are any travel expenses away from home and costs such as typing, printing, copying, postage, and so on. Remember that you *can't* deduct the cost of finding a job in a different line of work.

172. How about deducting unreimbursed job expenses related to my job?

Employees are entitled to deduct certain nonreimbursed expenses (such as union dues and work clothes) as ordinary and necessary business expenses within the 2 percent limit of your adjusted income.

173. If I get a new job, are my moving expenses deductible?

Moving expenses are an adjustment to income, not a deduction. To get this adjustment, your new job must be at least fifty miles farther from your old home than the old job was. You can deduct the cost of moving your things from your old home to your new home at a rate of ten cents a mile, but you can't deduct meals, househunting expenses, or temporary living expenses. There are no limits on the amount of moving expenses.

174. When I do charitable work such as Meals on Wheels, can I deduct the miles I drive? If so, how much?

The standard charitable mileage deduction is fourteen cents a mile, plus any tolls or parking fees. You should use your odometer for each trip and keep a log sheet to document when and how far you drove.

175. How should I keep track of donations to Goodwill for tax purposes?

Gifts of property to charity are usually deductible at their current fair market value. You must ask for a receipt when you drop off your donation, showing the charity's name and a description of the property. You should also keep a list of the property you gave, along with its market value. If the fair market value is more than $500, you will need to file Form 8283 with your tax return. If the value of the property is more than $5,000, you need a formal appraisal for the gifts to satisfy the IRS.

176. Is a canceled check enough documentation to satisfy the IRS on charitable donations?

Obviously, for cash contributions you need a receipt from the charity. A canceled check will satisfy the IRS unless your gift to a specific charity is more than $250—then you need a written acknowledgment from the charity. This documentation can be a receipt, letter or card, or computer-generated form.

177. Can I deduct work I do for a charity?

No, you can only deduct the donations you provide the charity or the mileage you drove doing service for the organization.

178. Can I deduct gifts I give to individuals who need help, such as blankets or clothes to help a family after their home has burned down?

Contributions made to or for an individual are not deductible. Usually a charitable organization can earmark money you give for a specific purpose (such as to buy blankets for a needy family); then the contribution is deductible.

CHARITABLE DONATIONS RECORD

CASH CONTRIBUTIONS

Charity	Check#	Date	Amount

NONCASH CONTRIBUTIONS

Charity	Check#	Date	Amount

179. Are tax adviser and tax preparation fees deductible?

You can deduct any fees you pay to have your tax return prepared. You would list these fees on line 21 of Schedule A under Miscellaneous Expenses.

180. How about investment management fees?

You can deduct the fees of a financial planner. Expenses related to investments that are ordinary and necessary for the production or collection of income, or for the management, conservation, or maintenance of property are deductible.

Home office expenses allocated to nonbusiness investment activities are deductible as are the costs of seminars, conventions, and so forth. These expenses must be allocated between tax-exempt and taxable income because the expenses associated with tax-free income are not deductible.

181. How about deducting medical miles—driving to and from the hospital for chemotherapy?

You can itemize transportation expenses up to ten cents a mile for mileage, tolls, parking fees, plus plane or train fare. You should use an odometer and a log book with dates and destinations. As with all medical deductions, you can't claim these deductions unless they total more than 7.5 percent of your adjusted gross income.

182. What exactly is depreciation?

When property (such as a car or rental property) is used to produce income, the law generally gives you a tax deduction to recover some or all of the purchase price. The IRS has schedules that outline the "life" of the property; you depreciate it over the scheduled period of years.

Depreciation is really a form of tax *deferral*. If you depreciate a car you use for business, for example, and then sell it, you may have to pay income taxes on the money you earn from selling the car if you make a profit.

183. If I work out of my home, can I deduct expenses?

Working at home for convenience is not deductible. I often work at home because one of my children is sick, or for the convenience of my clients, but I can't deduct home office expenses because the portion of the house I use for business is not exclusively nor regularly used for business. I have an office outside my home and only work at home for convenience. If you aren't self-employed and you want to deduct home office expenses, your home office must be for the convenience of your employer.

If you have an office in a room of your home used only for business, and that is your only office, you can deduct a portion of the utilities and the real estate taxes. You also can depreciate a portion of the costs of your home.

There have been many court cases fought over the home office expense deduction during the past few years. Although the rules have been eased beginning in 1998, as a general rule the deduction is only permitted if your home office is your *only* place of business.

184. Is student loan interest deductible?

The Taxpayer Relief Act of 1997 allows taxpayers who pay interest on certain higher education loans for themselves or their spouses to deduct interest paid during the first sixty months in which interest payments are required on the loan. The amount of deduction increases from $1,000 in 1998 to $2,500 in the year 2001 and after. The interest deduction is available to taxpayers whether or not they itemize their other deductions. Married couples must file a joint return in order to claim the deduction. There are income limitations to the deduction.

185. Can I deduct the gifts to my grandchildren from my taxes?

No. The person who got the gift doesn't have to pay taxes on it, and so the person who gave the gift can't deduct it either. However, if you give more than $10,000 to anyone in one year, you must file a gift tax return. The gift is not reported on any income tax form.

186. To sell my home, my wife and I had to pay several of the points towards the buyer's mortgage. Is that an itemized deduction?

The buyer can deduct the points paid by the seller the year the house is purchased, as if they paid the points, but must lower the cost basis of the property by the amount of points paid by the seller. The seller cannot deduct the points paid as interest. The points paid are only used as an amount to lower the capital gain realized on the property.

CREDITS

187. What is the difference between a deduction and a credit?

A deduction is considered above the line and a credit is below the line. What this means is that a deduction *lowers* your income. By lowering your income, you are lowering the amount on which tax is assessed. A credit is a direct lowering of the *income tax* that you owe. Thus, you're better off with a credit than with a deduction.

188. What is the new Child Tax Credit?

As of 1998, taxpayers can claim a tax credit for each qualifying child. The credit is $400 per child in 1998, $500 per child in 1999 and beyond. A qualifying child is one who is the taxpayer's child and dependent, under the age of seventeen by December 31, and a U.S. citizen (a national or legal resident). As with so many of the credits and deductions, there are income limits to this credit, and if you exceed the income limit, the credit is phased out.

189. What is the Child and Dependent Care Credit?

The IRS is giving you credit for money you have to spend to care for your family while you work. The Child and Dependent Care Credit is a credit for money you paid to someone to care for your child under age thirteen, or for your spouse or dependent who is not able to care for themselves. Based on income, the credit may cover up to 30 percent of the amount paid to the provider to a limit of $2,400 per dependent. (The limit is $4,800 for two or more dependents.) You must list your provider's Tax Identification Number or Social Security Number on the return if you want to get credit.

190. What happens if my care provider will not provide me with her Social Security Number so I can claim the Child Care Credit?

Your sitter can't legally withhold this information from you, although this often occurs. You can either lose a good sitter or not report the expenses.

If your provider refuses to divulge her number, you can complete Form 2441 (the credit form) as best you can and then in Part II of the form, explain that the provider refuses to provide the necessary information.

191. My employer provides Dependent Care Credit through my work. Which credit is better?

If an employer pays you or your provider for dependent care expenses through a qualified plan, this may be excluded in your W-2 amount of reportable income. This money comes off the top and is not taxed. This is known as using pre-tax dollars to pay for child care. If your employer has a qualified dependent care credit benefits program, I recommend you calculate both methods of taking the credit and review which is best for you. Usually, the IRS credit is most helpful to lower-income workers, while the company benefits program is more advantageous to higher wage earners. Only figuring the credit both ways will answer which is best for your situation.

192. What is the HOPE credit?

Starting in 1998, a new HOPE scholarship credit will be available against income taxes to be used for tuition and related expenses paid for a student's first two years of postsecondary education at an eligible institution. The student must be at least a half-time student during at least one academic period during the year. Subject to income limitations, the credit is 100 percent of the first $1,000 of expenses that were paid during the year, plus 50 percent of the next $1,000 paid—a maximum credit of $1,500.

193. What is the Lifetime Learning Credit?

Postsecondary education expenses that don't qualify for the HOPE scholarship credit may be eligible for the Lifetime Learning Credit. This credit is available for certain tuition and related expenses for courses to help you acquire or improve job skills. The credit is equal to 20 percent of expenses up to $5,000 (rising to $10,000 after 2003). You can take this credit to cover expenses for academic periods beginning after June 30, 1998.

194. I mentioned my high tax bracket to my broker and he recommended a tax shelter credit investment. What are the pros and cons of this?

Tax Advantaged Investments (tax shelter credit investments) changed dramatically in 1986. Basically, what we're talking about is purchasing low-income property. When you buy low-income property, you receive a credit on your tax that is usually considerable. It's a specialized, nonliquid asset, and you should only buy such a property knowing that it won't be very liquid and that there may be long-term tax consequences. The investment usually must be held for fifteen years. The government has rules about what property is considered low-income, and the broker who puts the deal together usually makes sure that the property qualifies. Tax Shelter Credit Investments should be reviewed by an independent accountant (one not associated with the broker's firm), and all pros and cons should be reviewed before you buy. Remember that this is an investment. Look at it from an investor's point of view, not just for the tax advantages.

INCOME, BENEFITS, AND CAPITAL GAINS

195. What is my adjusted gross income?

Adjusted gross income is the amount of taxable income you have left after you subtract the adjustments, including IRA contributions, moving expenses, self-employed health insurance premiums, Keogh/SEP contributions, alimony you paid, and penalties on early withdrawals of savings interest.

196. Are child support payments taxable?

Child support is not taxable; the person paying the support can't deduct the payments from his or her income.

197. My husband pays me alimony. Do I have to pay taxes on that money?

Yes. Alimony is a payment to a spouse under a divorce or separation agreement for spousal support, not for child support. You must pay taxes on the money from your husband, and he can deduct the payments from his income. On the other hand, child support is not taxable. If you are the custodial parent, you receive the exemption for the children, even if the other parent pays more than 50 percent for their support. This is why some people may prefer larger child support payments rather than big alimony checks. But keep in mind that child support stops at age eighteen.

198. My son received a scholarship for college tuition. Is this taxable?

You don't need to include scholarship funds in your gross income if the money was used for tuition, books, and fees. However, any funds used for room and board must be included.

199. I recently received money from a life insurance policy. Is this taxable?

No. Death benefits from a life insurance policy are not taxable. You would owe taxes on any interest earned on the funds from the date of death until you received the money.

200. What happens if you give more than $10,000 to an individual in one year?

If you give more than $10,000 a year to another individual, you must file Form 709 (Gift Tax Return) at the same time as your individual income tax return is filed —usually by April 15 of the year following the gift. The gift is not taxable income to the recipient.

201. Can I give dividends from my AT&T bond to my granddaughter?

You can't give away income earned on an investment to another person in order to lower your tax bracket. Of course, you can give your granddaughter the money, but you as the owner of the investment will be taxed on the funds—not the one who receives the gift.

202. I have a custodial account for my child. How is the income from a custodial account taxed?

A custodial account is an account for a child and managed by a custodian—usually a parent. Tax due on income from the custodial account is reported by the child. If the child is less than fifteen years of age, the first $650 of income is not taxed, the next $650 is taxed at the child's income tax bracket, and any income earned above $1,300 is taxed at the parents' income tax bracket. Once the child reaches age fifteen, all income earned on the custodial account is taxed at the child's bracket. The child's social security number should be on the account.

203. I earn a small income from Social Security. Are my Social Security benefits taxed?

Figuring out the taxable portion of your Social Security benefits is somewhat complicated. The government decides if you need to pay taxes on your Social Security by comparing your actual income—Social Security plus any other income you may have—to a standard base amount of income. If you make more than this base amount, you'll have to pay taxes on your social security. The government's base amount is $25,000 for single persons, head of household, or married persons filing separately (who must have lived apart for the entire year). It's $32,000 for married persons, filing jointly. In deciding whether or not you need to pay taxes on your Social Security, you take half of your Social Security benefits and add to this all your other taxable income (pensions, interest dividends, and so on) and then add all tax-exempt income. If this total is less than the designated base amount, none of your Social Security benefits are taxable. If the total is more than the government's base amount, you must continue on the worksheet to calculate the taxable portion of your Social Security benefits.

204. Should I invest so that my total income is less than the base amount, and thus my Social Security benefits are not taxable?

Income tax planning is an integral part of everyone's investment planning, particularly with the new capital gains rules. You *can* lower your income below the government's set base amount by using deferred annuities or tax-exempt investments, but each of these investments has pros and cons. Thus, before you take this step, you need to take into consideration your current and future income, the investments you have, and the investments you are planning to use to achieve your goal.

205. How are my disability benefits taxed?

Generally, you must report as income any disability benefit received from an insurance company paid for by your employer. If you paid for disability insurance (see question 327) yourself, then the disability benefits you receive are *not* taxable. If you shared the cost of the disability insurance with your employer, you only pay income taxes on part of the disability income. Social Security disability payments are only taxed once your income reaches the base amount. There is a credit for the elderly or disabled if income is under a specified limit.

206. How come I have capital gains on my municipal bond fund?

Although the income earned on municipal bonds is not generally taxed, any increase in value over your original cost when you sell the bonds *is* taxable. Therefore, if you buy a municipal bond for $9,000 and sell it for $10,000, you have a capital gain of $1,000. You'll have to pay tax on that amount.

207. What is the capital gains tax on a house?

If you buy a house for $100,000 and sell it for $200,000, you have made $100,000 profit—or a capital gain. When the government steps in and taxes you on this gain, it's called a capital gains tax.

208. How can I avoid paying capital gains taxes when I sell my home?

The Taxpayer Relief Act of 1997 made tremendous changes in the capital gains taxes you pay on the sale of your house. The new law says that you can take a $500,000 exclusion if your tax status is married filing jointly, or a $250,000 exclusion for married filing separately, single, or head of household.

This deferral is available to *everyone* of any age every two years for property held *at least* two of the last five years and used as a principal residence. What this means is that if you bought a house for $100,000 and sold it for $200,000, your capital gains would be only $100,000 and you wouldn't owe any capital gains taxes. You can continue to do this every two years. The downside: You may be required to pay a capital gains tax if you sell your home within two years. There is an exclusion for gains on a home within two years if sale is due to ill health, relocation due to a job, or other unforeseen circumstances. Also, new law permits proration of gain if sold within two years.

This new law is a great benefit to empty nesters who can now downsize their homes without paying capital gains taxes. Remember that you will still need to keep records for your state capital gains rules or possible casualty losses or depreciation.

209. Do I owe capital gains on my house if I sell the house when I am 62?

There is no age limitation for capital gains exclusion under the new law for homes sold after May 6, 1997. If you sold your house before August 5,

1997, you would have a choice of which format you wish to report the sale on your 1997 1040. The onetime exclusion for sales on a personal residence after July 26, 1978 disappeared with the Taxpayer Relief Act of 1997. The taxpayer now has an exclusion on every residence he or she sells, if held more than two years.

210. How does separation or divorce affect the exclusion?

If you are married but file a separate return from your spouse, you only have an exclusion of $250,000 for your capital gains. If you file jointly, you have the $500,000 exclusion.

211. What is the cost basis of property inherited from my mother?

The term cost basis for property that one inherits is usually the fair market value of the property on the date of the person's death. If you filed a federal estate tax return, the basis is on the return. If you didn't file a federal estate tax return, the basis is the appraised value of the property, as stated on the state inheritance tax return.

212. How do I keep track of the cost basis of my home?

You should give your tax preparer your purchase and sale settlement sheets along with any capital expenditures that will give the preparer the information needed if you sell your home.

213. What is the difference between short-term and long-term gains and losses?

The government defines a short-term gain or loss on property sold that was owned for a year or less. Long-term property is held more than one year.

214. I understand that the capital gains rules on investments have changed significantly. Is this correct?

As a general rule, for sales or exchanges of property, the maximum that a taxpayer can now pay for long-term capital gains has dropped from 28 percent to 20 percent. For property sold after July 29, 1997 but before January 1, 1998, you must have held the property for eighteen months to get the 20 percent capital gain tax rate. If you sold the property sooner than that, the rate remains at 28 percent.

HOMEOWNER'S TAXSAVER

Owner's Name(s) _____

Property Location or Description _____

Date of Purchase _____

Original Cost of Property $ _____

Closing Costs You Paid at Time of Purchase
(Itemize, and keep your closing papers.)

Sales Commissions _____

Title Insurance _____

Recording Fees _____

Legal Fees _____

Appraisal Fees _____

Survey Fees _____

_____

_____

_____

_____

_____

Seller-paid Points (if bought after 4-3-94) _____

Seller-paid Points you deducted (if bought before 4-4-94) _____

Amount Claimed as Moving Expense (pre-1994 moves) _____

Permanent Additions Since Purchase

Date	Description of Addition (Keep receipts)	Cost[†]
____	New Roof	$ ____
____	Storm Windows	____
____	Doors	____
____	Insulation	____
____	Carpets	____
____	Patios and Decks	____
____	Remodeling	____
____	Landscaping	____
____		____
____		____
____		____
____		____
____		____
____		____
____		____
____		____
____		____
____		____

[†]Include labor paid to others, but not your own labor.

Residential Energy Credit Claimed

Be sure to list the cost of these improvements on the front of this Home-owner's Taxsaver. The federal residential energy credit expired in 1985, but any credits claimed prior to expiration will affect your basis in your home.

19 _____ $ _____

19 _____ _____

19 _____ _____

19 _____ _____

19 _____ _____

Special Assessments

Curbs _____ $ _____

Sewers _____ _____

Street Paving _____ _____

_____ _____

_____ _____

Basis of Previous Residence

If you sold a residence before purchasing the residence described on the front of this Homeowner's Taxsaver, complete the following (or attach a copy of the Form 2119 that was completed when the previous residence was sold):

Sales Price (Date Sold _____) $ _____

Original Cost of Residence _____

Sales Commission Paid _____

Improvements _____

Depreciation Claimed _____

Gain Deferred Previously _____

Purchase Expenses Claimed as Moving Expense _____

Other (Describe) _____ _____

Seller-paid Points (if purchased after 4-3-94) _____

Seller-paid Points deducted (if purchased before 4-4-94) _____

_____ _____

_____ _____

Fixing-Up Expenses

Expenses of fixing up property for sale incurred within 90 days before the date of sale and paid no later than 30 days after the date of sale (itemize):

Date Work Performed	Date Paid	Description	Amount

Capital Gains Tax Rates

Personal Tax Bracket	Type of Asset	Holding Period	
		12 months or less	More than 12 months
All brackets	Personal residence	----- Special rules apply. -----	
28% or above	Most capital assets	Ordinary income rate	20%[A]
	Collectibles	Ordinary income rate	28%
15%	Most capital assets	15%	10%[B]
	Collectibles	15%	15%

[A]Rate decreases to 18% for assets *purchased* after December 31, 2000, and held for five years

[B]Rate decreases to 8% for assets *sold* after December 31, 2000, and held for at least five years.

NOTE: Special rules also apply to qualified small business stock held more than five years and to long-term gains on depreciated real estate.

215. One of my stocks became worthless. How can I take the loss on my return?

If one of your securities becomes worthless, the government assumes it has become worthless on the last day of the year. December 31 is then used as the security sale date to determine if the stock is a short-term or long-term loss. Your loss is the total amount you paid for the stock. It might be advisable to get a third party letter that states your stock is worthless.

216. How is the accrued interest earned on my EE bonds taxed?

Generally, EE bond interest is reported when the bonds are cashed in. You can choose to report the income annually so that you don't have so great an income tax liability when you redeem the bonds. You can change methods of reporting the income on your EE bonds. Changing from deferral to taxation of the income does not require permission from the IRS, though the accrued interest to date must be reported in the year of the change. Changing from taxing the income to deferral requires permission from the IRS, using Form 3115. Permission is automatic if you use the form.

217. How do states tax the income on EE bonds?

It is illegal for states to tax interest earned on Treasury bonds. Thus, the income on EE and HH bonds is not taxed for state tax purposes.

218. My EE bonds have matured, but I don't want to redeem them now because of the large amount of deferred income. Do I have another option?

Accrued interest on E or EE bonds, if traded for HH bonds, continues to be deferred until the HH bonds mature or are redeemed. HH bonds are savings bonds that pay interest semiannually directly deposited into a checking account. If you have bought EE bonds through your employer for years and are ready to retire, it's a good idea to trade them for HH bonds rather than be taxed on the entire accrued amount now. Interest paid on an HH bond issued in January will be paid in January and July, a February bond will pay in February and August, and so forth throughout the year. Therefore, I recommend you take the E bonds you want to trade into HH bonds to your local bank in six increments so you have a monthly check throughout the year. Then you can plan if or when you cash in the bonds and pay tax on the accrued interest. The problem with accrued interest on EE and HH bonds is that the liability for the tax on the accrued interest never goes away. The tax is owed by the decedent, the decedent's estate, or the heirs who receive the bonds. Thus, if you are in a nursing home or other situation where your income is lower, you might want to cash them in so your heirs won't have to pay tax on the bonds.

219. How is the income taxed on my EE and HH bonds if both my father and I own the bonds with joint ownership?

The person who bought the bond is usually the one who pays income tax on it when it is cashed in, even if the bond is given to the other co-owner to cash and that person keeps all the money from the sale. If both people pooled their money to buy the bonds, then the tax would be proportionally shared among the co-owners.

220. My mother is dying of cancer in a nursing home and is receiving money as living needs (accelerated death benefits) from her insurance policy. Is this taxable?

If a physician has ruled that your mother is terminally ill (with a condition that is expected to be fatal within twenty-four months) the accelerated death benefits received by your mother are not taxable.

221. Is my sick pay taxed?

Yes. Sick pay is money you earn instead of your regular wages while you are temporarily away from work due to sickness or personal injury. If your sick pay comes from an accident or health plan in which your employer doesn't participate, the benefits aren't considered sick pay and usually aren't taxable. If you are going to be getting sick pay from your job for a period of time, make sure your company withholds taxes from the checks (they don't have to) or you may have to pay a big tax bill at the end of the year.

"WHAT IFS" AND SPECIAL SITUATIONS

222. We've just adopted a child. Are there any special expenses we can claim?

Beginning in 1997, you could claim a tax credit of up to $5,000 in adoption-related expenses.

223. I called the IRS with a question and got wrong advice. What recourse do I have?

The IRS isn't perfect; they can make mistakes. If you call them with a question, be sure to take notes while you're talking to them to protect yourself if you get audited. Be sure to include the date, the IRS employee's name, your questions, and how the IRS answered them. Keep those notes together with a copy of your completed return.

224. If I file jointly with my husband, am I responsible for any wrongdoing on the tax forms?

Both of you may be held responsible, together and alone, for the tax and any interest or penalty due. Even if all the income was earned by your husband, if there is a problem on the form you may be held responsible for all the tax due. However, there is an innocent spouse exception. You must prove that you didn't know and had no reason to know that your spouse substantially understated tax due, either by omitting income or claiming a deduction or credit that wasn't permitted. Don't get yourself in such a situation. Don't just sign the tax return. Since you are responsible for your tax return, know your business, accountant, and the source of your income.

225. I was forced to take money out of my IRA to pay bills. Will this affect my taxes?

One of the most frustrating aspects of doing tax returns is that people don't realize there is a 10 percent penalty on early withdrawals from IRAs. Many people withdraw from their IRAs for vacations, living expenses, or a new car. Then they pay income tax on the money they withdrew. In addition to that, you will also pay a penalty for early withdrawal—10 percent on the withdrawal amount. This means that if you withdraw $15,000, you'll pay a $1,500 penalty that will be added to the bottom line of your tax liability. It is exorbitant and very greatly misunderstood, particularly when people take out the money because they need to pay bills and then they don't have the money at tax time to pay the income tax and penalty. Most banks withhold 20 percent tax on the early withdrawal and people assume that will cover their tax liability. However, if you are in a 28 percent bracket, you haven't withheld enough to cover your tax liability or withheld the 10 percent penalty.

226. So what should I do if I need the money?

You shouldn't withdraw IRA funds before age fifty-nine and a half. If you must withdraw the money, make sure the bank withholds enough tax, plus the penalty. If you withdrew $15,000 and are in the 28 percent bracket, make sure the bank withholds the $4,200 income tax due, plus the $1,500 penalty—a total of $5,700.

227. Aren't there new IRA withdrawal rules?

Beginning in 1998, the government will allow you to withdraw funds early from IRAs in some new situations. Now you can withdraw IRA funds early, without penalty, in these cases:

- You become disabled
- To cover first-time home buying expenses up to $10,000
- To cover qualified higher education expenses of you the taxpayer, your spouse, or any of your children or grandchildren for education obtained after 1997. Expenses aren't limited to tuition but include fees, books, room and board, and equipment.

228. How can I prepare for an audit?

Remember that the tax auditor is not necessarily a tax expert. It's a stressful, often unpleasant job and many auditors are young and inexperienced. They may well be unaware of the subtle tax intricacies in the tax code. You may well have the upper hand in the knowledge department, especially if you work with an experienced tax adviser, many of whom know more about taxes than the average IRS auditor. There are a number of ways to prepare:

- Gather all the documentation that you have for your return. Don't wait until the last minute to get your receipts in order.
- Get a CPA or enrolled agent to go with you. Bringing along expert help will cost you money, but it can save you time, stress, and maybe even more money.
- You only need to document those areas the audit notice mentions. You don't need to document parts of your return that are not audited.
- Make it as easy as possible for the auditor to review your materials. Be as organized as you can; don't dump your paperwork in a pile on the auditor's desk.
- Be polite. Remember that how you conduct yourself may have a bearing on how you fare during the audit.
- If your auditor intends to disallow something, or asks you to pay more and you don't agree:
    ✓ Disagree once, politely. If the auditor doesn't see it your way, don't persist.

✓ State your case later to your auditor's boss.
✓ If you work your way up the IRS as far as you can go without satisfaction, you can go to tax court and fight there.

DEFERRING TAXES

229. How can I avoid income taxes?

There is tax avoidance and tax evasion. Tax evasion is against the law. Evading, dodging, or not paying taxes you owe is illegal. You can avoid taxes by:

- deferring income into another year;
- directing money into retirement accounts—401(k), 403(b), SEP-IRAs, or Keoghs; or
- investing in tax-free money market funds and bonds.

230. What's the difference between tax-deferred and tax-free investments?

There are only two ways to avoid paying current income tax:

1. You can own assets that pay tax-exempt income. The best known of these is municipal bonds. The income from municipal bonds generally is not subject to taxation.
2. You can defer tax liability until later. Unfortunately, deferral does not mean tax free; you will have to pay the piper down the road. Deferral usually makes sense because you will most likely be paying taxes at a time in your life when your income tax bracket is lower, because your retirement income is lower than your current income.

231. How can I defer taxes?

You can defer taxes by investing in:

- deferred compensation;
- deferred annuities;
- IRAs;
- 401(k) savings; or
- depreciation on real estate and real estate investments (via limited partnerships).

232. Is there a better time of the year to buy a house for tax purposes?

You should always be thinking about tax planning. Unfortunately, I often see clients who buy a home in late November assuming they will have a big refund. This isn't always true. When you get a mortgage, you pay the bank points (often called loan origination fees or prepaid interest). Points are deductible as long as the amount you paid at settlement at least equals the amount of the points. Where I live, three points are normal when acquiring a mortgage; I would pay $2,400 in points on an $80,000 mortgage. This fee is deductible along with any interest paid on the mortgage for the year, charitable deductions, and all other itemized deductions. However, the government requires that your deductions be more than the standard deduction amount if you want to itemize deductions. If you only have points and paid a small amount of interest because your house was purchased near the end of the year, you probably won't be able to deduct the points. On the other hand, if you buy a home in the early part of the year, you have paid the points and interest for the entire year and will probably be able to deduct the money.

233. What is income shifting?

If you know you're getting a bonus and you can choose to receive it in December or January, look ahead. If you think you'll be making more money in the next year, you can shift your income by choosing to get the money in December so you'll have to pay less taxes.

TAX INFORMATION CARD

FOR THE YEAR _____

INCOME

INTEREST

Payer	AMT

Bring all statements showing interest, dividends, and other income.

DIVIDENDS

Payer	AMT	Payer	AMT

OTHER INCOME

TYPE OF INCOME	AMOUNT
Alimony	
Income from Self-Employment or Farm Activities	
Pensions & Annuities	
Royalties	
Estates & Trusts (bring Schedules K-1)	
Jury Duty	
Gambling or Lottery Winnings	
Partnership Distributions (bring Schedules K-1)	
S Corporation Distributions (bring Schedules K-1)	

TYPE OF INCOME	AMOUNT
Tips	
Prizes & Awards	
Hobby	
Commissions	
State/Local Tax Refund	
Federal Tax Refund	
Unemployment Compensation	
Social Security/Railroad Retirement	
IRA/Retirement Plan/Annuity Distributions	

GAINS & LOSSES FROM SALES OF PROPERTY

DESCRIPTION	DATE ACQUIRED	DATE SOLD	SALES PRICE	COST (OR OTHER BASIS)

RENTAL

GROSS INCOME

	Amount	Amount

EXPENSES

	Amount
Advertising	
Auto – Travel	
Cleaning – Maintenance	
Janitor – Yard Work	
Trash Hauling	
Pest Control	
Commissions	
Insurance	
Legal and Professional Fees	
Management Fees	
Mortgage Interest	
Other Interest	
Repairs – Improvements	
Carpentry	
Decorating – Painting	
Electrical	
Furnace/Air Conditioning	
Plumbing	
Roofing	
Supplies	
Tax Preparation	
Taxes	
Telephone	
Utilities	
Other	

TAX-RELATED DEDUCTIONS & CREDITS

MEDICAL

Item	Amount
Insulin & Medicines (Prescription Only)	
Reimbursement (Medicines)	
Medical Insurance Premiums	
Dr.	
Dr.	
Dr.	
Dr.	
Dr.	
Dentist	
Dentist	
Hospital	
Hospital	
Lab Fees	
Eye Exams	
Glasses & Contact Lenses	
Hearing Aids & Batteries	
Medical Supplies	
Transportation	
Lodging (while away from home overnight)	
Other	
Reimbursement (Other Medical)	

TAXES

Item	Amount
Federal Income Tax Balance Paid	

Federal Quarterly Estimates

Date:	
Amount:	

Item	Amount
State/Local Income Tax Balance Paid	

State Quarterly Estimates

Date:	
Amount:	

Item	Amount
Personal Property — State	
Personal Property — Local	
Real Estate — State	
Real Estate — Local	
City Earnings/Occupation	
Intangibles	

Business/State Tax Deductions and Credits

Item	Amount
Political Contributions	
Energy Conservation	
Auto License — State/City	
Rent	
Other (list)	

INTEREST

Item	Amount
Home Mortgage	
Investment	

LOSSES FROM FIRE, LIGHTNING, WIND, WATER, CAR ACCIDENTS, & THEFT

Item	Amount
Reimbursements	

Car Odometer Reading		
1/1		12/31
1/1		12/31

CONTRIBUTIONS

Item	Amount
Birth Defects	
Cancer	
Religious Organizations	
Disabled Children	
Goodwill Industries	
Heart	
Muscular Dystrophy	
Red Cross	
Salvation Army	
Scouts Boy/Girl	
United Way Campaign	
Other (list)	

VOLUNTEER WORK EXPENSES

Item	Amount
Supplies	
Uniforms	
Transportation	

CONTRIBUTIONS OTHER THAN CASH

Item	Date	Fair Market Value	Orig. Cost/Basis
Clothing			
Furniture			
Other (list)			

OTHER DEDUCTIONS

Item	Amount
Forfeited Interest (Bring 1099INT)	
Individual Retirement Accounts	
Keogh/SEP Plans	
Alimony Paid	
Moving Expenses	
Investment Expenses	
Safe Deposit Box	
Gambling or Lottery Losses	
Tax Return Expenses	
Medical Savings Account Contributions	

EMPLOYEE BUSINESS EXPENSE

Item	Amount
Auto	
Education	
Entertainment and Meals	
Job Seeking Expenses	
Professional Dues, Publications	
Qualified Office in Home	
Safety Equipment	
Supplies, Gifts, etc.	
Telephone (Business Use)	
Tools/Equipment	
Travel and Lodging	
Uniforms — Cost/Cleaning	
Union Dues	
Vocational Supplies	

CHILD & DEPENDENT CARE CREDIT

Amount	Name and Address of Provider	SSN/EIN

CHAPTER 4

INSURANCE

Insurance is a way to reduce risk by sharing financial losses within a group of people. There are many types of risks which can be either financial or nonfinancial, including: personal (disability or death), property loss, liability, risk from the failure of others (breach of contract), and speculative risks (the stock market). You must decide if the protection is worth the cost of the insurance. Many types of insurance are required. If you have a mortgage, your lender requires you to have homeowner's insurance for their protection, just as it's mandatory in most states to have auto insurance. In addition to required insurance, you must decide what coverage you need for your family and at what cost. Riders, options, and basic insurance itself all come at a cost so you need to review the price and the coverage as part of your total financial picture. You may be able to provide your own insurance for many types of risk by putting the funds aside on your own, such as money to pay dental bills, a nursing home stay, and so on.

INSURANCE 101

234. Where is the best place to buy insurance?

I recommend you review the insurance coverage provided by your employer. It's important when you start a new job that you understand both the salary and benefits. Disability, health, and life insurance are often provided and should be a base from which you build your coverage. Once you know your current coverage, you should locate a well-respected agent with a good insurance company. The agent should be designated both as a CLU (Certified Life Underwriter) and a ChFC (Chartered Financial Consultant). These initials are the best designations available in the insurance industry and are a sign of education and ethics.

235. How do I know if the insurance company my agent recommends is a good company?

Insurance companies are rated by five services: A.M. Best & Co., Duff & Phelps, Standard & Poor's, Moody's, and the newest—Weiss Research. *Consumers Report, Financial World,* and other financial magazines usually offer an annual listing of the top-rated companies. Some companies are tougher raters than others: Weiss Research is tough; A.M. Best & Co. gives more higher grades. Two or three credit ratings will give you a good idea of how sound your company is. You can get the current rating information for free from your agent. You should review the material and check on them yourself. Buying an insurance policy is an investment. Take the time for this that you do for your other investments.

236. What's your best advice about insurance?

Don't overestimate your risk and buy too much of the wrong kind of coverage. You do this whenever you buy plane crash insurance, when you take out a policy on healthy children, or when elderly people buy funeral insurance.

What you want to do is buy coverage to protect yourself against a broad range of risk with enough protection to insure what you can't afford to cover yourself.

237. What types of insurance should I avoid?

Don't bother insuring yourself against losses that would not be catastrophic for you. In general, if the policy doesn't cost much, it doesn't cover much. Here are a few to avoid:

- *Extended warranties:* Product manufacturers' warranties usually cover problems up to the first year. If you have to pay for a repair yourself, odds are that it won't be catastrophic.
- *Dental insurance:* Unless your employer throws this one in for free, it's not a good investment. Dental coverage usually only includes a few teeth cleanings a year and severely limits the expensive procedures.
- *Package insurance:* This doesn't cost much, but in general the U.S. Postal Service rarely loses or damages things.
- *Contact lens insurance:* You can buy contact lenses through the mail for less than the cost of this insurance.
- *Credit card insurance:* Buying a special policy to pay off your credit card debt if you die is extremely expensive because the benefit is so small. A good life insurance policy is a much better bet.

238. Do I have a grace period on missing an insurance policy payment?

Insurance companies permit, by contract, a thirty-day grace period on life insurance policies. Variable life insurance is a little longer and they have separate rules. After a premium payment is ten days late, the company sends out a late notice.

Auto and homeowner's coverage **do not** provide a grace period. Particularly on auto coverage, you don't want to be late in case you have an accident. The company can cancel you for nonpayment of premium. It's a good idea to have the premiums withdrawn from your savings or checking accounts so you know they are paid.

239. My husband has a cafeteria plan at work. What is this and how does it work?

A cafeteria insurance plan allows employees to choose among many options for their insurance needs (one of which must be cash). Noncash choices fall within the parameters of the employer's plan to meet the personal needs of each employee. With so many two-career couples, overlapping insurance benefits are common. Thus, if a couple's medical coverage is provided by the husband's employer, the wife—through her cafeteria plan—could opt out of health coverage and purchase extra disability or life insurance benefits.

LIFE INSURANCE AND ANNUITIES

240. How much life insurance should I have?

Your life insurance should protect your survivors with a replacement for your income or the caretaking services you provide. Generally, you should have life insurance to equal five times your salary to give your family what they need. Prepare a balance sheet by figuring out all your assets and liabilities, calculate money needed for your children's college expenses, survivors' living expenses, and so on.

241. Should I have term or whole life insurance?

If you have young children, buy term insurance which you can cancel when your children no longer need your support. Whole (or universal) life insurance generally requires you to pay higher premiums for years longer

Amount of Life Insurance Needed to Provide a Certain Monthly Income (at 3.5% interest)

Desired Monthly Income in dollars	10 Years	15 Years	20 Years
100	10,173	14,085	17,391
200	20,346	28,170	34,782
300	30,519	42,255	52,173
400	40,692	56,340	69,564
500	50,865	70,425	86,955
1,000	101,730	140,850	173,910
2,000	203,460	281,700	347,820
3,000	305,190	422,550	521,730
5,000	508,650	704,250	869,550

than you may need insurance protection. While many insurance brokers try to convince people that whole life is a good investment, your money will do better invested elsewhere. Half of all whole life buyers drop their policies within five years and never realize much buildup of equity. A $250,000 whole life insurance policy for a thirty-nine-year-old healthy woman costs about $3,220 compared to about $300 for a ten-year renewable level-term policy for a healthy thirty-nine-year-old woman.

242. What does renewable term insurance mean?

The renewable term contract requires that the policy *may* be renewed at the *option of the insured* for another term of equal length. This is an important option if the insurance purchased is a necessity (such as to provide college funds), if a parent dies, or if the purchaser becomes uninsurable. Obviously, this type of coverage is costlier than a regular term policy. This protection is the only way I would purchase a term policy because you never know if you will become uninsurable.

243. What does level term mean?

A term insurance policy becomes more expensive each year because as you get older there is a greater chance that the insurance company will have to pay a death benefit. Purchasers like to know how much the policy will cost for a certain period of time; in level term, the insurance company guarantees that the annual insurance premium will be the same for a specified period, such as ten years.

244. If insurance gets more expensive as you age, how does whole life/ cash value type insurance work?

Whole life policies provide insurance coverage for the entire life of the insured. If you buy this type of policy for yourself, you can borrow against the policy as interest accrues. Because you pay a higher premium in the early years for this type of policy than you would on a term policy, money builds up within the policy to pay the premium in future years when the insurance becomes more expensive.

On a cash value policy, the insurance company has calculated a fixed premium payment that guarantees the policy will continue throughout your lifetime. This type of insurance policy costs more than a term policy in the early years of the contract; however, good policies with good companies should provide dividends that can pay the premiums so the policy pays for itself in future years.

245. My sister has a variable life insurance policy. Is this better than my whole life policy?

Better is a difficult word to define. A whole life policy is like a Certificate of Deposit (CD) or a savings account. The policy earns dividends based on the policy's value and how the company performs. A variable life policy means that the cash value within the policy is invested in mutual fund investments or fixed payout accounts within the policy. This affects the policy's value—the performance of the funds determines how long the policy is to be paid as well as its cash value. If there is a bad year in the stock market or several poor years, you may need to pay a larger premium to continue the policy than the one initially quoted. Variable policies have been very popular the last several years when the stock market has been skyrocketing because the premiums are cheaper than standard cash value policies.

246. I have reviewed various types of insurance policies, but I don't understand universal life. What is it?

Universal life insurance was the industry response to high interest rates in the 1970s and 1980s, since it was hard to sell traditional insurance when you could earn 15 percent on CDs. With universal life, you get current interest rates in the cash value account instead of dividends.

247. I keep getting credit card insurance information in the mail. If I am carrying credit balances on my cards, should I have insurance to pay off the loans when I die?

Credit card insurance is expensive term coverage. The good news is that you can get the coverage without a medical exam, but you lose the coverage when you pay off the loan. Figure out how much life insurance you need and then buy coverage this way rather than piecemeal. A planned total insurance package is a more cost-effective way to buy insurance.

248. The mortgage agent offered life insurance to us when we applied for our mortgage. Should we take it?

Probably not. Insurance is important if you or your partner die prematurely, particularly if you are buying a home based on two incomes. You should definitely have enough life insurance (for both spouses) to cover the mortgage. However, where the insurance is purchased is another matter and the bank's policy is probably not your best choice.

Mortgage insurance is what is known as decreasing term insurance—you begin paying a monthly payment based on the initial mortgage amount and yet the premiums never decrease as you pay off your mortgage. Thus, if you have an $85,000 mortgage and you die during the first year you bought the home, the policy will pay off the full mortgage. However, if you die in the thirteenth year of the mortgage, the death benefits cover only the amount needed to cover the payoff, which might only be $40,000. This insurance might make sense if you have some reason to believe one of you may not live long and would not be able to pass a medical exam as required by traditional insurance.

The type of life insurance you get to cover a mortgage depends on how long you plan to live in the house. If you will be moving often, you should buy an insurance policy that you carry separate from the mortgage so you can carry the coverage with you to your next home.

My husband and I still have the coverage that we purchased on our starter home. Since the initial insurance purchase, we have moved once and refinanced twice. If we had bought standard mortgage insurance, we would have had to purchase new coverage at a higher cost each time we got a new mortgage.

249. Do I still need to carry life insurance if I'm over seventy?

Once your children have grown up and you have paid off your mortgage, you have less need to replace your income. It's a good time to review your financial picture to see if you can cut back on life insurance.

250. What's a child rider on my life insurance policy?

Many experts recommend a child rider on your life insurance policy so that your kids are able to buy their own policy by age twenty-five, up to five times the face amount of the rider with no questions asked. If you have a

$10,000 child rider on your policy, your son can get $50,000 of insurance at age twenty-five without a medical exam. It guarantees insurability if he can't acquire insurance on his own because of a health problem. People always assume that health problems won't occur in their family. This gives protection in case the impossible happens.

251. Should I have other kinds of life insurance for my child?

A life insurance policy for your child is not the best investment, but it can provide a current death benefit, cash value growth, and future insurability. Of course, you need to have the money to bury a child, if necessary. If you buy an individual policy on your child, this gives your child a way to save. One of the benefits of buying an insurance policy on your child's life is that when the child is old enough to buy life insurance for herself, she may be uninsurable because of a health condition. It doesn't often happen, but it certainly can. Your children will always have the benefits of any policies you have bought for them. Remember, of course, that the policy is not the total investment package for them—there are other investments that can earn more money. On the other hand, grandparents may find that a life insurance policy on a child is a wonderful gift to provide some cash value during the child's lifetime and for retirement.

252. My agent recommended a policy with a guaranteed insurability clause. What does that mean?

Guaranteed insurability for disability, health, and life insurance means that the option to continue the insurance is up to you, not the insurance company. This means that the company can't require a medical exam after an initial exam.

253. My insurance agent suggested that after a period of time my insurance policy would have a vanishing premium. What does that mean?

In a participating whole life policy where dividends are accumulated, the dividends paid to the policy are enough in time so that they will cover the policy premiums.

254. My husband and I signed up for term life insurance several years ago. But now we are earning much more than we were then. Should we add on more coverage?

Quite possibly. Your life and disability insurance needs will change as your family grows, you earn more money, and your children finish school and leave home. Too little protection is risky, but you don't want to hold onto too much of the wrong kind of insurance either. It's a good idea to audit your insurance needs each year.

255. My husband just died. I have the choice of taking the death benefits from his insurance policy in a lump sum payment or via a monthly payment for ten years, term certain. What does that mean?

The lump sum payment means you would receive the money all at once. A monthly payment ten-year term certain means that you will receive a fixed amount of money each month for the remainder of your life. If you die before the ten-year term, the beneficiary you designate will receive the monthly payment until the ten-year period is over.

As for how to take the death benefit payout, no one answer fits all situations. The first consideration is how the funds are to be used. If the policy was purchased for funds to pay for a funeral, death taxes, final expenses, and so on, the funds need to be paid in a lump sum. If the funds are to provide an annual income for a spouse or child, then the person buying the coverage must decide if the beneficiary is able to handle a large amount of money coming in at one time. If the beneficiary is able to invest the funds and will not spend the money, he or she should receive a lump sum payout. If the person buying the coverage wants a guaranteed income for the beneficiary's lifetime, the money should be paid as a monthly check.

256. I only want insurance until my children are educated. What is the cheapest kind of life insurance?

Term insurance is the cheapest when the insurance is first purchased and is usually bought for a specified time, such as until your youngest child is educated. The insurance company is obligated to pay a specified amount if the insured person dies within the policy period. Term life insurance becomes prohibitively expensive as the insured ages.

257. For estate planning purposes, my insurance agent recommended a second-to-die policy. How does that work?

As the name implies, proceeds from a life insurance policy are paid when the second spouse dies. These policies came into effect in the 1980s when the unlimited marital deduction came into effect. With the unlimited marital deduction, you can defer death taxes until the second spouse dies, so this is when funds are needed. Because you don't know which spouse will die first, the policy is on both lives. A second-to-die policy is cheaper than purchasing an individual policy on each spouse and provides insurability when one spouse is in poor health. You can also get a rider on a second-to-die policy for one or both spouses that provides some cash after the first death.

258. I have some money to invest. My broker advised me to buy term insurance and invest the rest. Is this a good idea?

Like so much in life, it depends. If the death benefit is to provide money to pay off the mortgage on your house if you die young or to guarantee college funds until your youngest child is educated, a term policy could be the best choice. You haven't paid too much for the insurance and your beneficiary will get the benefits. If you need the insurance for a legacy, to pay death taxes, or funds for your spouse, you will need a good cash value policy (or variable policy). If you buy a term policy and invest the rest as your broker recommended, you'll need lots of discipline. I have seen so many families in financial distress because they bought a term policy and did not invest the rest; at retirement they have neither insurance nor the savings they had planned.

259. Does the beneficiary of my life insurance policy need to be a relative?

No. You may name your church, a friend, a charity, your college, or a creditor; however, the original beneficiary must always be someone who has an insurable interest in you—someone who would suffer a financial loss if you were to die.

260. Can I change my beneficiary after the policy is originally issued?

Yes, unless this right to change beneficiaries has been given away as part of a divorce settlement or if you set up an irrevocable trust. Many things over your life may cause you to reconsider the beneficiaries of your insurance policies, so remember to intermittently review this information.

261. What happens if my designated beneficiary dies before I do?

If the designated beneficiary of your policy dies before you do, appoint a new beneficiary immediately. If your beneficiary dies before you do and there is no contingent (backup) beneficiary, the life insurance company must pay benefits to your estate. One of the benefits of insurance is that the proceeds are paid to a beneficiary at death instead of going through the probate process. You should always have a contingent beneficiary in case you and the primary beneficiary die before a new beneficiary can be named.

262. I borrowed funds from my life insurance policy to put a down payment on our house. How does this loan affect the death benefit if I die before the loan is repaid in full?

The loan on your life insurance is paid back from the death benefits of the policy before the death benefit is paid to the beneficiaries. Your beneficiaries would receive the life insurance amount minus all loans and any unpaid interest due. Because loans and interest always reduce the amount of death value available, loans need to be carefully considered when taken from a policy.

263. How much can I borrow out of my policy?

You should call your agent to find out the exact amount. It is generally 90 percent to 92 percent of the cash value of the policy. If you have a $100,000 policy with a cash value of $30,000, you could only get a loan of $27,000.

264. Can I get an unlimited amount of life insurance on my spouse?

You can't acquire an unlimited amount of insurance on your spouse. Insurance is purchased as a protection. Individuals must be able to afford the coverage and have a particular need. As a rule of thumb, insurance companies permit you to purchase life insurance up to six times the person's salary. The amount of liabilities (such as mortgages or business loans) combined with your income give you and your agent an idea of the maximum amount of coverage for your situation. Beyond that, you need to verify a reason for the coverage.

265. What happens if my insurance contract is lost or stolen?

You should contact your agent and ask for a replacement policy. Many people put their policies in a safety deposit box, but it's a better idea to have the policies at home with your important papers. However, you should keep a separate listing of all your policies in your lockbox so that your family has access to the information in the event of your death or incompetence.

266. I read about a living needs benefit. What is this?

A living needs benefit is a rider that enables you to use the life insurance benefits of the policy before you die. There are many limits—you must have a terminal illness and be within six months of death, for example—but this can be a great help during a time of need. This is a good benefit as a supplement to long-term care coverage because you or your family are guaranteed to receive benefits. Your beneficiary will receive the total death benefit if you don't use the living needs benefit and you will receive benefits in a nursing home. However, this is not a replacement for long-term care coverage; it is a supplement to coverage.

267. Why should I consider additional life insurance beyond what my employer is paying for?

Usually life insurance at work is based on your annual salary (one to four times your salary) and is only valid for as long as you are employed with that company. If something happens to your job, you could be left without coverage at a time when you are older and coverage is more expensive. Some employers allow a transfer of coverage, though this may be expensive. Knowing if your coverage is transferrable and at what cost is a question to ask your human resource department. Before buying more insurance, ask yourself:

- If I die, for what will the insurance benefits be used?
- If I lose this coverage, will I need insurance?
- Can I afford to replace it or will my new employer have life insurance for me?

268. I have the option to purchase a waiver of premium rider. Does this make sense?

You're less likely to die before age sixty-five than you are to become disabled. The disability rider means you wouldn't have to pay the insurance premium if you become totally disabled for six months or longer. You need to ask how much the rider costs and verify that the waiver stops if the policy goes on vanished premium.

269. I recently received a dividend statement from my life insurance policy. What are these dividends?

Dividends paid on classic life and some renewable term life policies are refunds of a part of the premiums you've paid on your policy—the part not used by the insurance company to pay expenses or contract benefits for the company as a whole. This is a benefit to cash value policies. Because dividends depend on the actual experience of the insurance company, the amount of dividends is not guaranteed. Before you purchase a life insurance policy, you should review the dividend history of the company because you want dividends to be paid on your policy.

270. When are dividends paid?

Once or twice a year. There is usually a selection of available options for you as the policyholder. Dividends may:

- provide additional insurance;
- earn interest (like a money market fund) at a variable rate;
- be paid in cash; or
- be used to reduce the annual policy premium.

You may withdraw any accumulated dividends, but you can't redeposit them with the policy later.

271. Can the dividend option ever be changed?

Yes and this is an important point to remember since your financial situation varies throughout your life. During certain stages of your life (such as when your children are in college), you will want the dividends to pay the policy premium; having the dividends pay for additional insurance can increase your death benefit later in life.

272. Is there an age limit after which you can not purchase a life insurance policy?

Because we're living longer these days, most companies have extended coverage until age eighty. Life insurance becomes prohibitively expensive as you age; only for estate planning or a special situation would it make economic sense for you to buy a policy so late in life. Some companies will insure a person after age eighty; however, there must be a special situation requirement for the coverage.

273. My broker recommended an annuity. What is it?

An annuity is a type of insurance/investment product. You don't have to pay income taxes on the interest earned in a deferred annuity until you withdraw the funds. They are kind of like a savings account that offers slightly higher yields and are backed by insurance companies. Unlike most other types of retirement accounts, such as 401(k)s, SEP-IRAs, and Keoghs, you don't get any tax deductions from nonqualified annuities. That's why putting retirement funds into an annuity doesn't make much sense unless you have already fully funded your tax-deductible retirement accounts.

274. What is the difference between a fixed and a variable annuity?

A fixed annuity generally pays a fixed interest rate that is usually related to an underlying fixed income security (Treasury notes, bills, and so on). The rate can be changed annually or quarterly or it can be guaranteed for a specific period, depending on the contract. A variable annuity permits investment in mutual funds—usually a series of funds in which the investor can choose the allocation.

LIFE INSURANCE

Company name
_____

Insurance agent's name   Phone number
_____

Address
_____
_____

Phone number   Fax
_____

Name of insured
_____

Policy owner
_____

Policy #   Policy location
_____

Whole life, variable, or term insurance?
_____

Monthly premium
_____

Renewal date   Dividend option
_____

Total cash value $ Total death benefits
_____

Loan against policy?   How much?   Date borrowed
_____

Primary beneficiary
_____

Secondary beneficiary
_____

HEALTH INSURANCE

275. I was recently turned down for a health insurance plan because I have a preexisting condition. What are my options?

If you've been turned down by a health insurer because of a current or prior medical condition, you can shop around to find another plan that might be willing to take you on. Most of these, however, will charge you more money than someone who is perfectly healthy. If you have a medical condition, you must really shop around to find the best financial deal. Check with an independent agent who sells policies from multiple insurers.

You may also try a few plans that don't discriminate in this way, including the traditional Blue Cross/Blue Shield and some HMO plans (such as Kaiser). Check to see if your state offers a plan for people in your situation; more than half the states are doing this now. Call your state's insurance department. You'll find the number in the phone book under the state government section.

276. What can I do if I'm not sure why I was turned down for health insurance?

You may not realize it, but you have a medical information report that is very similar to a credit report and is consulted by health and life insurers. There can be mistakes on this report and you have a right to see it. To get a copy of your medical information report, write to the Medical Information Bureau at P.O. Box 105, Essex Station, Boston, MA 02112, or call (617) 426-3660. If there is a mistake, you have the right to request a correction, but the burden is yours to prove the file wrong. You may need to contact doctors you've seen before to correct the problem.

277. My grandmother has a cancer policy. Are specific health insurance policies a good idea?

Specific health insurance policies aren't necessary if you have a good health insurance policy that covers you for any and all illnesses. These specific health insurance policies often have so many restrictions that even if you get the disease which you insured yourself against, they don't pay. A good health insurance policy guarantees that you are covered for any and all types of illnesses.

278. What is coinsurance?

This is a word heard bandied about a great deal with health insurance. It refers to a sharing of the cost between you and the insurance company. Typically, a health insurance company covers 80 percent of health care costs and you are responsible for the other 20 percent of the bill. (This coinsurance begins after the deductible is met.) Once a certain payout limit is reached, most policies require the insurance company to step in and pay 100 percent of the bills until the policy limits. The point at which the 100 percent payment begins depends on the policy.

279. What is major medical coverage?

A major medical policy is an insurance contract designed to provide protection from catastrophic losses. They usually contain high limits per loss and few exclusions with individual and family deductibles. Major medical coverage can be purchased as a stand-alone policy, supplemental coverage, or comprehensive coverage.

280. My employer provides dental insurance. Should I purchase it?

Is the coverage cost effective? You must decide if the cost of paying premiums is worth it or if it makes more sense to provide your own coverage by placing premiums in a savings account for use when needed. If you have several children who may need extensive dental work beyond simple fillings and checkups, this might be cost effective. Check the details about what the policy covers closely.

281. Is it true that an HMO (Health Maintenance Organization) doesn't have a deductible?

Yes. You pay a portion of each medical visit or prescription, which is known as a co-payment. The number of visits per year will influence whether you pay more than the standard deductible.

282. My employer is offering the choice between an HMO and an indemnity policy. Which is better?

There is no better policy; it's a personal choice. HMOs are the oldest form of managed care. You (or your employer) pay a premium and are covered under set guidelines by the HMO agreement. You are required to use an HMO doctor, hospital, and other providers. The good news about HMOs is there is no deductible, although you may have a small co-payment for pharmaceuticals and doctors' visits. HMOs are strongly supportive of preventive medicine and thus usually include coverage for annual physicals, checkups, and all shots for children. The problem is that you are limited to what hospital you can use and which doctors you can see, depending on which HMO your employer has. With an HMO, if you are unhappy with care locally you can't decide to go to a major medical center such as Johns Hopkins or the Mayo Clinic; you must be referred at the discretion of your physician and the HMO provider.

Indemnity policies (such as the traditional Blue Cross/Blue Shield) are usually more expensive and have deductibles. The insurance company pays the provider or reimburses you after submission of a claim. You have the freedom of going anywhere and getting any type of care, but premiums are usually more expensive.

283. My daughter is diabetic. If my husband loses his job, will his new employer's health insurance have a preexisting condition clause?

A preexisting condition clause means you won't be covered for any condition you have at the time you apply for the new policy. This limitation may last for up to two years. The clause usually requires you to hold two policies until the time limitation is met. Under the recent health care law changes, your husband's new employer must provide coverage for a preexisting condition if he can demonstrate he had prior coverage for that condition for at least a year.

284. Both my husband and I work outside the home and our employers both provide health coverage. Should we both get it?

It all depends on the insurance provided by your employers and whether the policies permit duplicate coverage. Often you can pick and choose coverage. It's important to know the benefits of both employers and know what your options are. In any case, remember you will not be paid more than the loss, so don't duplicate coverage if you can avoid it.

285. Does my health insurance coverage extend to services provided in another country?

Most companies do, but it is imperative to verify coverage if you are traveling to a foreign country. It's a good question to ask when you buy insurance, particularly if you are doing a great deal of traveling.

286. What is COBRA? Should I have it?

COBRA (Consolidated Omnibus Budget Reconciliation Act of 1985) requires your employer to continue your health coverage after a job loss, death of an employee, divorce, or age (as when a child reaches an age when he or she is no longer covered under the plan). Your employer is required to offer COBRA coverage for eighteen months after you quit your job or thirty-six months for other situations (such as divorce).

287. What are the problems with keeping my COBRA coverage?

COBRA was designed as a transitional insurance coverage. If you become ill while on the policy, you may not be able to get individual coverage elsewhere as the deadline approaches. Thus, it is strongly recommended that you acquire individual coverage as soon as possible after you leave your job.

288. My husband just died. Can I keep our health insurance that I pay for myself since I'm self-employed?

Yes. Be sure to tell the company that there is one less person on the insurance; your premiums should go down.

HEALTH INSURANCE

Company name _____

Address _____

_____

Phone number _____ Fax _____

Insurance agent's name _____

Address _____

_____

Phone number _____ Fax _____

Name of insured _____

Policy owner _____

Policy # _____ Group # _____

HMO, indemnity, PPO? _____

Premium _____ Policy location _____

Renewal date _____

Riders/exclusions _____

_____

Primary beneficiary _____

Secondary beneficiary _____

MEDICARE AND SOCIAL SECURITY BENEFITS

289. What is Medicare, Part A?

Medicare, Part A is mandatory health insurance that covers people sixty-five years of age or older, anyone who is on Social Security disability, or anyone who is undergoing kidney dialysis treatment. When you sign up for Social Security, you automatically sign up for Medicare, Part A. Part A covers hospitalization costs, some skilled nursing care, and home health care. Part A costs are paid by FICA (Social Security taxes) and not through premiums paid by individuals. More than two-thirds of the funds paid by Medicare, Part A are spent on people in the last six months of their lives.

290. How is this different from Medicare, Part B?

Part B coverage is a supplement to Medicare, Part A. Coverage is voluntary and must be purchased (the present rate is $43.80/month, but it is always increasing). Part B covers physicians' services, certain laboratory expenses, and so on. When you sign up for Medicare, you are asked if you want Part B. If you don't take Part B when you enroll for Medicare Part A, you are surcharged at a 10 percent per year penalty when you do sign up for the coverage. For example, if you don't take the coverage at age sixty-five and then you decide at seventy you do want coverage, the premiums will be 50 percent higher than if you had acquired the coverage at age sixty-five. Both Part A and Part B are subject to deductibles.

291. What is a Medicare supplement policy?

Medicare supplement policies are designed to cover the deductibles and coinsurances associated with Medicare. These policies can't contain exclusions, limits, or reductions that aren't associated with Medicare. Thus, if Medicare permits a particular coverage (such as chemotherapy), the supplemental policy also must cover chemotherapy.

In Pennsylvania, Parts A and B of Medicare and a good Medicare supplement policy are enough coverage because doctors and hospitals must accept what Medicare pays. For example, if Medicare feels that $1,000 is the reasonable and customary charge for a $1,500 procedure (the doctor's charge to all other patients), Medicare will pay 80 percent of the $1,000 (or $800) and the supplement will pay $200. If you live in a state that doesn't require doctors to accept what Medicare pays, then this may leave you responsible for $500 of your doctor's bill.

292. How do I find a supplement policy?

There are so many of these plans available that choosing one can be difficult. To make it easier on consumers, all states (except Minnesota, Massachusetts, and Wisconsin) limit the number of these Medigap plans to ten

Medicare Supplement Insurance Counseling

State	Phone Number(s)	State	Phone Number(s)
California	(800) 927-4357	New Mexico	(800) 432-2080 (505) 827-7640
Delaware	(302) 739-4251	New York*	(518) 455-4312
Florida*	(904) 922-3132	North Carolina	(919) 733-0111
Idaho	(208) 334-2250	Ohio*	(800) 686-1526
Indiana	(800) 622-4461 (317) 232-2395	Oregon*	(503) 378-4484
Iowa	(515) 281-5705	Tennessee*	(800) 252-2816 (615) 741-4955
Maryland	(800) 243-3425 (410) 225-1100	Texas	(512)463-6515
Massachusetts	(617) 727-7750	Vermont*	(802) 828-3301
Michigan*	(517) 335-1702	Washington	(206) 753-2408
Missouri*	(800) 726-7390 (314) 751-2640	Wisconsin	(800) 242-1060 (608) 266-8944
New Jersey	(800) 729-8820 (609) 292-4303		

*Note: These states either do not include extensive one-on-one counseling or are in the process of establishing comprehensive counseling programs. The 800 numbers cannot be used to go outside state boundaries.

standard versions, designated A through J. Plan A has the most basic coverage and Plan J has the most coverage. All of these plans cover specific medical coverages which aren't covered (or are only partially covered) under Medicare.

293. I'm still confused. Is there somewhere I can get more help in figuring out my Medicare information?

Yes. If you need help you can contact the local Office of Aging. For example, Pennsylvania offers a free service called Apprise. This service provides trained volunteers to help you make the right choice. To contact Apprise, in Pennsylvania, call (800) 783-7067.

What the Ten Standard Medigap Policies Offer

● Policy offers this benefit   ○ Policy does not offer this benefit

Policy Type	A	B	C	D	E	F	G	H	I	J
Basic benefits	●	●	●	●	●	●	●	●	●	●
Part A—hospital deductible	○	●	●	●	●	●	●	●	●	●
Part B—doctor deductible	○	○	●	○	○	●	○	○	○	●
20% coinsurance	●	●	●	●	●	●	●	●	●	●
Part B—% excess doctor bill	○	○	○	○	○	100%	80%	○	100%	100%
Additional 365 hospital days	●	●	●	●	●	●	●	●	●	●
Skilled-nursing coinsurance	○	○	●	●	●	●	●	●	●	●
At-home care	○	○	○	●	○	○	●	○	●	●
Prescription drugs	○	○	○	○	○	○	○	●	●	●
Preventive care	○	○	○	○	●	○	○	○	○	●
Health care abroad	○	○	●	●	●	●	●	●	●	●

294. What exactly is Social Security?

We all hope we will be receiving benefits from Social Security when we re-tire. However, Social Security is more than that. Known officially as Old Age, Survivors', Disability and Health Insurance, Social Security was created through the Social Security Act of 1935. Although it's been modified since then, the act was designed to protect eligible workers and their family against financial loss as a result of death, illness, disability, and retirement. Social Security benefits are funded through medical premiums and payroll taxes: 6.2 percent social security tax by you, 6.2 percent by your employer, 1.45 percent Medicare tax by you, and 1.45 percent by your employer—or the entire 15.3 percent is paid by you if you are self-employed.

295. Should I take my Social Security benefits before I reach normal retirement age?

This is a very individual question and each family situation is different. A review of your personal situation should be made with Social Security and a financial planner because of each family's unique income needs, health situation, salary, wealth, and so on. If you begin taking Social Security at age sixty-two, you have a lower monthly check than if you had waited until sixty-five (80 percent of what it would have been at age sixty-five). You also earn delayed retirement credits for every month after age sixty-five you wait until you take social security, up to age seventy. The delay credit is a percentage, and depends on your year of birth.

296. Do I always pay FICA (Social Security and Medicare Tax) from my salary?

The 6.2 percent tax that you pay and that is matched by your employer is required until you reach a salary maximum ($67,000 in 1998). When your earnings reach the limit, Social Security taxes are not taken from any more earnings for the year. You start over in the new tax year. The 1.45 percent Medicare tax paid by you and matched by your employer does not have a salary maximum. No matter what your income is, you are required to pay this tax.

297. If I die, does Social Security help my family?

At your death, your spouse receives a $255 lump-sum burial payment. To qualify for death benefits, at your death you must have been currently insured or fully insured. Currently insured provides some benefits; fully insured (as defined by your age and how long you paid in to Social Security) provides survivorship benefits to your wife and children. Your wife can collect on your account if she is a widow who is at least sixty.

298. What if I were married before?

Payments made to a first wife don't take away from a second wife. Each gets the full amount allowed. However, at your death your widow—not your ex-wife—gets the burial payment. In most cases, widows and qualified divorcees get 71.5 to 100 percent of their husband's full benefit, depending primarily on their age and when they claim benefits.

299. My husband and I were divorced and neither of us ever remarried or had children. He just died. Can I collect his Social Security benefits?

Yes. If your ex-husband died and your marriage lasted for at least ten years, you can collect on his account if you're at least sixty years old (or disabled and at least fifty). You could also collect if your ex-husband died and you are caring for a child from your marriage under age sixteen (or someone who was disabled before age twenty-two). In this case, it doesn't matter how long your marriage lasted.

300. I've worked all my life and so has my husband. Whose benefits can I get?

If you've held a paying job, you have your own Social Security account. But at retirement, you can collect on your husband's account instead of yours if you'd get more money that way. If you earned more money, your husband might get a better benefit from drawing on your Social Security.

301. Is there an income limit for Social Security survivors' benefits?

Yes. If your surviving spouse makes more than $20,000 a year, he or she won't get any coverage.

302. How do I find out what my Social Security benefit amount will be when I retire?

Contact the Social Security Administration at 1-800-772-1213 and request an Earnings and Benefit Estimate Statement for your account (Form SSA-7004-SM). This gives a record of your earnings and an idea of your monthly payment at normal retirement age, which for people born before 1938 is age sixty-five. For people born after 1960, the age has increased to sixty-seven.

303. Do the number of children I have affect the amount of Social Security benefits my wife receives at my death?

If your wife is under age sixty, she must have at least one child under age sixteen in order to receive a survivor benefit. Your child will also receive a benefit (75 percent of what your monthly Social Security benefit would have been) until age eighteen. There is a cap (called the maximum family benefit) on how much the family can receive and each member's benefit is proportionately reduced so the family does not go over the limit. Thus, having a large family doesn't guarantee a large monthly payment.

304. What is the Social Security blackout period for a widow?

If your husband dies and you have children under age sixteen, you will get 75 percent of his monthly Social Security benefit. In addition, each unmarried child under age eighteen also gets an equal share of 75 percent of his monthly benefit. Once the youngest child reaches sixteen years of age, your survivorship benefits end (unless you are disabled). When you reach age sixty, they begin again. At age sixty, your benefits are lower (the survivor only receives 71.5 percent of the age sixty-five amount). At age sixty-five, you would receive the full amount. The period of time between when the youngest child reaches sixteen and you reach age sixty and your benefits can begin again is called the blackout period.

HOME, AUTO, AND OTHER INSURANCE

305. What is bodily injury liability on my car insurance?

This provides insurance against lawsuits. Make sure you have enough liability insurance to at least cover your assets.

306. What about property damage liability?

This covers damage by your car to other cars and property. It's usually figured as a consequence of the amount of bodily injury level that you select.

307. What is uninsured/underinsured motorist liability insurance?

This very important coverage protects you if you are hit or hurt by someone who doesn't carry any or enough auto insurance. If you are in an accident that is someone else's fault, that person's insurance company should
pay for treatment or loss of income to you. If the at-fault person has inade-
quate insurance, your underinsured motorist coverage will pay you the
money you need up to the limits of your policy. You are protecting you
and your family with this coverage. In many states, uninsured motorists
coverage is required.

308. What is comprehensive coverage on my auto insurance policy?

There are two types of physical damage coverage on your auto insurance
coverage: collision and comprehensive. Collision pays for damage that
results from a collision with another object no matter whose fault it is. You
are often required by state law to have collision coverage for other drivers
in case you are at fault during an accident. If you have a loan or lien on
your car, collision coverage is usually required by a lender.

Comprehensive coverage is for losses that occur from accidents other
than collision and for legal representation for uninsured/underinsured motorists. Comprehensive coverage would apply if your car was stolen or
damaged by breaking glass, falling objects, trees, flood, fire, animals, and
so on. You should review how much the comprehensive insurance costs
and how this price drops with a higher deductible. As your car gets older
and is worth less, you can eventually eliminate your collision coverage alto-
gether. Remember that the point of insurance is to pay you for losses that
are financially catastrophic; it depends on what you're comfortable with.

309. What's the best way to save money on my car insurance?

There are several ways to save money:

- Raise your deductibles. You aren't likely to file many claims so there's
  no need to pay lots of money in extra yearly premiums.
- Drop collision coverage on older cars (or those worth less than
  $4,000)

CAR INSURANCE

Company _____

Agent's name _____

Address _____

_____

Phone number _____ Fax _____

E-mail _____

Policy # _____ Policy location _____

Annual premium _____ How paid _____

Cars Insured

Make _____ Model _____ Year _____

Vehicle ID # _____ Mileage _____

License # _____ Owned/leased? _____

Name(s) of insured _____

How many miles driven _____

Cars Insured

Make _____ Model _____ Year _____

Vehicle ID # _____ Mileage _____

License # _____ Owned/leased? _____

Name(s) of insured _____

How many miles driven _____

Cars Insured

Make _____ Model _____ Year _____

Vehicle ID # _____ Mileage _____

(continued)

License #	Owned/leased?
Name(s) of insured	
How many miles driven	

Cars Insured		
Make	Model	Year
Vehicle ID #	Mileage	
License #	Owned/leased?	
Name(s) of insured		
How many miles driven		

- Insist on discounts for insuring your car and home with the same company
- Increase collision and comprehensive deductibles; by raising from $200 to $500, you can cut your rates
- Comparison shop—prices for the same coverage can vary by hundreds of dollars
- Take advantage of low mileage discounts
- Take advantage of automatic seat belt or air bag discounts
- Ask about other discounts (such as a good driver discount, discounts for more than one car, no accidents in three years, drivers over age fifty, driver training courses, antitheft devices, antilock brakes, good grades for students, college students away from home without a car, and so on)

310. I'm thinking about buying a luxury car. Is there any easy way to find out what the higher costs might be for different models?

You're right to be worried. Cars that cost a lot to fix or are favorite targets for thieves have much higher insurance fees. For an idea of how different cars are rated, write to the Insurance Institute for Highway Safety, 1005 Glebe Rd., Arlington, VA 22201 to request their Highway Loss Data Chart.

311. Should I stack my auto insurance coverage?

Stacking takes the liability limits of each vehicle and stacks them on top of each other. Thus, if you have $50,000/$100,000 coverage and two cars, stacking will give you $100,000/$200,000 as your limits. Stacking costs more, but it's still cheaper than purchasing the higher limits for both cars outright.

312. When I rent a car, should I purchase the extra auto insurance?

Auto coverage isn't necessary if your personal car insurance provides coverage while driving a rental car. Remember that if you don't have comprehensive or collision insurance on your auto policy, you won't have it on the rental car either without extra (or credit card) coverage. If you are driving a rental car in another country, find out if your insurance company will cover damage outside the United States. Remember that if you decline rental insurance, you will have to pay a deductible if anything happens to the rental car while in your possession. To offset this problem and because rental car insurance is so expensive, some credit cards (such as American Express) will cover this deductible if you use their card when you rent the car. Check into your credit card policies before renting.

313. How long do I have to report a change in vehicles to my insurance company: twenty-four hours, forty-eight hours, or thirty days?

Although it's a good idea to notify your company as soon as possible in case you have an accident in the new car, you have thirty days in which to notify your company of a change. It sounds like a lot of time, but often people tend to forget to notify their company of the change. Keep in mind that you might need more coverage on the newer car than you had on the older car.

314. How much time do I have to notify my insurance company after an accident occurs?

You should notify your insurance company within twenty-four hours of an accident. If the accident occurred on the weekend, contact the company's 800 number and listen for instructions. Some insurance policies may have more lenient requirements, but most companies require notification within twenty-four hours.

315. What's the best way to save money on my homeowner's insurance?

Consider raising your deductible to $1,000 and insist on a discount for insuring both your home and car with one company.

316. What is replacement cost insurance?

This type of insurance means that your goods will be reimbursed at what the item would cost to replace today. This means if you have a replacement cost policy that covers a sofa you bought in 1960, you would receive not its actual value, but what it would cost to replace it today.

Without replacement coverage, you would only receive what the property is worth today, not what it will cost to replace it. You may have spent $400 on a TV but without replacement coverage, if the TV is stolen all you'll get from the insurance company is $100. With replacement cost coverage, you'll get enough to replace the TV at today's prices. The premium for replacement cost coverage increases your homeowner's premium about 13 percent a year, but it's money well spent.

317. Will my homeowner's insurance cover personal property I carry with me while traveling?

Property does not have to be in your house to be covered by your homeowner's policy. For example, your dependent child's stereo in her dorm room is covered. The amount of coverage on your personal property is usually 50 percent of the value of the home. If your home is insured for $150,000, your personal property is covered for $75,000. Replacement cost insurance means that your personal property may be covered up to 75 percent of the dwelling coverage. There are sublimits for certain types of luxury property, such as jewelry, furs, money, or silver. If you need coverage beyond the sublimits, you need to have an appraisal made on the property and purchase a rider that provides additional coverage.

318. How much homeowner's insurance should I have on my home?

Homeowner's insurance is designed to repair or replace your primary residence if damaged or destroyed. Coverage usually is based on the sale price of the home when purchased, but remember the sales price includes the value of the land. Coverage is based on replacement value and often this is less than the value of the entire property, but keep in mind that it can be more. One hundred percent coverage is required for replacement cost coverage. If your home is unique or historic or you don't have a clue of the replacement cost, you should get a replacement cost appraisal. Or ask your agent about the company's computer program that fine-tunes the replacement value of your home.

319. I live in a high-crime area and I can't find anyone willing to sell me a policy. What can I do?

The federal government offers a Crime Insurance Program to help you in this situation. For more information, call (800) 638-8780.

320. What kind of insurance protects me for liability?

Your homeowner's coverage insures you against liability for accidental damage (intentional acts aren't covered) in the event that:

- someone is injured on your property;
- someone is injured by you or a family member anywhere; or
- someone else's property is damaged or destroyed by you or your family.

People should have enough coverage for their socioeconomic state. If you are wealthy, you may need an umbrella liability policy or PCAT (personal catastrophic policy), too.

321. Should I have flood insurance on my home?

If you live in a flood plain, you should definitely have flood insurance through a National Flood Insurance Program. If you don't live in a flood plain, you can't purchase flood insurance.

322. I have a swimming pool at my home. Do I need extra insurance?

You should carry extra liability coverage, known as a PCAT (personal catastrophic) policy, if you have a swimming pool, aggressive dog, or are wealthy. If someone is injured on your property, will $300,000 coverage be enough if they know you are wealthy and have assets that can be taken in a lawsuit? Personal umbrella coverage is available at very reasonable prices. It covers not just accidents that might happen at home, but catastrophic car accidents—if, for example, your car went out of control and plunged into five others, the damages may well exceed coverage provided by regular auto insurance. An umbrella policy would cover this. You should verify that the umbrella coverage is supplemental to your homeowner's coverage. Also note that some companies' general liability policies do not provide supplemental auto liability coverage.

323. My agent recommends an inflation rider on my homeowner's policy. Is this a good idea?

Inflation riders attached to a homeowner's policy automatically increase the amount of coverage as the cost of replacement increases. They are designed for people who generally don't pay too much attention to their premium notices when they come for payment. The problem with an inflation rider is that you may be overinsuring your property. In one case, a family insured its home for twice its value. The homeowner mistakenly thought that if the property was damaged, he would have received the insured value rather than the replacement cost. Inflation riders take the responsibility for the insurance coverage on your home off your shoulders. If you don't have this coverage, you must review the value of your home compared with your coverage every few years.

324. I'm certain I don't need disability insurance since I'll be covered by Social Security disability. Is this accurate?

No. Seventy percent of all applicants for Social Security disability are turned down. Yet you have a better chance of being disabled before age sixty-five than dying. Social Security disability only applies if you become severely disabled and can't work before reaching retirement age. Note that the inability to work doesn't mean the inability to handle your current job—it means the inability to perform any job. Thus, if a surgeon could no longer operate, he wouldn't qualify for Social Security disability if he could still do office work. Also, remember that Social Security disability is only based on what your monthly Social Security benefit would have been. It has nothing to do with your current salary.

325. What about workers' compensation?

It doesn't pay you any benefits if you become disabled when you're not at work. You need disability coverage that kicks in no matter how and where you are disabled.

326. Is disability insurance a good idea?

Disability insurance is imperative if your family depends on your income to live, to maintain their current station in life, to keep your home, and so on. Remember that health insurance only pays your medical bills; it won't cover your lost salary.

    While disability insurance, in most cases, won't replace the full amount of your income, most will replace about 60 percent of your salary.

DISABILITY INSURANCE

Company name

Insurance agent's name

Address

Phone number   Fax

Name of insured

Policy owner

Policy #   Policy location

Monthly premium

Renewal date

Waiting period   Benefit period

Benefit amount $

Riders/exclusions

Primary beneficiary

Secondary beneficiary

---

327. Do I pay taxes on disability insurance benefits?

Not if you pay for your disability insurance yourself. If your employers pay for your disability, then you do have to pay tax on the benefits—so you need more benefits.

328. Where do I obtain disability coverage?

It is usually cheapest to buy disability insurance through your employer or a professional association because as a general rule group coverage is cheaper than individual coverage. If you can't obtain group coverage, you can buy an individual disability insurance policy through a commercial insurance company. Comparison shop for price and benefits since the differences in price and coverage can vary widely. Keep in mind when buying group coverage that you may lose coverage if you change jobs. Each association policy has its own criteria. You may get the best coverage by combining group coverage and an individual policy. If you have to buy disability insurance on your own, check with USAA (800) 531-8000; Wholesale Insurance Network (800) 808-5810; or Direct Insurance Services (800) 622-3699.

329. What features should I have in a disability policy?

Disability can be confusing. An ***own-occupation*** policy pays benefits if you can't perform the work you usually do. Other policies pay only if you can't do the job for which you are reasonably trained. Own-occupation policies are the most expensive because it's more likely that the insurer will have to pay you. It may not be worth the extra cost unless you're in a high income specialized job and you'd have to take a big pay cut to switch jobs. Here are a few things to look for:

- *Guaranteed renewable:* This guarantees that your policy can't be canceled if you get sick. If you get a policy that requires you to take physicals every so often, you could lose your coverage when you need it.
- *Waiting period:* This is the period of time between when you got disabled and when the plan starts paying. You should take the longest waiting period you can since the longer the waiting period the cheaper the policy. The minimum on most policies is thirty days and

the maximum can be up to two years. A good average to shoot for is ninety days or six months.

- *Cost-of-living adjustments:* This feature automatically boosts your benefits either by a set amount or in concert with inflation.
- *Future insurability:* This clause lets you buy additional coverage later on, but it's usually not necessary unless you're making much less today than you expect to earn in the future.

330. Should I have long-term care insurance?

Nursing home expenses have outpaced inflation for many years. The average cost of skilled nursing care in my area is $4,300 per month or $50,000 per year and this doesn't include medication, health insurance, and so on. Long-term care insurance is a trade-off and whether or not you should buy it could have a lot to do with your own attitudes. Do you have a spouse or relatives who could care for you in the event of a major illness? Then you may not want to pay the hefty bill for this type of insurance. However, if you worry incessantly about how you would pay for nursing home care, then go ahead and consider buying coverage. (But remember that Medicaid can pick up the cost of a home if you can't.) Medicaid will pay for your nursing home care if you don't have the money, but in order to qualify, there are very strict guidelines on what you own. For example, if you give away your property within three years of going into a nursing facility, Medicaid won't pay. When deciding whether or not to buy long-term care insurance, remember that most people die within a year of entering a nursing facility. However, long-term nursing home care can be financially ruinous. If you do decide to buy long-term care insurance, experts recommend that the best time to buy it ranges from one's late 50s to early 60s. After this, the cost becomes prohibitive. If you're interested, read the report on nursing home insurance policies carried in the October 1997 issue of *Consumer Reports* at your local library.

331. If I buy a policy, are there certain provisions I should guarantee the policy has?

Coverage should include custodial care, intermediate care, and skilled nursing care. Custodial care provides no medical treatment but includes regular assistance with day-to-day activities if needed. Intermediate care is a step higher, including some required nursing care. Many facilities base the levels on how much nursing care a patient needs each day, such as helping to

---

LONG-TERM CARE INSURANCE

Company name _____

Insurance agent's name _____

Address _____

_____

Phone number _____ Fax _____

Name of insured _____

Policy owner _____

Policy # _____ Policy location _____

Monthly premium _____

Renewal date _____

Exclusions _____

---

wash and dress. A long-term care policy should have coverage for all three types of care.

I recommend a respite care/home health care/home nursing care provision as well. Many people, particularly the first spouse to get sick, stay at home until they need skilled care, but the family may need some medical or home care help. Be very careful about these provisions. Check with a neighboring nursing facility administrator to find out his or her opinion of good long-term care companies and policies.

332. What waiting period should I have if I get a long-term care policy?

A waiting period is like a deductible. The longer the deductible period, the less your premium will be. Some people advise that the waiting period should be no less than 20 days and no longer than 100 days, but I recommend the waiting period should be longer since this makes the premium noticeably lower. You'll need to have the funds available to pay for your care within whatever waiting period you decide. A shorter waiting period is important for the home health care provision. Compare cost with need.

333. What benefit level should I have with a long-term care policy?

The benefit level is usually paid on a daily method from $50 to $300 per day. Review your current income, Social Security, pension, investment income, and so on to decide how much you need to supplement your income so you can cover your monthly costs. Many policies offer an inflation rider, but it is an expensive addition to your premium, particularly since nursing home coverage has outpaced inflation. A $100-per-day benefit payment will supplement your income yet keep the policy premium reasonable.

334. Are there other provisions or features of long-term care that I should know to consider a policy?

Review the preexisting conditions clause. No illnesses or diseases should be exempted from eligibility for long-term care payment. If they do, find another company that does provide coverage for all illnesses. You want a policy that covers Alzheimer's disease, dementia, and other chronic illnesses that require years of long-term care. It is ironic to have a nursing home policy that doesn't cover Alzheimer's disease or dementia.

Review the eligibility requirements carefully. With hospital stay limits, you don't want a policy that requires a three-day hospital stay before benefits will kick in. Try to have a policy that requires a physician's statement, not hospitalization, to trigger benefits. Many people today are living in retirement homes and go directly from an apartment or room to the nursing section. If they had a long-term care policy that required prior hospitalization, they wouldn't receive benefits.

You can have a policy that pays benefits for two years, five years, or for a lifetime. Obviously, the annual premiums are dependent on the choices you make—the longer the benefit, the higher the premium.

335. I attended a seminar where the speaker recommended giving all my assets away to my children so I can go on Medicaid when I go into a nursing home. Does this make sense?

Medicaid is a government-subsidized program that is available to individuals who don't have the assets to pay for their nursing home care. You get

Medicaid by applying with your local welfare office. In the past, some people have spent their assets and then applied for Medicaid. You can't receive Medicaid benefits within three years of giving away your property. As of 1997, knowingly disposing of assets to become eligible for Medicaid is a federal crime.

If control is important to you and you want to control where you go and who will take care of you, remember that this control is only available if the assets are yours. These long-term care decisions are major lifetime/financial decisions for each individual and family situation and need to be reviewed with the utmost care.

INSURANCE CONSULTANTS

Health insurance agent

Assistant's name

Company

Address

E-mail address

Phone (   )   Fax (   )

Disability insurance agent

Assistant's name

Company

Address

E-mail address

Phone (   )   Fax (   )

Life insurance agent

Assistant's name

Company

Address

E-mail address

Phone (   )   Fax (   )

Car insurance agent

Assistant's name

Company

Address

E-mail address

Phone (   )   Fax (   )

Homeowner's insurance agent

Assistant's name

Company

Address

E-mail address

Phone (   )   Fax (   )

CHAPTER 5

MARRIAGE, DIVORCE, AND MONEY

Marriage involves many lifestyle changes, not the least of which is financial. You're combining your assets with another person's, perhaps for the first time. You may be opening joint checking accounts, applying for joint credit, making joint investments, and maybe buying a home together. On the other hand, there are many other financial issues to consider when the marriage ends.

There are only two ways to legally terminate a marriage: by death or divorce. The financial considerations of divorce are extremely complicated and very important to understand. However, divorce is a creature of state law—there is no such thing as a common law divorce. For that reason, the information in this chapter is very general because each state has different rules for divorce. For example, Nevada has a very short residency requirement—you only have to live there six months before you can file for divorce. Nine states have community property rules that are quite different than the rest of the states (Arizona, California, Idaho, Louisiana, Nevada, New Mexico, Texas, Washington, and Wisconsin).

MARRIAGE

336. My partner and I aren't married. What financial benefits are we missing out on?

While there is an IRS "marriage penalty," there are plenty of other financial benefits when two people are legally married that others can't take advantage of. This includes:

- Health and dental insurance: A spouse gets employer-provided group health coverage; a non-married partner at most companies can't participate.
- Life insurance: Most employers provide some amount of life insurance; a married spouse gets the benefit automatically if the employee dies. The unmarried partner gets a benefit only if he or she is named as beneficiary.
- Bereavement leave: Many companies provide up to three days paid leave for the death of a spouse or close relative. No paid time off is guaranteed for the death of an unmarried partner or a member of partner's family.
- Pension: An employee can name anyone as beneficiary, but if the employee dies before retirement, many companies will pay a surviving spouse some amount of pension. An unmarried partner is not usually eligible.
- Social Security: If an employee dies, a spouse upon reaching age 60 could receive monthly benefits. An unmarried partner is ineligible.
- Club memberships: There are often much cheaper "family" memberships not open to unmarried people. For example, one exercise club charges married couples a $2,500 initiation fee and $101/month. Two unmarried people each pay $2,000 and $91/month, nearly double the family membership.
- Auto Club Road Service: Married couples pay a "family" rate, but two unmarried people must each pay the single fee; together, it costs more.

337. Is it better from an economic point of view to live together and not get married?

When it comes to taxes—you bet. It's a fact that if you both work and you're married, you will usually pay more in taxes than you would if you were single. If each of you earns $45,000 a year, you'd pay about $1400 more in taxes once you tie the knot.

338. So is there no financial benefit to getting married?

Most states no longer recognize common-law marriages. In most states, if you aren't married and you split up, you may have a hard time dividing up your assets. No matter how much you acted like a married couple, including joint accounts at the bank, you won't be able to claim anything you can't clearly prove is yours.

339. Do I have any financial rights under a common-law marriage?

A few states still recognize common-law marriage. Common-law marriages occur when two people make a decision to be married, but don't have a judge or clergy officiate. You can't have a common-law marriage if one partner is legally married to someone else. To have a common-law marriage you must:

- not already be married to someone else;
- intend to be married now; and
- have the capacity to be married.

340. If I marry, should I have a prenuptial agreement?

A prenuptial agreement is a means by which people about to be married can change what would happen if they get divorced and could outline how property will be divided in the event of a divorce. An agreement also may be written to exclude you from support or alimony upon divorce. However, you cannot legally waive away your child's right to support.

If you are married without a prenuptial agreement and then die before your spouse, another issue that could arise is that your widower has a right to a portion of your property whether or not he is named in your will. In some states, a disinherited spouse can contest the will and receive a share. This can be done if a spouse is totally disinherited or if he receives less than the share to which he is legally entitled. A prenuptial agreement could mean you agree to give away your legal marital rights of contesting the will. These agreements are usually prepared by those who have been through the divorce process.

341. How do we go about drafting a prenuptial agreement?

Between six months and a year before you get married, each of you should hire a separate attorney, who will draft an agreement and review it with you before you sign. List every single thing that's important to you that you own, especially items you want your kids to inherit. This is also a nice way of making a complete inventory of all of your assets. It's important to sign the prenup at least three months before the actual wedding date, so your future spouse can't later claim that he or she was forced to sign "under pressure" (that is, right before the wedding), which could invalidate the agreement.

342. Talking about money and prenuptial agreements is so unromantic.

Agreeing to property division and understanding each other's rights is imperative to a good marriage. Discussing how you'll handle money is as important as planning for a wedding, knowing how both people feel about children, deciding whether both partners will work once children are born, and so on. Remember that prenuptial agreements can always be amended after marriage if both partners agree.

343. Can my husband and I have the same attorneys when we put together our prenuptial agreement?

A prenuptial agreement is like any contract. Both parties must fully disclose all their assets. Although a prenuptial agreement can be drawn up by one spouse's attorney, that attorney can't really represent both prospective spouses.

344. Why would anyone want to change a prenuptial after marriage?

After several years of marriage, a spouse may consider his wife's children as his own. Both partners may become more secure about each other's ulterior motives in becoming married. As in everything else in life, you can't anticipate the future and how your feelings might change.

345. I'm getting married for the second time. Is a prenuptial agreement a good idea? We each have children.

Yes, it's probably a good idea. In second marriages, your surviving children may come to blows if there are no legal provisions for what each of you brought into the marriage. And since half of all marriages end in divorce, it's a good idea to enter the union with a clear understanding of who owns what.

346. What is a postnuptial agreement?

A postnuptial agreement is not an amendment to a prenuptial agreement. A postnuptial agreement is really just another word for a comprehensive document that sets down in writing a couple's agreement to end their marriage. It is a very technical document that you should seek counsel for before signing.

347. We've been married for 10 years, but we're not getting along very well. My husband is threatening to change his will. Can he really disinherit me?

No. Most states will allow you to take a "forced share" in the estate, which can amount to up to a third of the total.

348. I love my fiancee, but she ran up a lot of bills before our engagement. Will I be liable to cover those debts if she can't pay after we get married?

No. In most states, creditors can't come after you unless you set up joint accounts; once you do (this is called "commingling funds") then your wife's creditors can come to you for the money. Most debts your wife incurs after you get married will be your responsibility, too, in most states.

349. I'm about to get remarried. How shall we reorganize our finances?

Look over this checklist as you are about to get married for a second time:

- Set up a joint bank account.
- Rent a safety deposit box in both names.
- Update your W-4 form at work, showing the new number of dependents.
- Review your insurance coverage (disability, car, and home). You may need more life insurance to protect your new spouse; you may need to maintain a policy naming your former wife as beneficiary.
- Change beneficiaries. Check over your bank accounts, life insurance, pension, and profit sharing.
- Coordinate medical and dental benefits. Eliminate duplicate coverage and maximize your benefits.

- Notify everyone of your new status. Inform Social Security, the IRS, the Department of Motor Vehicles, employers, credit card companies, and so on of your new address or name changes.
- Think about your taxes. Make adjustments to minimize the tax bite.
- Look at investments. Understand each other's investments and review your combined portfolio to make sure you have diversity and liquidity.

DIVORCE

350. My husband just left me. We have three children. How can I live?

Yours is the most common question. Fear of the unknown, fear of the future. Here's how to start getting a handle on your life:

- Retrench immediately.
- Stop all discretionary spending.
- Start a plan to build a life of your own.
- Talk with your husband about support for the children while you talk about separation and/or reconciliation.

As the months go by, you will know whether you will be able to stay where you are living or will need to move. It's best not to do anything rash unless you are in an abusive situation.

351. Should I clean out my savings accounts before I leave my husband?

One of the important things to consider when you contemplate leaving your husband is what your income will be while the divorce is pending. If you don't work outside the home or are retired, how will you pay your bills during a divorce? Withdrawing all your savings doesn't mean you will necessarily keep all that money—you will be accountable for it during the settlement process.

352. My husband died while we were legally separated, but not yet divorced. Can I still collect on his will?

Yes, you'll still get whatever he has left you in his will. If he had cut you out of his will, you could go to court and claim your spousal share, which can range from $50,000 to half the assets, depending on the state you live in and how long your marriage lasted.

353. Where can I get the best divorce?

Define best. Best can mean different things to different people: The best property settlement for the wronged party, the best property settlement for the divorce filer, the quickest divorce, the best alimony payments, the least alimony payments? There are many different aspects to a divorce and I recommend you speak with an attorney who specializes in divorce law.

It's also interesting to note that just because it may seem better to file for a divorce in New York rather than Pennsylvania doesn't mean you can. There are residency requirements before you are permitted to file for a divorce.

354. My wife moved in with her parents who live in another state. I think she will file for a divorce. What should I do?

If you think your wife is going to file for a divorce or you think your marriage will end in divorce, begin the process now. While your wife lives with her parents, she is in a position to meet the residency requirement of that state. Once she is a resident of the state where your in-laws live, she can file for divorce there. While the state in which you file may not make any difference in settlement awards, it will certainly be less expensive for you to have your divorce filed locally.

DIVORCE ATTORNEYS

355. Will I get a fair financial deal if I use a mediator instead of a lawyer?

A mediator can be cheaper and faster than having a lawyer. However, remember that mediation by definition means to "occupy a middle position." This means that the mediator is trying to find a happy medium for both partners. The person is neither party's advocate and may not have your best interests at heart. Furthermore, the mediator may not take into account legal considerations that might be very important when the agreement is reviewed by an attorney.

356. How do I pick a divorce lawyer?

You should take the same care in choosing a divorce lawyer that you would in selecting a doctor. Call someone you know in the legal profession for several recommendations. Tips from people who have been satisfied with their divorce lawyer are often an excellent guide as well as recommendations from your local bar association. Then you should interview the recommended individual and call his or her references to check for compatibility.

357. What are some of the qualities I should look for when I'm interviewing a prospective attorney?

A good divorce lawyer is one who looks for a solution to the conflict while protecting your rights. An overly aggressive attorney may cost you much more emotionally and financially than an attorney who works with you and your spouse's attorney to find solutions. Your attorney should have experience in divorce law. Ask about past successes, and how the person defines "success." Note the attitude and approach to the divorce process. Do you feel the attorney will be confident and supportive for you through the process? Is she interested in your situation? Does he listen rather than talk about himself? Does she offer mediation? Will he answer your questions? You want someone who will talk with you and ease your concerns.

358. Can my spouse and I use the same divorce lawyer as a way of saving money?

No. Divorce is an adversarial process. You should have independent counsel.

359. Can I use the same lawyer that my spouse first talked to about our possible divorce?

No. Even if your spouse only interviewed an attorney, that person cannot then represent you.

360. Should I hire a lawyer on an hourly basis or on a percentage of the settlement?

Some lawyers have a flat fee. Most cases are done on an hourly basis, although contingency fees (the fee is based on the amount of the settlement) aren't illegal.

361. I'm ready to meet with my divorce attorney and I know I'll need to get organized, but I don't know where to start.

Start by putting together a financial profile:

- How much money are you living on now?
- Where does it come from?
- What investments do you have?
- Could you turn your investments into cash quickly if you needed to?
- Who administers your pension or other retirement plans?
- Do you and your husband have wills? Where are they?
- How much do you owe and to whom?
- What are your life and health insurance arrangements?

362. After my attorney and I decided upon how he will be paid, he asked for a retainer. Is this typical?

Yes. The divorce process entails paying filing fees and court reporter fees and a retainer is often requested. It is appropriate as long as it isn't too exorbitant. You can curtail some of the costs associated with an attorney by compiling your own records and doing a lot of the paperwork yourself. You should receive billing reports and time records of the work that's been done on your behalf—work is often done that you don't see. You certainly should be receiving copies of paperwork that should keep you up-to-date about what is going on.

363. Is there a way to lower my attorney costs?

Yes. First you need to understand the three stages to a divorce:

- The pleading process: where the petition is filed and the process begins.
- The discovery phase: where attorneys learn what they don't already know about the case.
- The trial phase (if necessary).

The first phase involves lots of forms and most divorces don't go to trial. The most expensive part of a divorce is the second phase: discovery. If you can gather financial information together, this can save a lot of money. Get your lawyer what he needs to know and organize it so he doesn't need to spend a lot of time on it. Whenever you save your attorney time, you're saving yourself money. The best way to save money in attorney's fees is to take responsibility, be an active participant, cooperate with your attorney, and provide all the information.

364. I'm afraid my lawyer won't get me a good financial deal. Can you fire a lawyer who isn't working out?

If your attorney isn't answering your calls, isn't working with you through the process of divorce, and continues to do this after you have pointed out these problems, you can sever the relationship with a phone call. I'd follow up with a letter of dismissal terminating the lawyer's representation. Terminating an attorney's services isn't pleasant; you should take extra care in the beginning of the process to guarantee this won't be necessary later.

365. What if my spouse and I agree to a settlement and my lawyer doesn't like it?

Remember who is working for whom. You have hired your attorney. Her job is to counsel you, but you need not follow that advice. Because of guilt or expediency, often one partner will agree to give up more than is required by law and that might not be what an attorney would advise. Remember that you can fire your attorney any time and you should always make your own decisions. Listen carefully to your lawyer's advice and the reasons given before you reject it.

366. Should I consult an attorney before I separate from my spouse?

No harm is done by speaking with an attorney so you know your rights. You can pay your bill in cash so your spouse is not aware of the meeting. Speaking with an attorney does not mean you will separate, it just gives you an idea of what you may or may not do with regards to your property, learn what is the process of a divorce, and so on.

EXPENSES

367. I'm worried about paying for my divorce. Any advice?

If paying for the divorce will be difficult and your ex-husband isn't paying the bill, try to receive enough cash through the settlement so you can pay your lawyer's bill.

368. Can my husband pay for the expenses of my divorce?

Certainly. This can be part of the divorce settlement. Normally, however, each person pays for his or her part of the divorce.

369. Is it really harder to maintain a lifestyle now that I'm on my own?

Yes, it is, especially for women who most often find themselves losing out financially. The reality of the emotion of separation and divorce can only be compounded by the reality of discovering that two cannot live as cheaply as one. Each spouse must pay for a residence as well as food, insurance, transportation, electricity, telephone, and so on. For many, at least initially, the financial reality will make the situation seem horrible. Very few couples break up and maintain the lifestyle they had together. Many women must go back to work after a divorce. Often they move to smaller homes. The noncustodial parent may find that after paying support, there is little or no discretionary income. There isn't an easy solution to the situation except to be frugal with your finances.

PROPERTY

370. What financial information do we need to take into account as we divide our assets after we separate?

Before you separate and before you discuss separation with your spouse, you should compile your financial records. You will need:

- Your tax returns for the last three to five years
- Copies of current bank statements
- Copies of current brokerage statements
- Most recent pension, 401(k) statements
- Any accounts in spouse's name alone
- Records of inherited property
- Copies of deeds
- Financial statements
- Canceled checks
- Credit card numbers

371. How is property divided during a divorce?

It depends on the state in which you live. For example, in Pennsylvania (a state with no-fault divorces), property may be divided in a variety of ways ranging from one spouse receiving all the property (not likely) to a straight 50-50 split. Knowing the division rules of your state should help alleviate some surprise, frustration, and anger.

Before meeting with your lawyer, make a list of your property, the title to the property, what was owned prior to the marriage, and present value of all the property. Most problems in property division occur with property that one partner owned before marriage and to which money was added after the marriage began. For example, if you had a brokerage account before you were married, it was worth a certain amount. After you got married, you may have added and subtracted money to and from the account. This makes it hard to figure out what is marital property and what was brought into the marriage. It's the responsibility of the spouse who wants to retain this property to go back and figure out what's what. After you've gathered the information, you should prepare a "his," "hers," and "ours" pile. The "his" and "hers" is usually easy to divide—it's the "ours" that gets sticky.

372. What property is considered when dividing the assets at divorce?

There is community property and marital property. Marital property is property that a couple acquires while married. In the nine community property states (Arizona, California, Idaho, Louisiana, Nevada, New Mexico, Texas, Washington, and Wisconsin), marital property is defined as anything that is acquired during the marriage. In most cases, it's divided equally. However, future income isn't property and is not subject to division. This is why there is often such a difference between the financial situation of a man and woman after the divorce. Because women often earn less, their lifestyle often suffers upon divorce.

373. What is marital property and can I hang onto all of it during a divorce?

Generally speaking, marital property means any property that you acquired during your marriage regardless of title. During a divorce settlement, property that is considered part of a marriage is divided between the two former partners. If you acquired property before your marriage, how it would be divided at settlement would depend on when you bought it and how it has increased in value during your marriage.

374. So how is property divided if one or both partners have brought property into a marriage?

When the property was acquired before marriage, its growth while the partners were married affects how it will be divided. For example, if you worked for ten years before you got married and you had a pension plan, that wouldn't be considered marital property. However, while you were married, the fund increased due to contributions from your employer and by the fund's investments. The growth and contribution from the time you were married until you were separated is considered marital property.

375. What happens if we don't agree to the property division?

If you can't agree on how to divide the property, the court can resolve the problem, but bear in mind this takes more time and money. Moreover, the court may not have the same sense of fairness that you and your spouse do. When you turn over the property division to the court, you lose control. The processes available:

- *Alternate Selection:* Both spouses take turns choosing one item at a time until everything is divided.
- *Judge's Choice:* The court decides how everything will be divided.
- *Auction:* Everything is sold and the proceeds are divided.

376. If I inherit property from my parents while married, must I divide that with my spouse when we get divorced?

In this case, the property was not a gift so it is not considered part of the property settlement. However, if you put your spouse's name on the property, the court considers that you gave your spouse half this property as a gift and that can be part of the settlement. In addition, if you inherited a house and it has increased in value during your marriage, that increase may be considered marital property when the final division of property is made. Inherited property is not considered marital property even though it might have been inherited during the marriage.

377. Should I be concerned about my husband's feelings rather than worrying about getting the best settlement? We have to work together raising the children until they are out of school.

It's important to keep a civil relationship with your husband; however, once the divorce is final, so is your property settlement. There is no guarantee that you will remain friends through the process and once you've given up assets, you can't ask for them back. Therefore, decide upon a fair settlement and stick to it.

378. I don't want a divorce because I don't want to lose my house. Can I refuse to give one to my husband and force him to remain married?

No. No-fault divorce states allow a divorce if either of you wants out of the marriage. You can delay the divorce from proceeding promptly; however, after a period of time the divorce is reviewed and property division is ordered by a judge.

379. Should my spouse and I talk about splitting our assets before we talk with an attorney or wait until we meet with counsel?

It is always more expensive to use attorneys for anything in a divorce. However, it's also important to understand your rights and to know what you are possibly giving up. You might want to talk to an attorney before discussing how you will split assets.

380. Will I lose our house if I leave our home until my spouse has been served with the divorce papers?

Divorce is an emotional as well as an economic decision. Living in your home during an adversarial transaction is often too difficult for people to handle. Check the law in your state; in many states, you aren't penalized for leaving the marital home.

381. If I'm living in our house while we're separated, who pays for major maintenance and repairs?

While you are undergoing the divorce, the house is still considered owned by both of you. Daily expenses, utilities, lawn care, and so on are your obligation. However, the big-ticket items (capital expenditures) are your joint responsibility. The payment of the expenses will need to be discussed by both of you.

382. During the division process, are the tax consequences of future liquidation of the funds taken into consideration?

Yes, it can be important.

383. How do we figure out the value of our home?

By appraisal or agreement. If both of you agree how much your house is worth, fine. If not, a qualified independent appraisal should be commissioned to give a true value of the house. Many people overvalue their homes because of the sentimentality involved.

384. Once the value is calculated, how do we split it up?

There are several ways to settle on the division of real estate. They include:

- Sell the property and divide the net proceeds in half.
- Rent the property and share the income and expenses until the real estate is sold. This is often done so that the property isn't sold too quickly at a loss. The problem with this method is that you are essentially in business with your spouse until the property is sold.
- Buy out your spouse.

385. How do I buy out my spouse?

There are several ways:

- Refinance and increase your mortgage so you have enough cash to pay off your spouse.
- Take a note from your spouse and have him pay you monthly.
- Pay your spouse his portion in cash from other property you received in the settlement.
- Trade your home for other property in the settlement.

386. My husband spent a great deal of money on his girlfriend the last year before our separation. Do I have to help pay off that debt?

No. Equitable division doesn't require that you pay off debts your spouse incurred. Although most states don't use infidelity as a factor in determining who gets what, economic misdeeds are taken into consideration when it comes to dividing property.

387. What type of information is used to determine an equitable splitting of our property?

Remember that equitable doesn't always mean equal. It often can mean a two-thirds-one-third split with the wealthier partner getting the smaller chunk. Here's a partial list of factors often taken into consideration during a division of property review:

- Job skills each spouse has or could develop
- The probability of acquisition of more funds in the future (inheritance, stock options, and so on)
- Retirement benefits of both spouses and when they begin
- Health and age of both spouses
- Property brought into the marriage
- How long the marriage lasted
- Alimony awards
- Child care and support
- Tax consequences of the property
- Responsibility and care of minor children

ALIMONY

388. Are modern-day courts still awarding alimony?

Yes. Alimony is a sort of allowance paid to a spouse for support pending or after a legal separation or divorce. The spouse may voluntarily pay alimony or it may be awarded by the court, which decides how much, how often, and for how long it will be paid. The court makes these decisions based on a number of factors, including:

- Length of time the marriage has endured
- Whether one spouse has not worked outside the home
- If one spouse is "at fault"

389. Which is better—getting alimony or a bigger chunk of the property division?

It depends. You have to pay taxes on alimony and the person who pays it gets to deduct it. Alimony usually ceases at death. It's often a means to financial security when a division of property can't be totally equitable. The purpose of alimony is to support the spouse who doesn't earn as much, giving that person the time to become self-supporting.

390. Can my husband ask for support?

Certainly and it happens more often than you might think.

391. I've only been married for a year. Will I get alimony?

The likelihood of alimony is very unlikely unless there are young children or health considerations that limit your ability to work.

392. I discovered my husband cheating on me. Will I get alimony?

Alimony is not punishment; it's support.

CHILDREN AND CHILD SUPPORT

393. How does the court decide who will pay child support and how much it will be?

While divorce is governed by state law, child support is subject to federal law. Basically, it's the parents' duty to support their children. Each state has a child support model and the courts are available to resolve disputes if parents can't agree. Pennsylvania uses an Income Shares Model; each spouse is responsible for child support based on income and earning capacity. You still have to pay child support even if your spouse doesn't let you see your children. There is an adjustment for a shared 50/50 custody situation.

394. I don't want my ex-husband to be near the children; he's not the best of fathers. Can I agree not to make him pay child support in exchange for staying away?

You and your husband can agree to this; however, you can't legally sign away your child's support obligation. If you die or change your mind, the children's father would need to begin paying support.

395. What if my spouse won't work and can't pay child support?

With national unemployment rates so low, it's hard to tell the court that you can't find a job, although earning capacity is taken into account when awarding child support. Your spouse may not find the job he wants or dreams of, but children need support based on his capacity. If he refuses to pay, the court can send him to jail.

396. My ex-husband quit his job and now states that he doesn't have any money to pay child support. Can he do this?

Although your children's father can quit his job, not having a job won't end his obligation to pay child support. Support is based on earning capacity, not actual earnings—particularly in this time of low unemployment. The court frowns upon delinquent child support payments just because someone isn't employed. Although the job may not be what he wants, your children's father should be able to find a job. The court doesn't care whether you like your job or it isn't what you've always wanted. They want your children to receive support. It is recommended that noncustodial parents look for a better job while they keep their old job, since they will be assessed support payments even if they don't work.

397. My sister's husband wanted her to take a lump-sum payment as child support. Is this legal?

Parents can't waive their child's right to support. Property given in lieu of support is inappropriate.

398. My husband is claiming that he's not the father of our son, so he doesn't have to pay child support. Can he do this?

It's possible today to determine paternity using blood and DNA testing. However, it is assumed within an intact marriage that the husband is the father of the wife's children. Thus, unless a husband is sterile or distant (meaning he was out of town at the time conception occurred), the husband is assumed to be the father of the children and must pay child support.

399. If my ex-husband magnifies his expenses, can that lower the support payment for the children?

Yes. It is important to note that living expenses can be manipulated to control support and you should review this matter with your attorney. Child support is based on a percentage of your income, taking into consideration your living expenses and other things. If your ex-husband spends all his money on living expenses (such as spending $2,000 a month for rent), he will still be obligated to pay you a certain amount of support for his children.

400. My husband refuses to pay me child support. Do I have any recourse?

Your husband's wages can be garnished. While divorce is governed by state law, child support is mandated by federal law. Under the Family Support Act of 1988 and the Uniform State Reciprocal Enforcement of Support Act, the federal government will try to collect delinquent child support payments no matter where the nonpayor is located. Half of all child support payments that are due are either not paid or not paid promptly. The Personal Responsibility and Work Opportunity Reconciliation Act of 1996 requires states to set up a program to locate noncustodial parents to enforce child support orders. It's a way to try to locate deadbeat parents.

401. My wife called my employer and asked for a W-2. Can she do that?

She is trying to acquire information that you should already be giving her. Your employer can only give your W-2 to her unless there is a court order. Employers are now being advised to give duplicate W-2s only if requested in writing. If your wife wants to have this information, she should contact the Domestic Relations Office concerning your total support situation.

402. I was ordered to pay a specific amount of child support and now my wife makes more money than I do. Can the support agreement be modified?

Yes, a support agreement can be modified if your incomes go up or down. Thus, if your wife's income has increased, it might be time to review the agreement. However, always remember that if you reopen a support agreement, the agreement modification can go against you—you could end up paying more.

403. If I take on large debts, will that lower my child support?

Taking on more debts won't necessarily lower your child support. You have an obligation that must be met.

404. My ex-husband just died. What happens to my child support?

Unless stated otherwise in the divorce decree, support ceases at death. That's an important consideration in the property division since child support and/or alimony payments will cease at death.

405. If I remarry, is my new spouse's income taken into consideration when calculating child support?

A new spouse's income is not directly taken into consideration in calculating child support payments. However, her income will help decrease your living expenses and this is a basis for changing child support. Living with another adult can decrease your expenses and this is a factor in calculating child support.

406. What if my wife can handle paying all the bills on her salary? Do I still have to pay child support?

Even if your spouse can afford all the bills on her own, you are obligated to pay support for your child based on your income and hers.

407. How will a divorce affect getting financial aid for my children's college expenses?

Most college financial aid offices require a financial statement from both the custodial and noncustodial parent. Colleges feel that before aid (grants and loans) is given, both parents should give some support. If a parent remarries, income from a stepparent can be used in figuring out how much money you need to contribute toward college when applying for financial aid.

408. What does legal guardian mean?

Legal guardian is the person you appoint in your will to take care of property and/or your children.

409. How does this compare to being a custodial parent?

The custodial parent is the parent with whom the child lives. Unless the custody is joint (or shared), one parent is usually known as the custodial parent and the other is the noncustodial parent. The legal guardian (both parents can be legal guardians) has the right to decide the child's religion, medical care, and so on.

410. If I die before my children are twenty-one, I want my children to live with my brother and his wife rather than their father. He doesn't see them and is behind on his support payments. Can I do that?

No. Unless your husband has signed away his parental rights, you can't have your brother appointed as your children's guardian. They still have a parent. You *can* have someone besides your children's father handle your money for the children. This person would either be called a guardian of the property or an appointed trustee.

411. If my ex-husband takes the children, will he receive my survivor Social Security benefits?

Ironically, if your children's father is their legal custodian after you die, your Social Security benefits for their care will probably go to him. Social Security requires that someone file for benefits and be appointed representative payee. Although you might like the person handling the benefits to be the trustee you've appointed in your will, the government usually appoints the custodial parent to receive the payments.

412. After I die, if my ex-husband is custodian for the children does he have to handle my money that I leave for my children?

Definitely not. It's not a great idea to have any guardian of the children also be a guardian of their money because it's often difficult for their legal guardian to deny a child's requests for money if they've been caring for them. If you appoint a separate person to handle their money, the job of handling requests for money is handled by someone other than the care-taker. It creates a sort of check-and-balance to protect your children from themselves.

PENSIONS AND BENEFITS

413. I want to begin receiving Social Security (I'm sixty-five); however, my ex-husband is still working. Can I begin to receive benefits?

If you were married for more than ten years, you are eligible to receive benefits on your ex-husband's account. You will be able to review the benefits based on your earnings history and compare it with the benefits based on your ex-husband's earnings history to decide which is more advantageous for you. You can apply for these benefits when you become eligible for Social Security as if you were applying on your account.

414. If my ex-husband's benefits increase due to increased earnings, will my benefits increase (even though I am already receiving a monthly check) as well?

If your ex-husband's benefits increase, your monthly benefit check will increase. This increase occurs even if you are already receiving benefits.

415. After the divorce, can I remain a beneficiary of my ex-husband's pension plan at work?

If your ex-husband does not remarry, he can keep you on as beneficiary of his pension plan. You also can receive a portion of his pension plan through the divorce. If you have the option of keeping your portion of the benefits with his current employer, you should review your options with your financial planner about whether it is better to pull out your share of the benefits and roll the funds into your own IRA or keep them with the employer.

416. If I keep the benefits with the employer, will they provide me with the information annually, like they have been while we were married?

If, as part of your divorce settlement, you will receive a portion of your husband's pension—and his employer allows you to maintain a portion of that benefit within its plan—the employer is obligated to provide you with information about your account as if you were an employee.

417. One of the settlement options my husband's attorney recommended is that I remain beneficiary of his large life insurance policy in exchange for giving up some current benefits. How do I guarantee that my ex-husband doesn't change the beneficiary designation after the divorce is final?

The beneficiary designation can be made irrevocable so the designation cannot be changed by filling out a form provided by the insurance company. You should also worry about whether your husband will continue to pay the premiums, who is responsible for paying the premiums, what will happen if the premiums aren't paid, how many years do the premiums need to be paid, and so on. Although the idea of being beneficiary of a policy is interesting and a consideration in a settlement, you will need an agreement and possibly a sinking fund to guarantee the policy stays in force.

418. Apparently my husband never removed his first wife's name as beneficiary on his retirement plan. Is it true she can still collect?

Yes and no. If a husband dies before removing his first wife's name as beneficiary on a life insurance policy or living trust, she can still legally collect even if he has remarried. This is why you must make sure the first spouse's name is removed from all these plans when you remarry. However, if you are legally married, even though your husband never changed the beneficiary designations, you will receive the benefits from his employer's retirement plan as his wife.

419. My husband and I are getting divorced. Should his pension plan be part of our financial settlement?

Yes. You're generally entitled to a share although not necessarily half. If you both have pensions, then both of those plans should be part of the financial negotiations. You may want to settle for taking property instead of a piece of your ex-husband's future pension allocation. However, it can be complicated to ensure your rights to pension plan money so be sure your lawyer follows all the regulations. If you're already divorced and you didn't include your husband's pension in the divorce agreement, it's too late now.

420. My divorce was just finalized. What should I do about estate planning?

Even while you were undergoing the divorce process, you should have been considering who will handle your estate when you die or become incapacitated. Who will handle your assets if you have minor children? Who will take care of the children's investments and when will they receive their money? The paperwork should be changed as soon as possible. You need to change the beneficiaries and contingent beneficiary designations for your life insurance policies, pensions, IRAs, and everything else you own. Do this as soon as possible. Delay can create a financial nightmare for your family if you die before completion of the changes.

421. Where do I get health insurance after we're divorced?

There is a federal law (COBRA) that requires your husband's employer to offer thirty-six months of health insurance coverage to you (you pay for it) after a divorce. Some states require the insurance coverage to continue until you remarry or you become eligible for Medicare. However, COBRA is usually transitional coverage until you can obtain coverage on your own. There could be a negative side to this coverage. If you take your spouse's coverage for the thirty-six months and don't try to get your own health insurance until the coverage is almost ended, you run the risk that if you get sick it may be hard to find your own independent coverage. Therefore, it's a good idea to get your own health insurance policy as soon as you can.

422. My attorney talked about a QDRO. What is it and what does it accomplish?

A QDRO (Qualified Domestic Relations Order) is an order of the divorce court that requires your husband's retirement plan give you (the non-covered spouse) your legal interest in the retirement plan. The court directs your husband's employer to set up a separate account for you. You can never have more rights to the retirement plan than your husband had. The QDRO is established after reviewing the assets that need to be divided.

423. Do I have to take a QDRO lump-sum payment or can I roll over the funds into an IRA?

You can roll over the funds into an IRA and thus retain the tax-deferred status of the funds until your retirement if the plan permits this. This may be a good idea because, while there is no 10 percent penalty for early withdrawal on QDRO retirement funds, the money would be taxable the year you take the payment unless you roll it over into the IRA. Make certain before you agree to a QDRO what rights you are acquiring.

424. How do we work out the debts that we incurred while married?

You'll have a problem if there are more debts than assets or if you have joint credit cards and other nonsecured debts. They are usually put into categories of husband, wife, and joint debts.

425. What if my spouse agreed to pay the debts and now isn't, and it's ruining my credit?

Creditors don't care if you are going through a divorce. If you have joint debts, you're both responsible for the debts. You have some recourse but it's wiser to plan ahead while you are going through the divorce. Some of the things you can do to neutralize the debt situation is:

- Pay off the joint debts during the divorce process so there are no debts when the divorce is final. (Of course, this can't be done with a house, but you can at least pay off all credit cards.)
- Get a release from the creditor so that the debt is no longer your responsibility.
- Take on the debts with an increase in assets as your portion of the property settlement so that you have control over the payment of the debts.
- Take security for repayment, such as a second mortgage on the house.
- Ask creditors to send late notices so you can keep abreast of late payments and nonpayment.

426. What recourse do I have to make my husband pay the bills?

There are several options and although you may not like any of them, the situation needs to be dealt with. Several of your alternatives are:

- Pay off the debts if you can and have your ex repay you when possible.
- Pay the debts and go back to court and ask for relief.
- Bring an immediate court action against your spouse to pay the bills.
- File bankruptcy (as a last resort).

427. I discovered that my husband planned for months to leave me, hiding assets and changing over credit cards. What can be done to fix this?

It's always amazing to me that people who wouldn't consider stealing from anyone attempt to hide assets from a spouse—which is, of course, stealing. Your husband may be required to return this property, which will cost both of you money (attorney fees, investigative expenses, costs of retrieving information, and so on). Like yourself, he would be accountable for assets taken. Little can be done if the property isn't found or discovered after it's given away. It often costs more to get it back than it's worth. You can only hope there are other assets available so you can receive a fair division. Your best defense is often a good offense—have a list of all the assets that you have as a family. Make sure you know whenever there is a change.

PART II

INVESTING WHAT YOU'VE SAVED

CHAPTER 6

HIRING A PROFESSIONAL

A financial adviser is a professional who advises you on how to spend your money, how to save your money, and how to make more money. Your financial adviser can be your accountant, stock broker, insurance agent, banker, financial planner, or even an attorney or real estate agent. Choosing an adviser is one of the most important financial decisions you can make. This chapter will answer questions on how to select the right adviser for your situation and how to work with the adviser you have chosen.

GETTING STARTED

428. When do I need a financial adviser?

You'd probably benefit from financial planning when you are undergoing life changes that can dramatically affect your finances. You may not need a total financial plan, but a review of your situation may be a comfort to you and you would be surprised how often a review can save you money. Having a structured financial plan is important to your financial well-being.

429. What can a financial adviser do for me?

A financial adviser helps you manage your money better and helps you develop a financial plan and choose investments to make it work. An adviser can set up a budget, open a life insurance trust, or guide you with retirement planning. Plans can be short term, but lifelong planning is both common and important. You can have a plan for a specific goal, such as retirement, or you can have a plan that encompasses every aspect of your financial situation. Common financial concerns are:

- Retirement
- College savings
- Estate planning
- Divorce
- Income taxation
- Eldercare
- Starting your own business

430. What are the different kinds of financial advisers to choose from?

There is a long list of the various types of financial advisers. They are:

- Bank customer service representative
- CPAs (Certified Public Accountants)
- Financial planners (CFP and ChFC)
- Insurance agents
- Private money managers (asset manager, personal banker, and trust officer)
- Stockbrokers/financial consultants

431. With the different types of investment advisers, how do I know whom to use?

The type of planner depends on your goals and the kind of relationship you want to develop through implementation of your plan. Some planners define your goals, provide a plan, and then send you elsewhere for the plan to be put to work. Other professionals specialize in buying and selling products for your plan. Still others work with you through every stage of your plan.

432. How much experience should a planner have?

A designation of financial planner indicates the person has an education and at least three years of experience. I'd look for at least five years of experience. Financial planning is a very complex process. Knowledge isn't acquired overnight.

433. Is a planner's reputation important?

A planner's reputation is of utmost importance. Referrals from others who have been pleased with the planner's service or referrals from other professionals, friends, or your employer are all ways to verify the person is honorable and capable.

434. Is it important to work with a planner who is affiliated with a major firm?

Planners may work independently or they may belong to either a local or a national firm. (Experts don't agree which is best.) There is no right or wrong affiliation for a planner. Large firms are known for their education of personnel, access to research, and their deep pockets. Local or independent planners probably can offer more independent advice. The reputation of the planner is what is most important. After that, decide if you feel comfortable with the person's affiliation.

435. Should I get a total financial plan or take it a step at a time?

A total financial plan can be expensive. It's a wonderful gift and every so often it's a good idea to have one. However, particularly with a new planner I'd take it a step at a time, focusing on one aspect of your plan and then continue if you're satisfied with the service provided.

436. As a single woman, I want to be taken seriously as an investor. Where can I find a financial adviser I can trust?

Look for a financial adviser who has experience working with single women. You might choose to seek help in an investment discussion seminar designed for women (check out your library, civic center, or university for information). Women-oriented professional groups may offer leads. Contact local or national women's groups for referrals or check out the Older Women's League at 661 11th St., Ste. 700, Washington, DC 20001; call (202) 783-6686.

437. My financial planner recommended I use an investment adviser/money manager. What do they do?

A money manager is not for everyone. It's for people who have a great deal of money that requires individual management. Money managers handle your funds, make trades on your behalf, and buy and sell the stocks and bonds in the account for you. They manage the funds within the management account for you.

438. Why would you use a money manager?

The nice thing about this type of financial adviser is the personalization of your investments. Your portfolio is designed for you with your tax situation in mind. You have the performance of individual stocks with the safety of individual bonds in your portfolio, and you can talk with the person who's making your investment decisions.

439. My money manager gave me a contract to sign. Why?

A money manager is a financial adviser who has total discretion to handle the funds you want to have managed. You sign an agreement so the manager can provide services to manage your money. The contract will outline the conditions of management, services rendered, fees, and how the relationship can be terminated.

440. My stockbroker/adviser wanted me to leave everything up to him. I felt uncomfortable with that.

Leaving everything up to him is setting up what is known as a discretionary relationship. Only in a money management situation would I feel comfortable with a discretionary situation. As a money manager, fees are based on the amount of assets under management, not on what is bought and sold. You should not have a discretionary account with a stockbroker or financial adviser unless this person is working within a money management account.

441. I saw an ad in the paper for a free seminar for financial planning. Should I go?

Certainly. You can always gather information that may be useful to you. However, you need to understand that these types of seminars are a way to attract potential clients for the planner presenting the information. You may learn helpful information at the seminar and after you have reviewed the education, experience, and fees involved you can decide whether you want to work with that planner any further.

442. How about adult education classes on finances at local universities?

The problem with these is that many of the instructors are really brokers or financial planners trolling for clients. You probably won't get many specifics, but you'll be encouraged to see the instructor if you contact him after class (read "hire" here). Sometimes colleges hire these people because the school knows the brokers want to sell financial products and therefore the school doesn't have to pay the instructors as much. However, there are also ethical instructors at these classes. Ethical instructors will be there to teach, not to solicit clients. They may discourage their students from hiring them.

443. Is cost the best way to pick a financial planner?

Look for a good, qualified planner, not a cheap planner. Although there are several types of planners/advisers who do not receive payment for their services from you, they definitely receive compensation for their services from someone. Look for an adviser with experience and education and one who will give you the most information for your money. Overpaying doesn't make sense, but neither does looking for the cheapest expert.

444. My adviser recently received the CFP designation. What is this?

Certified Financial Planner (CFP) is a national designation from the College for Financial Planning in Denver, Colorado, given to those who have completed a two-year program in tax planning, investments, and other aspects of personal finance. They also must pass a ten-hour exam. Before a planner is awarded a CFP license, he or she must have three years of work experience and promise to adhere to a Code of Ethics. CFPs agree to undergo thirty hours of continuing education every two years.

445. How does this differ from a ChFC designation?

Chartered Financial Consultant (ChFC) is awarded by the American College in Bryn Mawr, Pennsylvania, after designees pass ten courses in financial planning, wealth accumulation, and estate planning. ChFCs also must have three years of work experience before they are awarded the designation. ChFCs agree to thirty hours of continuing education every two years. A major difference between the designations is that ChFCs do not have to take the ten-hour exam and the ChFC ten-course study program includes five core courses and an additional five courses chosen by the designee. This way a person on the ChFC track may take five courses with an emphasis in insurance, investments, and so on.

446. Isn't there a designation for CPAs?

The American Institute of Certified Public Accountants gives the PFS (Personal Financial Specialist) designation to CPAs who have passed a six-hour test and have three years of experience in financial planning. CPAs have a rigorous continuing education requirement of eighty hours every two years.

447. How can I find a good CPA?

Contact the American Institute of Certified Public Accountants, 1211 Avenue of the Americas, New York, NY 10036. The AICPA is the professional association of CPAs and can give you names of those who have completed the Institute's Personal Financial Specialist program. Many CPAs can provide financial advice on a fee basis.

448. What qualifications should I look for in a financial adviser?

The general rule of thumb is to work with a planner who has received one of the three designations (CFP, PFS, or ChFC) and who has at least three to five years of work experience in the financial planning field.

449. Where can I go to begin searching for a financial adviser? Should I just pick up the Yellow Pages?

The best way to find any type of adviser is through a personal reference. Ask a friend or respected individual whom he or she recommends. Another option is to ask a professional for a personal recommendation. If this isn't possible, you could contact a professional organization. The next step is to call and discuss scheduling an appointment to meet with the planner.

450. How much should I expect to pay for good investment advice?

That's a very difficult question since different advisers earn their fees in different ways. A banker is salaried, an insurance agent receives a commission, and a money manager receives a percentage of assets under management. There are hourly fee-only financial planners, as well as plans with set prices (often provided through brokerage firms). Ask the International Association for Financial Planning (800-945-4237) for the average fee-only financial plan hourly cost for your area and use this to gauge all financial services.

451. What are the ways I can pay for financial planning advice?

You pay for financial advice and for the investments you make in one of four ways, depending on the adviser you use and the products you buy. Sometimes the cost is built into the price of the investment, sometimes it is added to the cost, and sometimes you pay for it separately. The four ways are:

- *Fee-only or hourly:* Planners charge by the hour or by the plan and you are billed for services rendered.
- *Fee-based:* Fee-based planners charge a fee for the plan and may also earn commissions on the products they sell.
- *Commission:* Advisers work on commission earned, receiving a percentage of the sale as payment.
- *Salary:* Advisers are paid by their employers.

452. Tell me more about a commission-based planner.

When you hire a commission-based planner, you're not really getting a financial adviser or counselor—you're getting a salesperson. In fact, people who used to call themselves stockbrokers or insurance brokers are now referring to themselves as financial consultants, which really cloaks the fact that they earn their fees via commission. That's rather like a vacuum cleaner salesman calling himself a home beautification consultant. Would you expect a Bissell representative to tell you how great the Electrolux is? The Bissell salesman is going to push his Bissell, and if he mentions the Electrolux at all, it will be to tell you what's wrong with it.

453. Tell me more about fee-based planners.

A fee-based planner is a financial planner who charges you a percentage of the assets being invested. This way there is no incentive to sell you on investments with high commissions (such as limited partnerships) or to generate lots of transactions as a way of producing more commissions. However, there are drawbacks to this type of planner. If the person's income is based on your total amount of assets, it's not likely that the planner would recommend investments that would deplete your investment capital (such as real estate ventures). There would also be a strong incentive for such a person to caution you against paying down your mortgage for the same reason. Finally, most fee-based advisers require six-figure minimums.

454. Is the best bet an hourly-based planner?

Yes. Because this type of financial planner doesn't sell products, the person can be objective. Some people find that it can be helpful to do their own research and then hire a fee-based planner for one or two sessions for advice. You can then implement the advice on your own.

455. Is it rude to ask how much commission my adviser will make?

No. You should ask how much an adviser is making on a product you purchase. It's the only way to decide whether the cost of an investment is justified by its value to your plan. Commission on a stock transaction shouldn't be more than 1 percent of the trade, but can typically range from .5 to 2 percent, even 3 percent, depending on whether you use a discount or full-service broker. Commission on a mutual fund can range from zero to 8.5 percent. Different funds have different fees.

456. I've heard about some dishonest advisers. What kind of things should I be on the lookout for?

Be skeptical of a planner who guarantees that you are going to make a lot of money, insists that an investment has little or no risk, and seems to oppose CDs, stocks and bonds, and even known mutual funds. Advisers should not:

- recommend that you put all your funds in one type of investment;
- recommend investments you don't understand;
- fail to explain investments clearly;
- state the investments are too complicated to explain;
- argue with you;
- ignore you; or
- be vague about the amount of commission or fees he or she will earn.

457. I received a call for a fantastic investment on the phone. What should I do?

Never send money to someone you transact business with over the phone. Meet in person, if possible. Find out for whom they work, their experience, and their credentials. Ask to be sent information about the investment for your review and perusal. Never transact business on the spot; no legitimate adviser would expect you to do so.

458. I'm not certain how much my adviser is charging me. How do I find this out?

Ask your adviser. If she is a registered investment adviser, attorney, or accountant, she is required to give you a disclosure notice/engagement letter disclosing fees. Brokers, realtors, insurance agents, and bankers usually provide you with a menu of products with their fees. You may or may not be paying the fee for their services; they may receive compensation for the service they provide you from the products they sell. It's a good idea to ask your adviser how much he or she will make on the transaction. Also, initially request an estimate of the cost of the services provided, although this is often hard to figure out until the planner begins the process.

459. Do I need a CPA? Aren't they for the rich?

A CPA (Certified Public Accountant) will prepare your income tax returns and offer tax advice if you wish. You need a CPA if your tax return is complex, you're self-employed, a first-time home buyer, or you've been audited by the IRS. A CPA can look at your tax picture long term and recommend a tax planning strategy which can be a considerable savings to you. Their expertise is the income tax code; however, they may be able to offer information on estate planning, deferral, and how to minimize income tax liability. For more information about the experts and tax planning, see Chapter 3.

460. How does a CPA get paid?

Generally, a CPA will bill you by the hour. Out-of-pocket expenses (long distance calls, faxes, and copies) are often additional costs. You can save money if you ask the CPA what you can do to help. You should receive an engagement letter after your first meeting which outlines fees for services rendered.

461. Should I consult a tax attorney or a CPA?

Unless you are involved in a serious tax dispute with the IRS and need to go to court, a CPA is a better choice because of the lower cost. A tax attorney is a specialist. A CPA can prepare your tax return, but a tax attorney doesn't prepare returns; he or she deals with tax law.

462. Is my lawyer considered a financial adviser?

Your attorney can be one of the people who saves your family the largest amount of money in your total estate plan. She can negotiate prenuptial agreements, divorce settlements, adoptions, custody matters, and writing a will. Attorneys charge on an hourly basis and you should receive an engagement letter after your first meeting.

463. Should I hire a lawyer who specializes in estate planning?

You will need to hire an attorney who specializes in estate planning to prepare your documents so your plans will be implemented at your death. In our litigious society, attorneys will know their limitations and should refer you to someone else if they can't do the proper planning for your situation. Attorneys charge on an hourly basis; the more specialized their practices, the higher the fee.

464. How can I save fees when I deal with my attorney?

There are several ways to save money when dealing with attorneys:

- Do as much of the work yourself as you can. Gather documents, compile names and addresses of witnesses, make phone calls, and copy materials. All this helps save fees.
- Keep conversations with your attorney as brief as possible. Don't chitchat. Discuss your case, explain what you've accomplished or need, and go from there.

- Be up front with your attorney. Give her all the information at the beginning. This saves time and money later.

465. I'm very dissatisfied with the services of my attorney. What can I do?

You should first terminate your relationship with your attorney before you proceed with another adviser. Although you will be charged for services rendered to date, ask for any documents and copies of all paperwork in your file to take elsewhere. The material is yours—you paid for it.

466. I want to buy stock. Do I need a stockbroker?

You can purchase a no-load mutual fund directly from the fund; however, you need a stockbroker to purchase stock and make the trade for you (you can purchase directly through the Internet, though that is really with a broker). You have a choice between a full-service stockbroker or a discount broker; the difference is cost and the amount of service provided.

467. What can I expect from a full-service broker?

A full-service broker will recommend which stock you should purchase and will advise about long-term investment strategies and risks. A full-service stockbroker should review your portfolio, provide periodic updates of your account's performance, and send you research material of investments as well as economic updates. These brokers make their fee by charging you a commission on the transactions you make with them. There are national, regional, and even local full-service brokerage houses.

468. I feel that my broker is required to sell certain products to me. Is he?

Your investment interests are to be considered first; however, the reality of the brokerage industry is that the account executives (brokers) are required to sell. About twenty-five years ago, entry-level brokers were finance and business majors in college. In today's world, the person who sells best is considered the best broker. Brokerage houses demand a certain level of commission income. Many firms have bonuses for overall sales production as well as trips and gifts for exceptional sales.

469. Besides the commissions, what other fees are there in my brokerage account?

Because the brokerage business is more competitive each day, not all firms charge all these fees. Comparison shop. Often, you pay a fee for:

- making a trade. Generally, commissions run higher for more complicated and risky investments because they are more difficult to sell. You pay a commission when you buy a stock as well as paying a commission when you sell a stock (1–3 percent on average).
- postage and handling.
- annual account fees, termination fees, and ancillary fees. Many firms charge you an annual fee, particularly if your account is below a specified minimum. Many firms charge you a nonactivity fee, if you haven't made enough trades in your account.
- transferring the account to another brokerage house.

470. I saw an ad on TV about a discount broker. What do you think about this type of service?

A discount broker is a great choice for someone who picks her own stocks. This is a no-frill service. Often you can receive the same research as you would with a full-service broker but you won't receive a recommendation for a stock to buy nor will she offer general investment advice. You are paying for a transaction and you pay about 45 to 70 percent less than most full-service firms.

471. Can I use automated services to make a trade?

Many discount brokerage houses permit automated trades that permit you to make a trade or get stock quotes at any time.

472. Is a discount broker different from a deep discount broker?

Yes. A deep discount broker is even cheaper than a discount broker. You will receive no investment research material and you may be limited on the products you can purchase. Deep discount brokers make their money on volume so investment advice and a personal relationship with clients is frowned upon.

473. What are the negatives to a deep discount broker?

The way your trades are made may not always be the most advantageous to you. Some deep discount brokerage orders may not shop around for the best stock price. Ask the deep discounter if his firm is paid to take orders to particular exchanges. Recent rules require that they tell you this in writing on your statements and confirmations, if you ask. Many discounters charge you an annual IRA fee, termination fees, and margin account fees that are often higher than you would pay with full-service brokers. Dividend reinvestments may not be available, or if they are, you may be charged for this.

474. How do I receive investment advisory information if I use a discounted broker?

Besides *Value Line* and *Morningstar* (two of the largest investment advisory services), investment information is available through magazines, newspapers, and investment advisory newsletters. Some of the well-known investment newsletters are *The Zweig Forecast, Granville Market Letter,* and *Dow Theory Forecasts.*

475. My broker isn't a registered investment adviser. How do I review information about his background?

Information about a broker can be obtained from CRUD (Central Registration Depository) Report. It will tell you how long the broker has been registered as a broker, whether he or she has been sued or ever convicted of a crime, what firms he or she has worked for, and whether he or she ever had to pay damages in a suit.

476. What is my broker not permitted to do?

There are several things brokers can't do:

- *Churning:* Making too many trades within a period of time solely to generate sales commissions.
- *Unauthorized trading:* Execute trades you didn't order.
- *Unsuitable investments:* For example, selling limited partnerships (a long-term investment) to an eighty-five-year-old investor.

- *Theft:* This happens more often than you think. Keep track of your account.
- *Misrepresentation:* Either your broker lies to you or omits information.

It's imperative to know the pros and cons of any recommended investment.

477. What questions should I ask the broker at our first meeting?

- What is your education and work experience?
- How much will you and your firm earn on my business?
- How often will we discuss my portfolio? How often will you review my account?
- How quickly can I get out of this investment? How liquid is the asset?
- How have your other accounts performed?

478. My local bank branch manager recommended I meet with one of the bank's financial advisers to review my situation. What do you think?

There are two types of bank advisers: customer service representatives and personal bankers. The customer service representatives (CARS) are the frontline people who open savings and checking accounts, sell you a Certificate of Deposit (CD), and so on. They know about the products their institution provides, and while they can be helpful they are limited in what they can advise. Financial advisers are personal bankers. These bankers provide personal, consolidated service. They can lower fees charged to your account and verify that you are getting the best account for the amount of money you have invested. A personal banker can expedite loans and consolidate service to you.

479. How does a personal banker differ from a private banker?

A private banker provides a high level of service to the wealthiest customers and customizes the bank's products and services. Service is often in conjunction with the bank's trust department.

480. How is a private banker different than a trust officer?

Generally, a private banker defers part of the service he or she provides to a trust officer. The trust officer will handle the investments and tax planning aspect of your portfolio. The general difference between a private banker and a trust officer is that the private banker can make loans. You can truly do one-stop banking with a private banker.

481. Can my banker also act as my broker?

Yes. As the investment business changes, insurance agents sell investments, bankers sell investments, and insurance brokers sell insurance and CDs. It becomes difficult to know who does what. Your bank can have a broker-age arm (a subsidiary) that will help you buy an investment. Many banks who don't have such a brokerage arm have employees who can sell annu-ities and mutual funds through an outside service. Comparison shop for cost. Having your banker act as a broker can have benefits. You can trans-fer money to pay for trades directly from your bank checking account, you can deal locally, and it's often a way to begin investing.

482. Why don't more brokers and brokerage houses recommend when to sell a stock?

Brokers and/or brokerage houses can't recommend selling stock in a com-pany in which the brokerage firm may be bringing out new issues of the company in the near future. They can't recommend that you sell and then recommend that you buy new issues of the same company. If you review the literature and the research material of your brokerage house, you'll find there are many more buy than sell recommendations.

483. My broker recommended that I set up a wrap account. What is this?

A wrap account is a fairly new concept. It is a brokerage account where all costs are wrapped into one fee—the cost of the broker-consultant, money manager, and transaction costs are consolidated and should never go above an agreed-upon percentage. Although wrap fees are positive in theory be-cause they eliminate the payment and transaction commission basis of the broker/client relationship, the percentage charged on wrap accounts is gen-erally quite high. Some wrap accounts are as high as 3 percent; they should be priced at a third of that.

484. I'm planning to retire next fall. My neighbor recommended I meet with a local annuity service financial planner. Is that good advice?

Why would you limit your financial advice to a recommendation from a provider/financial adviser who sells only one type of package? Annuities are one type of retirement product. Annuity service planners such as the one you're considering are brokers for various annuity companies. Many annuities have performed well in the recent past. By limiting your planning to an annuity provider, you are almost assured of being told that an annuity is the answer to your retirement needs. In fact, this may not be the **best** answer. Annuity companies pay their salespersons on a commission basis, which can be as high as 8 percent of the value of the funds you roll over from your retirement account.

485. How about retirement planning experts? Should I meet with a retirement planning expert when I'm ready to retire?

There are certainly questions you need to answer as you approach retirement. For example, should you take a lump-sum payment at retirement and roll the funds into your own IRA account or take the monthly lifetime payout from your employer? The answers as to what's best will vary, depending on your financial goals. Most financial planners have software to provide you with the facts that will help you make the decision so you shouldn't need a retirement expert. What's most important is to get advice from an independent adviser, such as an accountant, a fee-only or fee-based financial planner or even a banker. These experts won't give advice based on whether you're buying a high-commission product. If you do use a retirement specialist, make sure you know how he or she will be paid.

WORKING WITH YOUR ADVISER

486. How do I avoid any misunderstandings with my financial adviser?

Have the adviser put the plan in writing. The plan should summarize your goals, state your risk tolerance, list your assets (your current financial condition), and how the adviser will implement your plan. After reviewing the information, if you feel something is missing, tell the planner so there are no misunderstandings from the beginning.

487. Can I work with more than one planner?

Certainly, whatever makes you comfortable. Make certain that you aren't duplicating services (particularly if you are paying both advisers); however, many people are comfortable with advice from several advisers. Actually, no planner can do everything so you need to review what your planner can do and supplement his or her services elsewhere. Whatever format you decide to choose, share the information about your plan with all your advisers. It doesn't make sense to withhold information from one planner. A good planner needs to know about all your finances.

488. I want to begin working with a new investment adviser; however, I don't want to give her all my assets to manage at this time.

There is no harm in giving a new adviser only some of your assets at first, particularly if it makes you comfortable. Start with a portion of your accounts, such as IRAs, a stock portfolio, and so on. It's not advisable to do this with too many advisers, but testing one or two will help you evaluate how they are following your plan and their recommendations.

489. My financial adviser is registered with the SEC. What does that mean?

The Securities and Exchange Commission (SEC) is a federal agency that has been commissioned to administer the Securities Act of 1933, the Securities Exchange Act of 1934, and other federal laws. The SEC regulates investment advisers and their activities under the Investment Advisers Act of 1940. To register with the SEC, an adviser must have funds set aside for security, show educational and/or professional experience in the investment field, and disclose any disciplinary actions, complaints, or investment misconduct. Many states require that registered investment advisers file with their Security Regulatory Commission before they may practice in their state.

490. What do I ask the financial adviser at the interview meeting?

During the initial telephone interview, find out if the planner is taking new clients, explain how you were referred, ask for credentials and costs, and explain your needs. From your conversation you should have a feel for the person—you will know if you want to proceed with a meeting. Although most initial consultations are free, verify that at the beginning.

491. What do I do at the first meeting?

Get written disclosure of the individual's education, background, and fee schedule. Then:

- Ask questions that you have written down and brought along.
- Take notes of the answers, your opinion about the planner, if the planner took notes.
- Evaluate your meeting; write down your impression for future reference.
- Choose the planner with whom you felt most comfortable. Did he or she treat you with courtesy and respect? Did he or she listen carefully to your questions and answer them to your satisfaction?

492. What questions should the planner ask me at our first meeting?

The planner should have asked:

- what your financial goals are;
- your income and your assets (and how they are titled);
- about your risk tolerance;
- your current age;
- the age you plan to retire; and
- your marital status.

493. Should I ask the financial planner to see a sample of a plan she has done?

Definitely. There are formal plans and informal plans and what you want depends on your financial situation and the amount of money you wish to pay for a financial plan at the current time. A formal plan usually describes your current financial situation and goals and provides an overview of investing strategies. It usually proposes different types of investments as well as insurance, tax planning, and other strategies. Advocates of an informal plan feel that a memo or report outlining your assets, goals, and willingness to take risk is enough to serve as a foundation for building an investment strategy.

494. Once I have implemented a plan, are there follow-up consultations?

If you need them, they are certainly recommended. With the fee-only and fee-based planners, there will probably be an additional charge for follow-up consultations. Commission-based advisers should not charge you a follow-up consultation fee. An annual review of your plan should be made with your adviser, if you want. This will give you an idea of how your assets have performed and how you and your plan are proceeding toward your goal.

495. I feel uncomfortable asking if my planner has ever been suspended or reprimanded for poor business practices.

Although you have a right to know this and should ask it, you also should be able to have that question answered by the professional organization that licenses the planner. Walk away from anyone who has been suspended or reprimanded. There are too many good people to risk working with someone who has a checkered past.

496. What do planners consider a good client?

Planners describe the ideal client as someone who:

- defines goals and sticks to them;
- has realistic expectations;
- measures success in terms of how well his or her investments are meeting his or her goals; and
- is easy to work with.

497. My adviser won't give me any references because he stated it's breaking confidentiality.

Obviously the adviser can't disclose clients' names without first getting permission to do so. However, he should have clients whom he can use as references (upon their approval). If not, that could be a warning sign.

498. What do I ask the references my adviser has given me?

There are some basic questions you should ask:

- What did the planner do for you?
- What part of the work were you dissatisfied with?
- What was most satisfactory?
- Did the planner accomplish everything promised?
- Are you still using the planner's services? If not, why?

499. What recourse do I have if I'm unhappy with the financial adviser?

If you signed a contract and the adviser didn't provide the agreed-upon services, you can sever your relationship by following the contract termination clause. If the service is with your accountant, attorney, or fee-based financial adviser, you only need to sever your relationship by calling and discussing termination with them and then follow up with a termination letter.

If you are unhappy with your stockbroker, you can speak with his supervisor and ask for a change in account executives or you can find a broker with another agency. This can proceed with the transfer of your account.

If you feel your adviser has made inappropriate or dishonest transactions or representations, speak with the person's supervisor. If this is unsatisfactory, you can send a notice of complaint to the governing body that licenses the adviser's particular profession. If none of this works, you can consult an attorney.

500. My broker speaks very quickly and I feel dumb asking basic questions. What should I do?

Would you permit this from your doctor, dentist, or car repair shop? I would hope not, but so many of us are timid with financial advisers because we are afraid to appear ignorant. You are paying for a service and you should understand what you are receiving for that service. If you are purchasing a product that you don't understand, don't buy it. Part of the adviser's job is to provide clear explanations about how the investments perform and how they fit into your financial plan.

501. I have been working with my insurance agent concerning financial planning. How does she get paid?

Insurance agents are paid primarily on a commission basis from the insurance products they sell. An experienced, knowledgeable agent will know how to present you with information on your policies, your death benefits, paying your premiums, and so on. If you get general financial advice from your insurance agent, chances are that insurance will somehow figure into the solution.

502. What is the difference between an insurance agent and a broker agent?

An insurance agent works directly with the insurance company and is usually an employee of the company. Agents who work for Prudential, Northwestern, Allstate, or State Farm insurance companies, for example, are direct agents. A broker agent (most frequently seen in business insurance situations) works independently of the companies and brokers the policies to you. As far as financial planning, the knowledgeable planner is the person you want. A direct agent should have access to other company policies so you can be given a comparison of several policies. Shop the agent and then the policy.

503. What is meant by conflict of interest when working with an investment adviser?

Some advisers just do financial planning and then send you to others when you are ready to put your plan into action. Others incorporate planning into the services they provide. The advisers who provide products or services beyond the planning stage can have a conflict of interest if they don't disclose the relationship or if they don't give you an alternative to their products.

504. My adviser and I disagree about my investment plan. What happened?

You either misunderstood or were misled; you'll know better next time. Whether your adviser misinterpreted or ignored your wishes or made an honest mistake, you should correct it as quickly as possible.

505. My broker bought the wrong stock for me. What should I do?

You should always review your confirmations when they arrive. When you catch the error, call your broker immediately (as soon as you receive the confirmation) and insist you want the matter resolved. If it was a misunderstanding, the trade can be broken or busted. If the broker won't break the trade, talk with his or her supervisor. If you don't get satisfaction, talk with an attorney. It is imperative to keep track of stock trades that are discussed with your broker. Understand what you discussed, what you are purchasing, the cost, and why you are purchasing the asset.

FINANCIAL ADVISERS

Accountant's name

Assistant's name

Company

Address

E-mail address

Pager/beeper (   )   Work phone (   )

Mobile phone (   )   Fax (   )

Financial planner's name

Assistant's name

Company

Address

E-mail address

Pager/beeper (   )   Work phone (   )

Mobile phone (   )   Fax (   )

Banker's name

Assistant's name

Company

Address

E-mail address

Work phone (   )   Fax (   )

OTHER ADVISERS

Attorney

Assistant/paralegal

Firm's name

Address

E-mail address

Home phone (   )   Work phone (   )

Mobile phone (   )   Fax (   )

Copy of will in office?

Executor/Trustee

Assistant's name

Company

Address

E-mail address

Home phone (   )   Work phone (   )

Mobile phone (   )   Fax (   )

Benefits officer at work

Company

Address

E-mail address

Work phone (   )   Fax (   )

Lender's name

Assistant's name

Company

Address

E-mail address

Work phone (   )   Fax (   )

Spiritual advisor's name

Address

E-mail address

Home phone (   )   Work phone (   )

Mobile phone (   )   Fax (   )

Other name

Assistant's name

Company

Address

E-mail address

Fax (   )

Other name

Assistant's name

Company

Address

E-mail address

Fax (   )

Chapter 7

Saving for Retirement

We all know we should be putting money into retirement plans, but far too many of us aren't doing that. In fact, less than half of Americans have put aside money specifically for retirement. As of 1993, one third of workers who had access to a 401(k) plan didn't participate. Retirement planning can be an intimidating subject, but it doesn't have to be. While the topic is too broad for a comprehensive examination here, this chapter answers questions on the most common methods of saving for a secure retirement. You'll be wise to learn all you can about the rules of any retirement plans in which you participate.

GENERAL GUIDELINES

506. How long is the average person retired?

The average number of years a person is retired is between twenty and twenty-five years.

507. When do most people retire?

Half of U.S. workers retire by age 60. However, many of these people return to the work force in part-time positions.

508. How soon do I need to start saving for retirement? I'm twenty-five.

If you invest $2,000 into an IRA at age eighteen and never add any more, averaging 10 percent a year, you will have $176,400 at age sixty-five. If you invest $2,000 each year from age eighteen to age sixty-five, you will have $1,744,000 at age sixty-five. Although these numbers seem unreal (and they are not adjusted for inflation), they are accurate and will help provide a nice retirement. It is never too soon to start saving for retirement. You should begin no later than age thirty-five.

509. What are some ways I can prepare for retirement?

There are many ways:

- Know your retirement needs—about 70 percent of your preretirement income. Lower-income earners need up to 90 percent or more of their preretirement income to maintain their standard of living once they stop working.
- Find out what your Social Security benefits are. You'll only get about 40 percent of your preretirement earnings. Call the Social Security Administration for a free statement of your estimated benefits at (800) 772-1213.
- Understand your employer's pension or profit-sharing plan. For a free booklet on private pensions, call the U.S. Department of Labor at (800) 998-7542.
- Contribute to a tax-sheltered savings plan, such as a 401(k).
- Ask your employer to start a plan if he or she doesn't have one. For information on simplified employee pensions, ask for Publication 590 from the IRS by calling (800) 829-3676.

- Put money into an IRA.
- Don't use your savings; you'll lose both principal and interest and you may have to pay more taxes. If you change jobs, roll your IRA over into your new employer's retirement plan.
- Set goals and stick to them. The sooner you start saving, the more time you have to gain interest.
- Ask questions. Get information from your employer, bank, credit union, or financial adviser.

510. How much of my current income do I need at retirement?

You should earn between 60 to 80 percent of your preretirement income to maintain your current lifestyle. This income is known as your wage replacement ratio (WRR).

511. I have been offered a position at a company without a retirement plan. Should I consider the job?

Obviously you would consider a new position if the total benefits are better than your current job. Don't forget that an employer-paid retirement plan is money in your pocket. If the job is so good you can accept the fact that there is no company retirement, you can set aside your own funds every year for retirement—posttax except for an IRA. Compare the retirement plan you now have and all the benefits provided by both companies including salary and the nonfinancial considerations and then decide.

512. How much do I need to contribute to a retirement plan to guarantee I'm comfortable at retirement?

Since you can't contribute more than 15 percent or $30,000 of your income into a retirement plan, you usually don't have to worry about having too much money available for retirement. Obviously, too much is better than too little. A financial adviser should have the software to help guide you with this dilemma. The Vanguard investment firm has software available at a very reasonable cost so that you can do the projections yourself (800-523-7077), but remember the projections are based on assumptions.

513. Isn't there a penalty tax if I have too many retirement funds?

The Taxpayer Relief Act of 1997 removed the penalty tax for having too many funds in your retirement account. Now there is no limit on money set aside for your retirement.

514. Won't my Social Security benefits help replace my current income?

Social Security was never designed to be a retiree's full wage replacement and it probably won't meet all your retirement needs. That's why it's important to plan how you will supplement your benefits. Social Security provides up to 45 percent of the wage replacement ratio for a single low-income worker who retires at the normal retirement age of sixty-five. If this lower-income worker is married to someone who never worked outside the home, the wage replacement ratio increases to 76 percent of the preretirement income. If you're a high-income person, this ratio is quite different. In this case, Social Security will only replace 13.5 percent of your preretirement income. The ratio increases to 20.25 percent if you have a nonworking spouse.

515. I'm worried that Social Security won't be there when I retire. How can I find out what my current benefits are?

All of us should check our Social Security accounts every three years to make sure that everything is accurate. The government keeps records of how much money you've invested in Social Security from every job you've ever held. You can get a copy of this valuable record by calling the Social Security hotline at (800) 772-1213. You'll be guided by a taped message into leaving your name and address, and within two weeks you'll receive a form to request your records. If the information in your records is incorrect, you need to know about it so it can be corrected and your benefits will be correct.

516. My employer talks about ERISA. What is ERISA?

ERISA, which stands for Employee Retirement Income Security Act of 1974, provides the regulations that guide retirement plans. Enforced by the Department of Labor, ERISA (along with half a dozen other laws) outlines the rules and guidelines to administer the plans.

IRAS

517. What is an IRA?

An Individual Retirement Account (IRA) is a personal pension account to set aside money for retirement. You can contribute up to $2,000 in pretax income into a deductible IRA each year if your employer doesn't offer a pension or a tax-deferred retirement/savings plan if you meet certain income limits. You pay federal income tax on the funds only when you withdraw the money. There are numerous rules and regulations set up by the government. Growth and income on an IRA grows tax deferred until withdrawal. People whose adjusted gross income does not exceed the earnings ceiling may contribute after-tax income into a nondeductible IRA, even if they *are* covered by a retirement plan at work.

518. What is the new Roth IRA?

More affluent wage earners who didn't qualify to deduct contributions to an IRA will now be able to get their tax break with a Roth IRA. They are available to:

- Singles with an adjusted gross income less than $95,000
- Couples filing married filing jointly earning less than $150,000

The major difference of the new Roth IRAs is that there is no tax of any kind on withdrawals as long as some money has been in the account for at least five years and the account holder is fifty-nine-and-a-half. No tax of any kind. Let's reiterate that—no tax of any kind! While you must take distributions from a traditional IRA account by age seventy-and-a-half, there is no mandatory distribution date for a Roth IRA. You can leave your money in place as long as you live. The biggest bonus is that death benefits are not taxable income to heirs. (See Question 527.)

519. Do you recommend I have an IRA if I already have a 401(k) at work?

Yes, but first you should make sure you maximize your 401(k) matchable contributions. After that, if you can afford the extra $2,000 a year, I would definitely recommend an IRA. If $2,000 is too much, contribute what funds you can afford. Remember that by setting funds aside, you are contributing to your financial security at retirement. The type of IRA (standard versus Roth) depends on your individual situation.

520. Which type of IRA should I purchase in 1998, a Roth IRA or a regular IRA?

Higher-income investors who aren't eligible to make tax-deductible IRAs because they earn too much money should open Roth IRAs, if they are eligible. Deciding the type of IRA you get is a more difficult choice if you are eligible for a tax-deductible IRA. Since saving income tax on the contribu-

Roth Decision Checklist

	Yes	No	
• Do you currently have an IRA?	____	____	
• Is your adjusted gross income (AGI) $100,000 or less?	____	____	*This income limitation is set by law, and it's the same for singles and married couples.*
• Do you expect to be in a higher tax bracket when you retire?	____	____	*If you expect to be in the same or lower tax bracket when you retire, it may not make sense to pay the conversion tax today.*

If you do roll your existing IRA into a Roth IRA:

	Yes	No	
• Will you be able to pay the resulting income tax with cash from *outside* your IRA?	____	____	*If you must tap into your IRA to pay the tax, conversion to a Roth IRA is unlikely to pencil out. But remember: You can reduce the potential tax bill by making a partial conversion. Also, if you convert in 1998, you can spread the resulting tax payment over four years.*
• Will you be able to leave the money in the rollover IRA for at least five years?	____	____	*You could incur tax and a penalty if you tap your Roth IRA in less than five years.*

If you checked "Yes" to all questions, you could be a good candidate for a rollover Roth IRA.

tion to these IRAs is a major benefit, you need to go a step further and review other options. Generally, Roth IRAs seem preferable if you must wait a long time until retirement, since your buildup in earnings will be tax free. The Roth IRA is better for persons who feel their income tax bracket will stay the same or even increase after retirement. T. Rowe Price (800-IRA-5000) has prepared an analysis to help you decide which is better.

521. What do I do with my current IRAs if I like the Roth IRA idea?

Anyone whose adjusted gross income is less than $100,000 can transfer funds from a current tax-deferred IRA to a Roth IRA, making all future growth of that retirement account permanently tax free. This makes sense if you are young and have decades to allow your Roth IRA funds to accumulate. The difference can add up to thousands of dollars of extra income in retirement. You can transfer the funds by paying income tax on what is in the current IRA (payment on this can be made over a four-year period) and transferring the funds. You need to carefully consider this move, and you should have your financial adviser analyze whether or not this is the best move for you.

522. Can I have an IRA account?

Anyone younger than age seventy-and-a-half by year end can have an IRA if you meet the rules:

- You have earned income.
- You can defer up to $2,000 a year if you earned that much in wages.
- If you are married, your spouse (even unemployed) can contribute $2,000 to a spousal IRA.

523. What determines if the IRA can be deducted on my income tax return?

You can contribute up to $4,000 ($2,000 each) if your family's income is less than $150,000 and you don't have a retirement plan at work. IRA contributions are deductible up to the $2,000 maximum per spouse. If you have a retirement plan at work, but your income is below $50,000 in 1998, the contributions are deductible. Single taxpayers can contribute if their income is less than $30,000.

524. Should I designate my estate as the beneficiary of my IRA?

You need to assign a designated beneficiary for your IRA at the time distribution is made, but you shouldn't name your estate as beneficiary—name an individual or individuals. If you have too many beneficiaries, make the beneficiary a trust.

525. Are there investment limitations within an IRA?

You can't:

- Borrow money from it.
- Sell property to it.
- Receive unreasonable compensation for managing it.
- Use it as security for a loan.

526. When I begin withdrawing funds from my IRA, how is it taxed?

The income from an IRA and most pension plans is taxed as current income. There is no differentiation between capital gains and current income. You will get a 1099-R at year end advising you of the amount you received from your IRA and how much is taxable. You then place the figures on your tax return.

527. When I die, how is my IRA taxed?

Few people realize that the deferred income tax liability on their IRAs follows through to the beneficiaries. Only your spouse gets a break. Thus, if your $200,000 IRA is payable to your spouse at death, he can choose to roll the funds into a current IRA or set up a new IRA. This permits the deferral to continue until he withdraws the funds. However, if you are a widow when you die, your children are liable for the income tax on the funds received and they can't defer the payout longer than five years—unless you have planned properly. If you have two children and a $300,000 IRA, your children can be zapped with taxable income of $150,000 each the year you die. With luck, your beneficiaries have a good tax planner so they can have up to five years to withdraw the funds; this means they could take $30,000 a year (in taxable income) for five years rather than all in the year of your death, if beneficiaries so choose.

528. Is there another way to defer the accumulated income tax besides taking the funds over five years?

As owner of the IRA, you may designate your beneficiaries to receive a payout of the IRA based on their ages. The beneficiaries will receive a lifetime payout, monthly or yearly, based on this minimum requirement. They can always withdraw more than the minimum; however, this plan helps alleviate the terrible tax burden of a lump-sum IRA payout. This ability to continue deferral with proper planning is one of the least-known secrets in retirement planning.

529. If I retire before fifty-nine-and-a-half, can I withdraw funds from my IRA to use to live on without incurring a penalty?

Payments won't be subject to a penalty if they are part of a series of substantially equal periodic payments made at least annually. The payments must be calculated on your life expectancy. Payments are obviously subject to income taxation. A careful review of your withdrawal plan must be made. If you change the withdrawals within the time period, all the previous payments will be subject to the 10 percent penalty. You won't have to pay a penalty if you are fifty-five and the money from the IRA distribution covers medical expenses, whether or not you itemize deductions.

530. When must I start withdrawing funds from my IRA?

You are required to take your first IRA withdrawal by April 1 of the year *after* you are seventy-and-a-half. If you reach seventy-and-a-half in 1998, you must withdraw a minimum amount from your IRA by next April 1. The problem with deferring payment until then is that you are then forced to take two payments that year, increasing your annual income. Deciding when to take your first payment should be made after reviewing your entire financial planning scenario.

531. How much must I take?

You can, of course, take all of it. Because of the tax liability of withdrawing the funds, people like to continue deferring funds as long as possible. There is a minimum that you must take based on your life expectancy, the life expectancy of you and your spouse, or the life expectancy of you and the nonspousal beneficiary of your IRA. The penalty for taking too small a distribution is 50 percent of the amount not distributed.

532. I have about five IRAs. Should I consolidate them?

Consolidation will let you easily know what assets you have. However, an investor is often unable to consolidate IRAs due to segregation of the funds. By increasing the number of accounts, you are increasing the amount of work it takes to keep track of your asset allocation, increasing the work to keep current on the mutual funds philosophy of your investments, increasing fees, and so on.

533. Can I use my IRA as collateral on a loan?

If you use a part of your IRA as security for a loan, that part is treated as a distribution and is included in gross income, along with the penalties that apply to early withdrawals.

534. Can I withdraw funds from my IRA to help pay for my son's college education?

The 10 percent penalty for early withdrawals is waived for funds used for education from all IRAs, even current IRAs. However, you still have to pay income tax on withdrawals for education. The amount of the withdrawal is unlimited.

535. How about for my first home?

If you withdraw funds from your IRA to pay for your first home, you won't have to pay a penalty for the first $10,000 you take out. However, the withdrawal is subject to income tax liability.

536. What is the difference between a deductible and nondeductible IRA?

A deductible IRA means that any contribution made to an IRA can be deducted from your adjusted gross income. You can't deduct nondeductible IRA contributions from your tax return. Within both types of IRAs, the income earned and any capital growth are deferred until you withdraw the funds.

If you have kept track of the nondeductible contributions using Form 8606, you will not have to pay tax on the nondeductible contributions made over the years. This paperwork is imperative.

537. Should I invest in stocks or bonds inside my IRA?

With the lowering of capital gains taxes, this is a hot topic of debate. Stocks grow with a historic return of 10.5 percent while bonds have had a 5 percent return. Bonds are secure; stocks have a greater risk. Bonds give you liquidity that stocks often do not. Therefore, it is important to have cash and bonds held personally for use towards current emergencies rather than in an IRA.

OTHER PLANS

538. If I have a retirement fund at work and IRAs, should I also set up a nonqualified annuity?

It is great to have retirement funds, but don't put too much money aside with restrictions. Once you have contributed as much as you can in your retirement fund and IRAs, look at how much money you have for current expenses, college for your children, and funds for emergencies. A nonqualified annuity defers income tax liability on the income earned and capital gains within the fund, but you can't withdraw the money in the annuity until fifty-nine-and-a-half without a penalty. I would only contribute to an annuity after I had plenty of nonqualified funds available.

539. I'm interested in a SEP-IRA. How do I find out more about it?

Many banks, mutual fund companies, and insurance companies, offer SEP (Simplified Employee Pension) services and should be able to help you sort through your options. Call your local IRS office for a copy of form 5305-SEP or 5305-SIMPLE.

540. What is a KEOGH plan?

A Keogh plan is set up by people who are self-employed. This type of plan requires more paperwork to set up than does a SEP, but it lets you put away a higher percent of your income (20 percent) up to a maximum of $30,000 per year. All types of Keoghs allow vesting schedules which mandate that employees must stay with the company for a number of years before they earn the right to their retirement account money. There are several types of Keoghs, including:

- *Profit-sharing plans:* These plans have the same contribution limits as SEP-IRAs, but they interest owners of small companies who want to minimize the contributions to which employees are entitled.
- *Money-purchase pension plans:* You can contribute more here than you can to a SEP-IRA or a profit-sharing Keogh. The maximum contribution here is either 20 percent of your income or $30,000, whichever is less. You can contribute more, but you don't have any flexibility on how much you contribute each year—the amount is fixed. These plans are designed for high-income workers who are comfortable enough to know they can continue making large contributions.

541. What can we expect Social Security to offer us in the year 2012?

When most of us pay employment taxes, a part of that money goes to Social Security (the part of your paycheck that refers to FICA). This money is kept in a trust fund that is presently invested in Treasury obligations. At the moment, the system has enough funding until 2020. People are concerned about the state of Social Security because, as Baby Boomers retire, the government will have to pay out more than it will take in. I am assuming that in twenty years, Social Security will only be available if your income is below a certain level. Social Security's biggest problem is the cost of living allowance that was instituted twenty years ago. That is what is bankrupting the system along with the fact that they invest only in government bonds.

EMPLOYER PLANS

542. My employer offers investment opportunities at work. Are they a good idea?

Called a defined contribution plan, these plans are popular and a good opportunity to invest. They may include:

- Employee stock option plans (ESOPs)
- Money-purchase pension plan
- Profit-sharing plan
- Thrift/savings plan

- 401(k) plan
- SEP
- Target benefit pension plan
- Tax-deferred annuity (TDA)
- Hybrid (combination of two or more plans)

Your employer maintains an individual account for each participant and contributions are made annually. Your retirement benefits depend on the amount in your individual account, how it has increased over the years, and so on. Your employer sets up rules for the plan, such as your eligibility to participate, whether or not you can take a loan from your account, withdrawals, and so on within ERISA's guidelines.

543. At retirement, I must roll over my funds. How do I go about doing this?

Your employer wants you to take your individual account and have it invested elsewhere. Thus, to keep the funds from being taxed, you need to roll over the funds in the individual account from the current trustee to a new custodian. Therefore, you will need to locate a financial adviser who will be able to guide you through the process of the transfer to a new custodian.

544. When must my employer permit me to go into the company's retirement plan?

If you are older than twenty-one, ERISA requires your employer to cover you in their plan after one year.

545. If that's true, why don't I get any benefits if I leave the company within five years?

You will always receive the funds you have invested in a retirement plan, no matter when you leave your job. However, the funds contributed by your employer can be paid out under different rules. Coverage by a retirement plan doesn't mean you are vested (that you have the right to your accrued benefits in your employer's plan).

546. What is a thrift plan?

A thrift or savings plan is a defined contribution plan where both employer and employee are able to contribute funds. In most thrift plans, the employer typically matches the employee's contribution either dollar for dollar or in some ratio. The employee's contribution can be only posttax dollars.

547. My company said it would match my investments. What does this mean?

If you put 3 percent of your salary into a retirement vehicle, then your company will match your 3 percent. It's a wonderful way of increasing benefits since you get an immediate 100 percent return on your investment. You should always contribute to your plan at least the amount your employer matches. It's lost money if you don't contribute.

548. What do you mean by pretax and posttax dollars when it comes to retirement investing?

Pretax dollars are funds that you contribute from your salary into an account before federal income tax is taken out. This lowers your current tax bracket. This money will be taxed when you withdraw it at retirement. The contributions are still taxed for Social Security purposes and state and local income tax. Posttax contributions are monies deposited into a retirement plan after federal income tax is taken out. The earnings (growth) of both funds are tax-deferred until they are withdrawn. Posttaxed dollars are segregated so you aren't required to pay tax on the funds again.

549. What is a profit-sharing plan?

A profit-sharing plan is a kind of benefit in which your employer determines the amount of annual contribution—there is no set annual contribution obligation. Employers can decide if and when to funnel money from the company into the plan. The total amount contributed to the plan is then allocated among the individual accounts. Many companies choose profit-sharing plans so they are not forced to contribute in years when they have not made a profit. The maximum contribution is 15 percent of eligible participants' compensation.

550. What is a 401(k) plan?

All 401(k) plans involve salary deferrals as an add-on to a profit-sharing plan. Its main feature is to allow for pretax employee contributions which are sometimes matched by employers. They have become very popular in recent years because of the employees' ability to take their funds with them (upon severance) from employer to employer or employer to IRA. Employees also like the choices of internal funds usually allowed by the plan.

551. What is the maximum contribution to a 401(k) plan?

The maximum contribution made to a 401(k) plan is $10,000 in 1998, but this maximum can be lowered if there are more higher-salaried employees contributing to the plan than lower-salaried employees.

552. How much should I contribute to my 401(k) at work?

It's easy for everyone to spend what they make. It's often difficult to save, but your 401(k) is your security for retirement so you should contribute as much as you can. It is imperative that you contribute enough so that you get all company matched funds. Beyond that amount, you should contribute so much a pay period, gradually increasing the contribution with raises and so on. It's amazing how little you will miss money from your paycheck if you don't see it.

553. What if I can't afford to contribute to my 401(k) or an IRA?

You can't afford not to contribute if you want security in your retirement. A $1,000 contribution for a 28 percent taxpayer is really only a $720 contribution. This is because you are saving $280 in tax by making the deductible contribution. I find that if people start with a small contribution and gradually increase it, the contributions are not as painful as if done all at one time. Thus, start at $50 a month and work up to the $2000 a year. Or start at a contribution of 3 percent of your income and work up to the 15 percent or whatever the maximum amount is for your plan.

554. My 401(k) has a choice of seven different funds. How do I choose which ones to be in?

The allocation is based on your investment objectives. Know the objective of each internal fund. If you don't know, ask the human resource department at your company. If you still don't understand, ask them to bring in someone who can help you. It's your company's responsibility to help you understand your investment choices. If you are still uncomfortable with choosing the fund allocation, schedule a visit with a financial adviser to review the asset allocation of your 401(k) as well as all your investments.

555. My 401(k) allows me to borrow against the plan. Is this a good way to get a loan?

Yes and no. All loans made from a 401(k), except those made for your home, must be repaid with interest within five years. The amount of the loan is generally limited to one half of the amount held in your 401(k) account, but it can't be more than $50,000. The amount of the loan can be more than 50 percent if your account balance is less than $20,000. Then, the loan can be as high as $10,000. The loan rate charged is the prime rate plus 1 percent. (You are paying yourself a nice interest rate.) The bad news is that the loan must be repaid if you quit your job, it must be repaid in five years, and you may be losing a higher return in equities investment in your 401(k).

556. When I leave my job, should I roll my 401(k) account into my existing IRA?

It's a good idea to keep the 401(k) account with your current employer until you become eligible for the 401(k) plan at your new job. Then you can transfer your current 401(k) balance into the new fund. This permits you to consolidate funds and your costs will be lower since your employer is already paying fee management for the 401(k). If you can't keep the money in your current 401(k) plan until you become eligible under your new plan, transfer the funds into a segregated IRA apart from all other IRAs you may have. Then you will be able to roll this IRA into a future 401(k), if available.

557. What is a 403(b)?

A 403(b) plan is similar to a 401(k) plan except the retirement plans are for employees of hospitals, schools, and nonprofit organizations. The assets of the plan are usually held with an insurance company in an annuity. Participants can contribute up to 15 percent of their salary to an annual maximum ($10,000 in 1998).

558. My company has a five-year cliff for vesting. Do I get any money if I leave in three years?

There are two ways for a company to vest employee's retirement benefits—graduated or cliff vesting. Cliff vesting is designed so that you don't get any of the contributions your employer made on your behalf if you leave before five years, although it's possible to have a three- or four-year cliff. If you leave before that time, the money goes back to your employer's pension fund. If you stay five years, you are 100 percent vested; you leave then, all the employer contributions follow you.

559. So what is graduated vesting?

Graduated vesting means that you are partially vested after three years, but you must work for seven years before you are 100 percent vested. The schedule goes as follows:

Years Employed	Percent Vested
3	20%
4	40%
5	60%
6	80%
7	100%

560. Can my husband take me off as beneficiary of his retirement plan at work?

No. If your husband dies before retirement, you will receive payment from his retirement plan under a qualified preretirement survivor annuity or in a lump-sum payment. Once vested, you have the right to an annuity if he dies. If he retires, you will receive a qualified joint and survivor annuity postretirement death benefit, as his wife.

561. Can I waive this right?

Yes (unless you are under age thirty-five), but you must sign a written waiver and have it witnessed by either a notary or official of the plan. Once you do this, the waiver is irrevocable.

The spousal annuities are designed in a way so that the retiree usually receives a lower amount at retirement because if he dies, there will be continuing payments to the surviving spouse. Thus, if you retire early, it might make sense for your spouse to sign a waiver so that you receive a larger sum for many years. If both spouses have excellent pensions, they could opt for each to sign a waiver and forego the death benefits so they would both receive larger amounts of their pensions. Whatever the reason for waiving, you should only sign it if you completely understand your rights and what you may be potentially losing. The information should be written for review from your financial adviser and/or accountant.

562. My employer gave me a choice between a lump-sum payment and a monthly check. How do I decide what is better?

Like taking monthly checks or a lump-sum payment from a life insurance policy, you must compare the amount of the monthly check with the monthly income if you invest the lump-sum payment, who will invest the funds, how they will be managed, and so on. This very important question *must* be reviewed with a financial adviser.

563. My employer gave me a lump-sum payment for my retirement benefits. Is there a way I can be sure I got all I was entitled to?

Yes. While most Americans assume that the lump sum they receive from their pension or the monthly payout they get is accurate, there is increasing evidence that they shouldn't assume so. According to one company that reviews these payouts, as many as half the pension payouts are not accurate. You can contact the National Center for Retirement Benefits, Inc. (NCRB) at (800) 666-1000. This company reviews payouts from pension and 401(k) and profit-sharing plans. If they discover an error, they keep 30 percent of any money they recover. If there is no error, there is no fee.

564. I left my employer after seven years of service and only received $4,200. Why?

Because you were covered by a defined benefit plan and you are not yet sixty-five. The plan is designed for your employer to guarantee you a retirement benefit at age sixty-five. The amount of the plan is based on an acturial figure, using investment return, time and your age to calculate what contributions are needed to provide a retirement benefit for you. If you leave before retirement, you receive only what is in the account. The younger you are, the less money you will receive when you leave.

565. When I left my job, my employer offered me my pension money directly. Is this legal?

If your accrued defined pension benefit is less than $5,000, your employer has the option of letting you roll over the money into an IRA or you may take the money as cash. This is permitted because of the small amount of funds available in the account. Employers feel it is too expensive to keep track of the small amounts in these type accounts.

566. My ex-wife got a Qualified Domestic Relations Order on me. What is it?

This order is a decree, order, or property settlement under state law relating to child support, alimony, or marital property rights that assigns part or all of your plan benefits to your ex-wife. This decree gives her a share or portion of your pension.

CHAPTER 8

SAVING FOR COLLEGE

When your children are first born, college seems so far away that it's hard to think of putting away money for their education. As time goes by, other expenses crop up and there never seems to be quite enough extra money to start those college funds. Now your child will be starting college in the fall and you're wondering how you're going to pay for it. Perhaps you have another child who'll be ready for college in a couple of years. What are you going to do? First, don't panic. There are many different ways to pay for your children's education. While it would be ideal to start putting aside $200 in a growth fund the day your first child is born, many people can't afford to do this. However, even modest amounts will grow over time, so it's a good idea to start putting some money aside. If the time has come to start paying, there are a variety of plans and programs available to help you. This chapter gives you a quick look at the overall process—from early college savings to financial aid, student loans, and payment plans once your child has been accepted at a college.

PLANNING AHEAD

567. College costs seem to be spiraling out of control. Is a college education still a good investment?

Census Bureau data demonstrate that the educational-income relationship is striking. Male and female college graduates earn significantly more than high school graduates; the gap is different for technical school graduates. (Acquiring a technical school degree may be the way to go for many students.) Income rises faster if you have more education. In the ten-year period before retirement, the difference between those who graduated from high school and those from college is nearly 6.2 percent.

568. What is the first step in planning for my child's college expenses?

First, you need to set realistic goals. A goal is not a wish but a statement of purpose; it should be as concrete and specific as possible. In order to set your goals, you need to:

1. Figure out what college will cost when your child attends (obviously this is a guess).
2. Divide this sum by the number of months from now until your child begins college. For example, $40,000 divided by 120 months would mean you need to save $333/month without taking into consideration any growth or earnings.

569. So financial planning for college is a good idea?

Yes. Planning for college will help you get the most out of the money you have saved to date, while helping you budget for increased savings towards the future. It also can help you obtain financial aid to help pay for your child's college education.

570. Do I need to have all the funds available when my child starts college?

Certainly not. Remember that college is a four-year process and you won't need to have all the funds available the September of your child's freshman year. You should also note that you can pay for college after your child graduates. This helps make the costs more palatable.

571. Is there a minimum I should consider when investing for my children's college?

Save whatever you can. If you can afford to save $300 a month, do it. If you can save only $50 a month, then do it. Too many people have an all or nothing approach to savings—unless we can put away at least $100 a month, we figure it's not worth it and we don't save anything. In fact, saving even the *smallest* amount is better than nothing. This savings will decrease the amount of loans you will need to incur when the time comes to pay for college. If your budget only permits $5 a week, put that aside. Five dollars a week is $20 a month. That's $240 a year. Save regularly; it's a statement of your faith in your children's future.

572. Is there a minimum total amount I should aim for when saving for college?

Of course it depends on whether your child eventually chooses a public or private school, but if you're earning only a modest income, aim for saving a third or a half of the total cost. You can make up the rest with scholarships, grants, loans, and having your child work while going to school.

573. So how do I come up with a sum?

First of all, assume that as of today the average public college costs $36,000 for a four-year education. The average private school costs $76,000, but this figure can go up to 30 percent higher for the most pricey schools. To figure out how much you'll need to save in today's dollars, fill out the following form. (Note: We use today's dollars on the assumption that the money you are saving is growing at the college costs' rate of inflation. You should increase the amount you need to save each year by the inflation rate—probably about 5 percent.)

574. I only have $100 a month to save towards college. Is it worth it?

If you invest $100 a month starting when your baby is born and invest at a conservative 8 percent, you will have $43,100 when college begins at age eighteen. Although this may not cover all the expenses, it will be a nice dent in the bill.

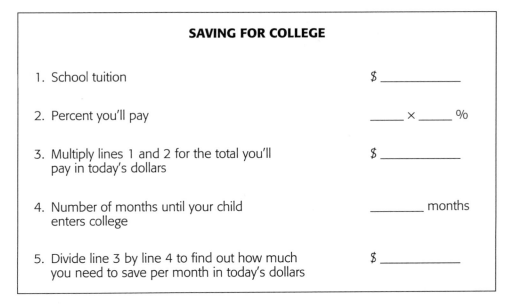

SAVING FOR COLLEGE

1. School tuition $ _____

2. Percent you'll pay   _____ × _____ %

3. Multiply lines 1 and 2 for the total you'll $ _____
   pay in today's dollars

4. Number of months until your child   _____ months
   enters college

5. Divide line 3 by line 4 to find out how much $ _____
   you need to save per month in today's dollars

575. It is so difficult finding the discretionary income to put towards a college fund for our new baby. What do you recommend?

If you are a two-income household, most likely you have child care expenses. Once your child is old enough to go to school, those expenses will stop. At that time, you could take what you were paying the provider before your child went to school and put the money in your child's college account. This can add up to a significant savings over the years. If one of you stays home while your child is small, and if you go back to work when she starts school, you can put some of that extra salary in a college fund. Since you won't be used to the extra income, you could spend only a portion of the funds and save the difference.

576. Is it possible to pay for college as my children attend school?

Yes. Many colleges do permit payment through the installment plan. You pay the annual college cost through a ten-month payment plan. This is a good way to go if you don't have the money to pay the entire tuition bill.

577. What's a tuition prepayment plan?

Such a plan allows you to deposit money into an account for education at one of your state's colleges with the guarantee that the money you deposit will cover your child's education when he or she is of college age. The problem is that your child will then be restricted to attending a college in your state.

578. My son was born in June and my parents are offering to fund a tuition prepayment plan implemented by the state we live in. Is this a good idea?

That's a hard question to answer. It depends on your resources and goals. To help assess the strengths and weaknesses of these prepayment plans, the College Entrance Examination Board has issued the following set of guidelines:

- Is there a minimum contribution required to enter the program? Are incremental additions possible?
- Is there a maximum annual amount that can be contributed? Will any such maximum restrict the accumulation below a realistic projection of future college costs?
- Can anyone in the family contribute? Are there exclusions?
- Can the proceeds from the plan be transferred to another family member if the child's educational plans change?
- Are there eligibility restrictions—can you only apply to a particular class of schools, such as only independent colleges? Are there penalties associated with these restrictions?
- Is the yield from the plan guaranteed? How? How are you protected from investment deficits below college cost levels?
- Is the plan insured? Can the investment be recovered if the plan sponsor ceases to exist?
- Does the plan cover all college costs or just tuition?
- Are there age restrictions or time limits on use? Do proceeds from the plan have to be used within a certain number of years after high school?
- Are there residency requirements for eligibility? What happens if you move during the plan years?
- How many years of study are covered by the proceeds? Is graduate school possible? Is part-time attendance possible?

- Are there restrictions as to who might match funds contributed to the plan? Could an employer or state contribute?
- What are the refund conditions if your child doesn't go to college for whatever reason?
- Do you benefit if there is more money in the fund than you need or is the profit a bonus to the sponsor?
- Will the plan benefits be taxable for either federal or state taxes? Will any tax accrue to the contributor, plan sponsor, or student?

579. I don't want a prepayment plan since that would restrict my child's college choice. Are there any plans that don't restrict my daughter's choice?

Yes. The prepayment idea was begun by the College Savings Bank of Princeton. Here you invest the amount in a CollegeSure CD and they will guarantee you will have enough to pay tuition when your child is ready for college. It's more flexible than state- or college-sponsored plans since you're not committing to any one college. The drawback: You need a large lump sum to contribute and if you've got *that* much available you can probably earn more with a different kind of investment, such as a stock mutual fund.

580. My child will start college in less than a year. Is it too late to start saving?

It's never too late to start planning. Verify that the accounts and investments you do have are earning the highest rate of return possible without risk. Make certain you are creditworthy and if you need to borrow funds, make certain your credit history is accurate. Be sure you have not exhausted your borrowing capacity; it's often better to pay off high-interest loans than save at money market rates.

581. We've saved up lots of money for our child's college education. But is it possible not to use our own funds and have college paid for with financial aid?

Financial aid is usually dependent on need, but there are grants for academic and athletic scholarships based on a student's ability, not need. A more detailed discussion of all the various financial aid packages is included in the latter part of this chapter.

582. If I do save, won't those savings mean I won't qualify for aid?

To a degree, yes. However, your annual income has a much greater influence on how much aid you qualify for than how much money you've saved. Although the family who has saved for college may be required to contribute more towards a child's college expenses, two families with comparable incomes will be required to contribute fairly comparable payments. Moreover, the family with savings won't have to borrow (or they'll have to borrow less) and thus have a more secure future after their children have graduated from college. At the moment, the maximum amount that parents can be expected to contribute in a given year is less than 5.6 percent of their total assets. Home equity is not included.

583. I have a new grandchild. How much can I give him to start a college account?

You don't have to pay gift taxes on gifts totalling less than $10,000 a year to any one person. You and your wife can give a joint gift (if you split the gift) of $20,000 per year to your grandchild, tax free. The $20,000 need only come from one spouse, but the other spouse must join in the gift.

584. Should I put the account in the name of my son or my grandchild?

To keep the funds set aside for your grandchild segregated and thus out of your estate, the funds should be placed in a custodial account. You should not be the custodian for the funds you gift or the funds are pulled back into your estate. Custodial accounts eliminate the need for setting up a trust. The money for the child is held in the name of a custodian. The custodian could be the child's parent, aunt, uncle, sibling, almost any other person. When your grandchild reaches age eighteen or twenty-one (depending on the state where you live), the funds in the account not used for college expenses are turned over to the child. Funds within a custodial account should be the first assets used to fund your grandchild's college expenses.

585. How can my parents help in sending their grandchild to college?

They could make a direct gift to the college your child attends without incurring any gift tax liability nor income tax liability since it's not considered income to you or a gift to the child.

586. Is it wise to borrow for education?

If you don't have the money for your child's education, you either need to liquidate assets, pay through monthly contributions, or borrow. The important point about borrowing is that you should know your limits. Non-student loans taken out in your name will need to be repaid. Any default can ruin your credit. There are other ways to save money on education: Send your child to a community college or have him pay for his education himself.

587. Are there any other ways to save money on college?

Yes, there are many other ways:

- Consider a program that lets you graduate in three years instead of four.
- Courses your child took in high school can save you a semester or two of tuition.
- Attend summer classes at a college near your home to supplement courses you take during the school year (make certain the courses are transferrable before you go to the time and expense of taking them).
- Consider a work/study program that helps provide funds for tuition while you go to school.
- Live at home and commute to classes rather than living on campus.
- Attend college while employed. Many employers reimburse some or all tuition expenses for their employees.

INVESTING

588. Our first child is three months old and already my husband is worrying about paying for college. Isn't this too early to worry about college investments?

No. The longer you put off saving, the more likely you're going to have to borrow a large amount of money when your child is ready to go to a university. If you wait too long, you will need to pay interest on loans required to meet college expenses. Most experts suggest you:

- set up education accounts separate from other investments;
- deposit money each month; and
- choose an investment that stresses growth in the early years and safety as the child nears college age.

589. Must I really deposit money each month?

The best way to save is to put funds into a college fund from every pay or make a contribution monthly. Looking at college savings as a type of fixed monthly payment guarantees that the money will be deposited. It's often hard to find money to contribute so the payments should be part of your monthly bill payment process. Another way of making contributions is to put any income tax refund into a college account. It's interesting to see how quickly the funds accumulate if the savings are made with each paycheck, each month, or annually when you receive a lump-sum refund. Start small, if necessary, and increase the savings as you can afford to do this.

590. What kinds of investments should I start so we'll be prepared to pay for college?

Most experts would recommend investments which gain value, such as stocks and mutual funds. You should limit potential risks by starting a college fund after each child is born to have as many years as possible for investing. You can minimize taxes by making growth investments which don't usually produce yearly income.

591. Should I change my investments as my child gets older?

As your child nears college age, you will want to start switching some of the portfolio into more stable investments, such as equity income funds and medium-term Treasury bonds. If the stock market is on the rise, you could sell some of your investments to protect the gains your stocks have made.

592. What about zero coupon bonds as a method of financing college tuition?

Zero coupon bonds are bonds in which the interest (coupons) has been stripped from the bonds. They work very similarly to EE bonds. You buy a bond from a broker at a substantial discount from face value and then collect the full value when it matures years later. With zero coupon bonds, the accrued interest is not deferred so you must in most cases report the interest each year even though you didn't receive it. Zero coupon bonds can be an excellent source of guaranteed growth if you purchase bonds that mature during the four- or five-year period when your child will be going to school. If you must sell them before they are due, you may lose money since the commission on selling bonds can be exorbitant. Unless you purchase tax-exempt zeroes, you will be responsible for the accrued interest on the bonds each year.

593. I want to start saving for my daughter's college costs. Aren't EE bonds the best choice since the interest is tax free if used for education?

It's true that some people don't have to pay taxes on interest earned on EE bonds if they are cashed in to pay for a child's education. However, not *everyone* can enjoy this tax-free bonanza. Remember:

- The bonds must be issued after 1989.
- They must be bought by a person over age twenty-four and the bonds must be in *your* name, not your child's name.
- The bonds can only be used for your education, your spouse, or your dependent children
- When you cash them in, the entire interest amount is tax free only if your joint household income is less than $74,200. If you and your spouse earn between $74,200 and $104,200, some of the interest from the EE bonds will be taxed and the rest will be tax free, depending on where your income falls within that range. If you and your spouse earn more than $104,200, none of the interest is tax free. Also, if you're a married taxpayer and you don't file jointly, the exclusion is not available to you at all.

594. My child is a junior in high school. Is it too late to buy Series EE Savings Bonds for college?

Remember that you must keep these bonds at least five years in order to collect the full interest. Thus, if you bought them now, you wouldn't be able to cash them in to their full advantage until your child is a junior in college. The interest rate earned on EE bonds is a percentage of the Treasury note interest rate adjusted semiannually. The advantage to EE bonds would be that if you qualify, the income tax might be avoided if the bonds are purchased as educational bonds and the proceeds at redemption are used for college.

595. When I sell my stocks or mutual funds to pay for college, is there a way to avoid paying lots of tax?

You can take advantage of your child's lower tax rate when he or she is college age by making a gift of stocks or stock mutual funds to the child just before they're sold to pay for college tuition. Since your child will be selling the investment, the taxes will probably be less. The capital gain liability is at your child's bracket, not yours. You won't owe any gift tax if the value of the stock or stock fund gifted is less than $10,000 (if the stock is in your name and your husband's, then the gift tax doesn't kick in until you give $20,000).

596. Should I put investments for my six-year-old's college into her name?

Children under age fourteen will pay taxes at your rate so there is no tax advantage to saving the assets in the child's name if her income is in the taxable range of more than $1,300 per year. If your tax bracket is above 28 percent, put enough money in your child's account to take advantage of the $1,300 annual income limitation. Keep the rest of the money in your own name. Once you put money into your child's name—called a custodial account—you give up the right to use it for your personal needs although you may use the funds for camp and other expenses of your child, if necessary. At eighteen (or twenty-one in some places) your child then has the right to spend whatever money has been saved in her name. Remember, if you want to apply for financial aid, a child is expected to contribute a higher percentage of his or her assets (35 percent) than you are of yours (5.6 percent).

597. How is the income from the custodial account taxed?

Income from the custodial account is taxed to the minor. If the child is less than fifteen years of age, the first $650 is not taxed, the next $650 is taxed at the child's bracket, and anything above this is taxed at the parents' income tax bracket. Once the child reaches age fifteen, the income earned on the custodial account is taxed at the child's bracket.

598. Should we use our retirement investments to pay for our child's education?

Not a good idea. It may leave you short of money later and any money you take out of a qualified retirement plan will incur an income tax liability to you. Under current law, there is no longer the 10 percent penalty for withdrawal for educational purposes. It seems wise to withdraw from an educational IRA since the funds were set aside for the purpose of saving for college.

599. Is that really a good idea?

Yes. If you can save in a retirement account and then separately borrow for college, you're going to come out ahead in the end because of the tax benefits that you get from retirement accounts and the increased financial aid you may get by not building up so much money outside retirement accounts.

600. So what should we do?

Consider a home equity loan. The interest rate is usually low, it's tax deductible, and if your original mortgage is almost paid off it won't be hard to arrange. Keep in mind that if you default, you can lose your home.

601. What's a baccalaureate bond?

A special tax-exempt zero coupon bond usually sold in small denominations. Because they're sold to come due on a specific date, you can time them to produce money when you need to pay college bills. Some may provide an extra bonus if you use the money to pay tuition at an in-state school. Remember that if you sell the bonds before they mature, you can lose money.

602. Is there some way to figure out how much I have to invest now to send my son to college in five years?

A guesstimate is to take the estimated cost of college and divide it by sixty months (twelve months times the five-year period). This will give you the figure you will need to save each month for your son's college.

603. What are the best investments for college?

The best investments are assets that are available for college. Of course, it would be wonderful to be in a fund that grows 35 percent each year for ten years; however, you need to review the risk/reward relationship of your investment plan. A common plan is to invest a portion of the portfolio in zero coupon bonds that will mature when the student is ready to attend school. The other portion of the portfolio should be in a blue chip or equity stock fund for long-term growth potential. This allocation should depend on your risk/reward relationship, the total family's assets, income, and the money you are able to set aside for college.

604. What are the worst investments for college?

There are several investments that seem inappropriate for college:

- *Limited partnerships:* They aren't liquid.
- *Tax-deferred annuity:* If you withdraw funds before the age of fifty-nine-and-a-half, there is a 10 percent penalty for early withdrawal.
- *Life insurance:* You have the loan interest to pay as well as the internal fees associated with the insurance.
- *Savings accounts:* These accounts often fail to keep you ahead of inflation; you need your money to grow faster than this.
- *Money market accounts:* Money market accounts have the same problems that savings accounts have.
- *Prepaid tuition plans:* Your child may not want to go to the school for which you've prepaid. Instead of prepaying, invest your own money, which is what the school is going to do.

605. Is it better to have a student loan or an equity line of credit on my house?

Before 1998, you could not deduct the interest on a student loan. Therefore, it was better to take out a loan on the equity in your home. With the Taxpayer Relief Act of 1997, taxpayers who pay interest on qualified higher education loans taken for themselves, their spouses, or any dependent (at the time the debt was incurred) may deduct the interest. The amount is up to $1,000 in 1998 to $2,500 in the year 2001 and after. This deduction is permitted whether or not you itemize your deductions. Married couples must file a joint return to qualify for the deduction. The best way to handle a student loan is to review whether or not you can itemize your deductions and then review the best loan interest rate and repayment schedule.

606. What about borrowing for college using my margin account?

A margin account is a type of brokerage account where you can borrow money at the prime rate. Your stocks within the account are collateral. Now that student loan interest is deductible, the use of a margin account isn't nearly as attractive as it once was. You can deduct the annual interest paid on a margin account up to the investment interest earned by you through the year. The bad news about a margin loan is that you may be required to contribute money towards the loan if the value of your account drops below a certain point because of a significant drop in the value of your stocks held in the account. You should consider going elsewhere for the funds. The margin account is great for quick access to money, but use it with discretion and understanding of the pros and cons.

607. I have a choice between increasing my 401(k) fund at work or placing the funds in my son's college account. Which should I choose?

Your 401(k) account is your retirement—your security for the future. There are grants, loans, and work programs to help you with your children's education, but there aren't loans and grants to help you with your retirement. Funding the 401(k) should lower your income tax bracket. These funds are not used when calculating your contribution for college aid.

608. If my son is a junior in high school, is it time to liquidate his stock portfolio?

With only two years to go before you need money for college, it is clearly time to place funds for the first two years' tuition into an investment that isn't going to fluctuate too much.

609. Should I set up an education IRA?

Under the Taxpayer Relief Act of 1997, you can now withdraw funds from an IRA for educational expenses without incurring a 10 percent penalty, but the money you withdraw can be subject to income taxation. You can avoid even this tax liability if parents invest up to $500 per year in an IRA in their child's name (if the child is under age eighteen) and then withdraw the funds for use towards college. Putting money into a child's educational IRA is a good idea because it's not taxed or penalized when it's withdrawn to pay for college. If the child doesn't use his or her education IRA, you could roll it over for use by another child.

610. Are there drawbacks to an education IRA?

Yes. They include:

- Income limitations.
- You can't have an education IRA and participate in a prepaid-tuition plan for your child.
- The IRA will be considered a part of your child's assets and thus be included in the 35 percent figure that must be paid from the child's assets before financial aid is considered.

The year you withdraw funds from an education IRA, you can *not* claim the HOPE Scholarship or the Lifetime Learning Credit.

FINANCIAL AID

611. What's the HOPE Scholarship?

The HOPE Scholarship (Higher Opportunities for Performance in Education) has been available since January 1998. It's a tax credit for qualified tuition and related expenses paid for a student's first two years of college. The student must attend postsecondary education courses at least half time. The credit is 100 percent of the first $1,000 of qualified expenses paid during the year, plus 50 percent of the next $1,000 paid for a maximum credit of $1,500.

612. I recently lost my job and want to go back to school. If I'm married, will I still qualify for the HOPE Scholarship?

If you are at least a half-time student in your first two years of school and you and your spouse file a joint return, you can apply for the HOPE Scholarship. Although you won't reap the benefits of the credit until you file your taxes in the spring of 1999 for the 1998 tax year, your husband might want to lower his withholding to benefit from the credit throughout 1998.

613. When does the HOPE Scholarship begin?

The HOPE Scholarship is for expenses and courses that start on or after January 1, 1998.

614. Aren't there any other credits to help me through school?

In addition to the HOPE Scholarship, there is a Lifetime Learning Credit. This may be helpful for expenses that don't qualify for the HOPE Scholarship. The Lifetime Learning Credit is available for any school year for courses to acquire or improve job skills. The credit may be for undergraduate, graduate, or professional degree courses.

The credit is equal to 20 percent of expenses up to $5,000 for a maximum credit of $1,000 per year. After the year 2003, the credit rises to 20 percent of $10,000 for a maximum credit of $5,000 per year. It should be used to cover expenses paid after June 30, 1998, for an academic period beginning June 30, 1998. The credit is for the taxpayer, spouse, and their children or other dependents and is intended to help towards tuition and related fees—not room and board, commuting, or other expenses. As with so many deductions and credits, there are income limitations.

615. Will I be able to deduct both the HOPE Scholarship and the Lifetime Learning Credit for my daughter's freshman year tuition and expenses?

Generally, you will not be able to claim both the HOPE Scholarship and the Lifetime Learning Credit in a given year for the same student: it's one or the other. Thus, if you qualify for both, choose the one that is the best for your situation.

616. What do colleges consider financial aid?

Federal student financial aid includes federal grants (which you do not pay back), loans (which you do pay back), and work-study money (which you earn and do not pay back). The aid can help you pay for most kinds of education after high school.

617. What about state aid?

Your state should have its own financial aid programs; you should check with your local high school or college financial aid officer to get these forms. Some colleges may want you to submit supplementary forms directly to them.

618. Must I be accepted for admission before I apply for financial aid?

You should apply for financial aid at the time you apply for admission.

619. How can I find out what the deadline is for applying for aid at the college I will be attending?

Review the college catalog and then verify the information with the financial aid office at the college. Many institutions have priority filing dates which you should meet if possible. The difficulty is that there is so much more financial need than funds available. An early application may help you receive more of the money you will need.

620. What are the requirements to be eligible for federal financial aid packages?

You must:

- be a U.S. citizen or eligible noncitizen;
- be registered with the selective service (if required);
- attend a college that participates in the programs;
- be working towards a degree or certificate;
- be making satisfactory academic progress;
- not owe a refund on a federal grant or be in default on a federal educational loan; and
- have financial need as determined by the F.A.F.S.A. (Free Application for Federal Student Aid) program.

You can't qualify for Federal Pell Grants if you already have received a bachelor's degree or if you have been convicted of drug distribution or possession.

621. My child works and supports herself, but she's only twenty. Will the school believe us that she is self-supporting?

No. It doesn't usually work to claim that your child is self-supporting and most colleges won't consider her independent until age twenty-four.

622. I'm twenty-five years old, I live at home, and I'm paying for my own college. Will my parents' income still need to be considered when I apply for college?

No. If you're over age twenty-four, their income doesn't count even if you live at home. You also qualify for the same federal grants and loans that a dependent student does.

623. My husband and I are divorced. Do we both have to fill out financial aid forms?

Since parents are considered to be responsible for their children's education, most colleges expect the noncustodial parent to contribute towards their child's education. Thus, both parents are usually required to fill out financial information forms for colleges before your child can be eligible for aid. If either of you has remarried, stepparents' income is also included. However, if your child is someone the college really wants to recruit, the college may make an exception. Eligibility for federal Pell grants may be based on the income of the custodial parent only.

624. What's the first step in the financial aid process?

You must fill out a FAFSA which your child's high school or college guidance office should have on hand. You don't have to pay anything when you submit this application. Some private schools also want to see a Financial Aid Form (FAF) which will ask you for more information than the FAFSA.

Both the FAFSA and the Financial Aid Profile (PROFILE) are due January 1 of the year for which you're asking for aid (usually the January of your child's senior year in high school and each following January).

625. After I fill out the financial aid forms, what happens next?

The information you've supplied on all these forms is then assessed via a financial needs analysis—a standard formula approved by Congress. The analysis looks at:

- parents' income (your 1998 income is used to determine your expected family contribution for the 1999–2000 school year);
- your assets (your home, money in retirement accounts, and annuities are not included);
- your child's investments and savings;
- age and need for retirement income;
- number of dependents;
- number of family members in college; and
- unusual financial problems (explained on your application).

The analysis will figure out how much the parents and the child need to contribute toward the child's education. This is called the expected family contribution (EFC).

Within four to six weeks of application, you will receive a Student Aid Report (SAR) which will list your EFC. The EFC is the percentage of the college expenses that the government expects you and your child to be able to contribute towards his or her education.

626. Will this figure change each year while my son is in college?

Parents get one EFC figure a year regardless of their child's college costs or the number of children they have in college. If a second child joins the first child in college, the EFC for each student is divided by two. Since you must reapply each year, the figure can change.

627. Does this expected family contribution change whether I go to a state college or an Ivy League university?

Your EFC is based on your family's income and assets. If the EFC is $9,000 and your state college costs $10,000 a year, you will qualify for $1,000 in aid. However, if your dream is to attend Yale at a cost of more than $25,000 a year, your EFC would still be $9,000. This means that you would qualify for $16,000 in grants and loans. The EFC figure doesn't change no matter how expensive the school.

628. Is my son expected to pay a minimum amount towards his college costs?

While there is no federal student aid rule that expects students to contribute a minimum towards their college costs, most colleges expect students to pay a minimum of $900 per year from summer jobs when it comes to awarding their private funds towards a financial aid package.

629. Is it necessary to apply for financial aid every year?

Yes.

630. How does the college advise me of the financial aid package we've been given?

It's interesting to see how a family may spend more to send a child to a less expensive college than to an Ivy League school due to the financial package put together by the financial aid office of the two schools. Notice of the packages is sent to you by an award letter. Note how much you're required to pay now, how much you will be required to repay down the road, and at what price you are borrowing the money. Compare the award letter from the colleges to which you have applied. Don't delay in responding because you are waiting to hear from other colleges. If you don't respond by the required date, your award may be canceled and the funds freed up for other students. Responding to the award letter does not commit you to attend the college, it just safeguards your award if you do decide to attend the school.

631. We're worried that the only school my daughter wants to go to is one we can't afford. What should we do?

You should have her apply to a school that you *can* afford, such as a small state college, in addition to her expensive dream school. Then if your other financial aid packages fall through, she will at least be able to afford to go somewhere. She can always transfer to the other school in the last year or two. Some colleges will reconsider or negotiate their initial financial aid offer if you ask. It can't hurt. If this still doesn't work, it is best to begin the student loan process.

632. Can you list some of the federal student financial aid programs available?

- Federal Pell Grants (Pell Grants)
- Federal Supplemental Educational Opportunity Grants (FSEOG)
- Federal Subsidized and Unsubsidized Stafford Loans
- Stafford/Ford Federal Direct Subsidized and Unsubsidized Loans
- Federal Perkins Loan
- Federal Work-Study (FWS)
- Title VII Public Health Act Program

For more information about federal student aid programs and how to apply for them, visit their website at: http://www.ed.gov/offices/OPE/Students.

633. What is a Pell Grant?

The Federal Pell Grant Program is the largest need-based student aid program in the country. Only students with an expected family contribution (EFC) of less than $2,300 are eligible for Pell Grants. The maximum Pell Grant for the 1998–1999 school year was $2,550. The amount a student receives depends on need, costs of education at the particular college, length of the program, and whether enrollment is full-time or part-time.

634. I'm going back to school because I lost my job. Will I still qualify for a Pell Grant?

Yes. You'll also qualify if your marriage has dissolved and you're going back to school even if you don't strictly meet the financial guidelines.

635. I have funds set aside for each of my children in separate college accounts. Will they assess all the children's funds for the 35 percent figure my son needs to contribute?

You, as parents, are responsible for contributing via a formula as calculated by the federal government. Each child is expected to contribute 35 percent; however, a sibling's funds are not used in this calculation. Thus, if you have $15,000 set aside for each of your three children, the $30,000 set aside for your two younger children is not included when the government figures out what your eldest child's contribution should be.

636. My son is in the beginning of his senior year in high school. Should he give all the money in his account to his siblings so he doesn't have to use 35 percent of his funds the first year?

You are required to use 35 percent of the funds he has when he begins college or any funds given away up to two years prior to his entering college. Thus, transferring money to a sibling while he's a senior won't work.

637. I understand that I must use 35 percent of my son's funds towards his college expenses in the first year, but if I use all his funds to pay our family contribution the first year, will that increase our aid package for the last three years of school?

Yes. However, check with your son's college financial aid office before you do this because there are schools that require 35 percent each year based on the funds available prior to the first year of college. If you spent this money, you wouldn't have it for use in future years.

638. Is money we have in retirement funds not counted when figuring up our eligibility for financial aid?

That's right. Only money you have outside your retirement accounts is counted when figuring whether or not you are eligible for financial aid. That's why it doesn't make sense not to contribute to your retirement plan in favor of salting money away for your child's education. If you don't save for your retirement, you're paying higher taxes on your income and the interest on savings, plus you will be expected to contribute more money to your child's education.

639. What about IRAs and KEOGHs? Are these values included in the information used to calculate financial aid?

No. Eligibility for financial aid does not take into account any of these assets:

- Your primary residence
- A family farm (unless it is an investment rather than a working farm)
- Personal or consumer loans or any debts that are not related to the asset listed

- The cash value of life insurance and retirement plans
- Student financial aid

640. The college financial aid office talked about our asset protection allowance. What is that and how is it calculated?

The financial aid formula depends on your assets; however, the government wants you to have enough money for retirement. Thus, the asset protection allowance is calculated based on your age. The older the parent, the more assets you may have protected from use for the college expenses of your children.

641. What if we didn't qualify for financial aid because we have too much money?

If you go through the aforementioned application process, you will still have access to loans that aren't based on need. This is why you should make sure to apply for financial aid.

642. We're thinking of applying for financial aid. Is it better to have money in the bank for college or pay off all our debts to lower our list of assets?

Except for something like a mortgage on a house, consumer debt is not taken into consideration when you are applying for financial aid. Thus, if you have $25,000 in credit card debt and $35,000 in bank accounts and stocks, from a financial aid consideration it's better to pay off the cards and keep only $10,000 in bank/stock accounts. This could possibly increase your financial aid. If you don't pay off the debt, it won't be considered in any way when it comes to deciding whether or not financial aid is granted.

STUDENT LOANS

643. What is a Stafford Loan and what's the difference between subsidized and unsubsidized Stafford Loans?

A Stafford Loan is considered an entitlement. The Subsidized Stafford Loan is awarded based on need; the Unsubsidized Stafford Loan is available to all students and their families regardless of income. In the subsidized loan, the government pays the interest for you:

- while you are enrolled in school at least half-time;
- during the six-month period after you stop attending school at least half-time; and
- during any authorized deferment.

When you have completed or stopped attending school and the six-month deferral period has passed, you are then responsible for both the interest and principal of the loan. The unsubsidized loans require you to pay *all* accrued interest. You may make the interest payments while in school or defer (and accumulate) the interest until repayment. The Stafford Loans are insured against the student's death or total disability. You may be charged a 1 percent fee as an insurance premium for this coverage.

644. My family isn't needy, but I want to apply for a federal student loan. Are there any loans that aren't tied to need?

Yes. There are a number of loan programs that are available even if your family isn't considered to be financially needy. These include Unsubsidized Stafford Loans and Parents' Loans for Undergraduate Students (PLUS).

Only Subsidized Stafford Loans (where the government pays the interest that builds up while you're still in school) are limited to those students who are financially needy. For more information on federal student loan programs, call the Federal Student Financial Aid Information Center at (800) 433-3243.

645. Will I be limited in the amount of money I can borrow through these loan programs?

Yes. Most loan programs will limit both the amount you can borrow each year and the total amount you can borrow for college and graduate school. If you need more than the amount you can get through these loan programs, the PLUS loans can fill in the difference (parents can borrow the full amount needed). Both of your parents will need good credit.

646. Is it better to take out a Federal PLUS loan or a private supplemental loan?

As with so much in life, there is no better. Federal PLUS loans have an interest rate cap which may be lower than standard loans, but standard loans may give you a fixed monthly payment plan. Your best bet is to comparison shop.

647. Do the federal loan programs require that I have established credit?

No. Unlike privately funded programs, the federal programs only ask that you don't have negative credit—recent bankruptcy, more than three debts more than three months in arrears, and so on.

648. Who is responsible for paying back school loans?

Most financial aid loans are made to students, not parents. It is your child's responsibility to repay them.

649. Is financial aid and a student loan the same thing?

No. A student loan is just one of the many types of financial aid you can use to pay for your education. The financial aid process is constructed on a commonsense premise: The less money you'll need to repay after college is finished, the better. Thus, the best kind of financial aid is gift aid—grants and scholarships—which need not be repaid.

650. How do you apply for a student loan?

There are various ways to apply. You can apply at almost all banks for a student loan package. The college where you will attend has a preferred list of lenders and there are national specialists where you can go directly for the loan. The loans differ in how the total package benefits the student. Because there are different origination fees, loan interest rates, and so on, you should comparison shop.

651. How is the interest rate on a student loan calculated?

The interest rate varies on student loans, depending on the economic environment during the period of the loan, but the maximum interest rate is 8.25 percent.

GRANTS AND SCHOLARSHIPS

652. I want to apply for only a scholarship. Do I have to fill out the FAFSA or the PROFILE forms to apply?

Check with the scholarship sponsor and/or the financial aid office at the college to which you are applying. Find out which forms should be completed and when they are due.

653. What about grants? Do I need to pay them back?

No. A grant is a gift and doesn't need to be paid back. There are many grant programs available from both schools and the government. You can apply for the federal government grants when you fill out the FAFSA (see question 624). You may need to apply separately for any state grants. Check your guidance office for information on grants from specific colleges and other private groups, such as employers, banks, credit unions, community groups, and so on.

654. Are these grants hard to find?

You'll find out about some grants simply by applying for financial aid through a college. Other programs won't come to you; you need to ferret them out. You can check for these grant programs by checking directories, your local library, and by simply asking local organizations, such as churches, employers, and so on.

655. Where do you find out information about the various scholarships available?

Several of the most common places are the financial aid office of the college you want to attend, your high school guidance office, your local library, or a bookstore. There are many scholarship search programs on the Internet; a good place to start is FastWEB (http://www.fastweb.com).

656. Should I sign up with a scholarship search service?

No. Most of the time they are a money waster and some are downright scams. Some may charge you lots of money simply to tell you about grants or scholarships that you'd be automatically eligible for just by signing up for financial aid at the college of your choice.

657. Must we pay taxes on scholarships that cover expenses other than tuition?

Yes. Grants to cover expenses other than tuition are taxable.

658. When looking at the EFC, does the government expect only the parents to contribute to the child's education?

No. Your child must contribute 35 percent of his or her own funds per year. You must contribute 5.6 percent of your funds. The college requires you to disclose both your and your child's assets when you apply for financial aid. Your child's assets are then multiplied by 35 percent and your child is expected to use those funds for college for the upcoming year. Thus, if your child has $35,000 set aside for his college in a custodial account or in his name alone, he would be expected to use $12,250 of that money to pay for his freshman year before financial aid kicks in. When he enters his sophomore year, he must kick in 35 percent of his remaining funds for the second year and so on.

CHAPTER 9

STOCKS, BONDS, AND MUTUAL FUNDS

There's so much happening these days on the investment front that it's both exciting and intimidating. On one hand, there are so many different ways to invest that you should be able to find the investment niche that's just right for you. On the other hand, the world of stocks, bonds, and mutual funds is growing increasingly more complex so it may be hard to spot the right investments in the forest of possibilities. The more you know about key investment concepts and strategies, the better you will be able to make informed decisions about putting your money into various types of stocks, bonds, mutual funds, and other investments. This chapter lays the groundwork for success by answering your essential investment questions.

STOCKS

659. What is a stock?

Stocks are the most common ownership investment traded on the securities market. When you buy stock, you are buying an interest in a specific business. Companies that issue stock include computer companies, car manufacturers, hotels, fast-food restaurants, and so on. You make money on your investment if the company pays a dividend or if the company's stock increases in value.

660. What is the difference between a stock and a bond?

Stocks represent ownership shares in a corporation and may pay dividends. Bonds pay interest over a specific period of time on funds lent to the issuer.

661. How do I buy stock?

You buy stock through a broker or sometimes directly from a company. Prices can range from less than $1 to more than $100 per share.

662. How do I find out information about a stock?

Information on individual stocks can be acquired by calling the company's shareholder services and requesting last year's annual report and the most current quarterly report. Information is also available through *Value Line* and *Morningstar,* investor services which provide a great deal of information about individual companies. Information is also available on the Internet.

663. What kind of return do stocks bring?

Over the past sixty-five years, common stocks have returned an average of 12 percent each year. For this reason, advisers believe that there's a good chance that a well-diversified portfolio, which includes average risk common stocks, will continue to bring in about 12 percent a year.

664. Is the key to making money in stocks knowing when to get out of the market?

There are some periods when it's better to own a greater percentage of stocks than other times. However, it isn't usually a good idea to dive into and out of the market frequently. In fact, a recent Harvard study found that someone who tries to time the market in this way would have to be correct 80 percent of the time in order to have even some success. Interestingly, the problem is usually not that you didn't get *out* of a failing market soon enough, but that you didn't get back into a rising market soon enough.

665. My broker suggested I put in a stop-loss order. How does that work?

A stop-loss order is an order to sell a stock when its market price reaches or drops below a specified level. It is held on the books of the brokerage firm until used, primarily to protect the investor against rapid declines in prices and to limit loss.

666. Is it better to use a discount broker or a full-service brokerage house?

Like anything in life, you usually get what you pay for. If you use a full-service house, do you feel that you get what you paid for? Is it worth the price? If you call your broker and tell him or her what you want (that person hasn't given you the information), you should use a discount broker since the firm is only doing the trading for you. On the other hand, if your broker gives you investment ideas or information or provides financial planning services, then a full-service broker is worth the money. Analyze what you are paying, shop around, and find out if your broker is giving you the right service for the fees.

667. What does it mean when a stock splits?

Stock splits are used when a company believes the price of its stock is too high and wants to enhance its trading appeal and activity by lowering the price. The company lowers the par value of the stock and increases the number of shares so that after the split you still have the same ownership (equity) in the company but you have more shares worth a lower price. Many of my clients believe they have increased their holdings when a stock splits, but at the time of the split ownership in the company is the same.

668. What is a reverse split?

A reverse stock split is used to reduce the numbers of shares of stock outstanding and will increase the price of a stock. Reverse splits often occur when a company is coming out of bankruptcy or financial difficulty or the company wants to control the number of smaller shareholders.

669. How does this work in a 2 for 1 split, if I own 100 shares of stock?

The company increases the number of shares outstanding via a stock split. A company announces they will exchange a specified number of new shares for each outstanding share of stock presently held. In a 2 for 1 stock split, you will have an additional 100 shares for the 100 shares you already own (200 total). In a 2 for 1 split, earnings and dividends are cut in half.

670. Since preferred stock usually pays a higher dividend than common stock, is it a better investment?

There are various types of preferred stock. As with so many investments today, hybrids are coming on the market as quickly as people can think them up. A standard preferred stock is considered a fixed income security because the level of income does not change. I consider investment in preferred stock to be the same as buying a bond without the maturity date. Usually, the value of the preferred stock correlates with interest rates. If interest rates are lower than the payout, the stock is worth more than you paid for it; if interest rates have risen since you purchased the stock, its value has decreased.

671. I'm thinking about joining an investment club. Is this a good idea?

It can be a great idea and a way to make new friends, learn a lot about investments, and make money. They are especially attractive to women, since many investment clubs are for women only. According to the National Association of Investors Corporation, here are the fifteen most popular stocks (as of 1996) owned by investment clubs in the United States:

- McDonald's
- Merck & Co.
- PepsiCo
- Motorola
- AFLAC, Inc.
- Intel
- AT&T
- Wal-Mart

- RPM, Inc.
- Coca-Cola
- Walt Disney
- Abbott Labs
- Rubbermaid
- General Electric
- Microsoft

672. I keep hearing about P/E ratio. What is it and what does it mean?

A company's P/E ratio is used to determine how the market is pricing the company's common stock. This ratio relates the earnings per share (EPS) to the market price of the stock. Earnings per share is a measure of profitability. If a common stock has a PE of 49 when the average PE of the market is 18, the stock is very expensive. A high P/E ratio is not necessarily bad just as a low P/E ratio does not necessarily mean the stock is a good investment. The investor needs to relate the P/E ratio to future growth of the company. Will the company's earnings continue to grow at a rate greater than the market to justify the high P/E ratio?

673. What is churning?

Churning means a broker is buying and selling securities in a client's account for the sole purpose of generating sales commission. Churning is a difficult charge to prove and what the brokerage industry considers excessive and what the average investor considers excessive is usually quite different.

674. Should I open a cash or a margin account with my broker?

A cash account is one where the customer can make only cash transactions. This is the typical brokerage account. You make a trade and the cash or security must be in the account within three business days.

A margin account means you have been given borrowing power by the brokerage firm. The securities within the account are collateral and you are permitted to borrow a prespecified proportion of the market value of the account. A margin account provides easy accessibility to money and interest is usually deductible (up to investment income earned by the taxpayer). However, the bad thing about a margin account is that you may be subject to a margin call. This occurs when the collateralized securities fall in value below the specified proportion previously discussed.

675. What is a discretionary account?

A discretionary account is one in which the broker can use his discretion to make purchases and sale transactions on behalf of the customer. I am adverse to this practice. If you want investment management, contract the services of an investment manager. Brokers receive payment on transactions; most investment managers are compensated on a fee basis.

676. What is the difference between the New York Stock Exchange and NASDAQ?

The New York Stock Exchange is an organization that was founded in 1792. Stocks are listed to trade on the exchange and traded on the floor of the exchange. The goal is to buy the shares at the lowest price and sell the shares at the highest price. Specific companies are listed on the exchange. The exchange is highly regulated.

NASDAQ is a computer system that connects buyers and sellers on over-the-counter stocks. The over-the-counter market is a mass telecommunication network where government bonds, mutual funds, and various size stocks are traded.

677. What is due diligence and what does it have to do with my financial adviser?

Due diligence, as outlined in the Securities Act of 1933, requires that investment advisers investigate any security before offering it for sale to a client. Additionally, the security must be suited to the client's needs and objectives.

678. What is diversification?

Diversification is the process of reducing risk within a portfolio. As the number of companies increase, the level of risk should decline. In addition to the number of companies, you also need to diversify your assets, buying a variety of stocks, bonds, and real estate. Talk to your financial adviser for help in diversification. You should buy at least twenty stocks of different companies in different industries. You should also diversify your total portfolio, holding real estate, bonds, stocks, cash, and so on. It doesn't make sense to own twenty pharmaceutical companies or twenty oil companies; however, owning a variety of common stocks should diversify your portfolio. Mutual funds are sold with the idea of diversification; however, as the types of mutual funds become more specific, you must keep aware of the diversification of your total portfolio.

679. Can I own too many stocks or mutual funds?

Yes. Unless you spend all your time reviewing financial information for your various holdings, owning too many stocks prohibits you from keeping track of your investments and knowing about the companies. There is no benefit in owning lots of stocks or mutual funds—you increase your portfolio expenses. My rule of thumb is to own no more than ten of any one asset.

680. *Morningstar* and *Value Line* have a figure called beta. What does it mean?

Beta is a measure of risk. The market has a beta of 1. Thus, a security with a beta of 1.25 would be considered to be 25 percent more volatile than the market. Stocks with a beta less than 1 are considered less risky than the market. Beta is calculated by a formula using historical returns of the given security and the historic returns of the market.

681. What is a "laddered portfolio"?

Laddered portfolios, also known as staggered portfolios, are individual bond portfolios that mature at different times. This method is designed to diversify interest rate risk from your portfolio as well as providing liquidity at maturity. An example of a staggered portfolio would be a $100,000 Treasury portfolio with a six-month Treasury bill, two-year note, three-year note, five-year note, and ten-year note, $20,000 each.

682. Are mutual funds better than individual stocks?

Mutual funds are liquid and they can provide professionally-managed diversification for people with a small amount of money to invest. A portfolio needs many individual stocks to reach this diversification; you can only invest in individual stocks with diversification when you've built up enough money. You must handle individual stock investment either by keeping abreast of the market or by hiring an investment manager to buy individual stocks. When you buy mutual funds you let the portfolio manger handle them.

683. What is dollar cost averaging?

Dollar cost averaging is the process of purchasing securities over a period of time by systematically investing a set amount at regular intervals. The goal of dollar cost averaging is to reduce the effects of price fluctuations.

684. Should I have dividend reinvestment?

Dividend reinvestment is the process of automatically investing the dividends. The down side of dividend reinvestment is that investors don't always keep track of the large number of shares they have accumulated over the years (so that they have too many shares of one stock or fund). Keeping track of the cost basis of dividend reinvestment is a nightmare.

685. My broker and I are in a dispute about the way he handled my account. Should we go to arbitration?

Arbitration is a process for handling controversies and disputes between investors and their brokers that does not involve the courts. There are no punitive damages, class action suits, and so on. The process is done within the Code of the National Association of Securities Dealers, Inc. Arbitration is the process the brokerage industry prefers since 60 percent of the cases are won by the industry. The requirement of an investor to go to arbitration is part of the standard brokerage new account form. Several brokerage houses will not take new customers who do not agree to arbitration.

686. What is hedging?

Combining two or more securities in a single investment to reduce risk; this is done with options and futures. There are even hedge mutual funds.

687. Since the commissions are cheaper, should I invest over the Internet?

Internet trading is cheaper than direct contact with an individual, and entails buying and trading via the computer. You get a status report when you make the order and execution is supposed to be made almost immediately if it is a market order and the markets are open. You will receive your monthly statement. Internet trading requires you to keep good records of your transactions.

688. What is the difference between a bull market and a bear market?

Market trends that move increasingly upwards are often referred to as a bull market while a continuously dropping market is often referred to as a bear market. A bear market is usually associated with investor pessimism, economic slowdowns, and government restraints. The bull market, on the other hand, is usually associated with investor optimism, economic recovery, and government stimulus.

689. I was advised that the stock market is volatile. Should I worry?

Volatility—the speed with which an investment gains or loses value—poses the biggest investment risk in the short term. The more volatile an investment, the more you can potentially make or lose in a short-term period. The volatility of the stock market is why it is not used for short-term goals. Investing in the stock market is for a mid-term or long-term investment.

690. I heard a TV announcer talk about timing the market. What is it and is it possible?

Timing the market is the process of predicting what the stock or bond markets are going to do next so you can be in the right place at the right time. Sell when the market is high and then reinvest when the market has dropped and the assets are cheaper. The problem with timing is that if you miss the best days of the market, it is difficult to catch up.

691. What are the different types of stocks?

There are many different kinds of stocks to buy:

- *Blue chip stocks* have a long and usually stable record of earnings and dividends. They are highly regarded investment quality companies and include Exxon, IBM, GE, and Procter & Gamble.
- *Growth stocks* normally pay little or no dividends because most of the profits are reinvested in the company and are used to at least partially finance its rapid growth. Sales, earnings, and market share are growing at rates that are higher than the average company or the general economy. Growth stocks are purchased for their capital gain potential.
- *Speculative stocks* lack a proven record of success, have uncertain earnings, are subject to wide swings in price, and don't usually pay

dividends. They are bought for the capital gain potential, usually held short term, and are not an investment found in most portfolios.

- *Cyclical stocks* generally follow the peaks and troughs of the general economy. They do well in an expanding economy and tend to do poorly when the economy retracts. Examples of cyclical stocks are Ford, Chrysler, and DuPont.
- *Defensive stocks* are not makers of weapons. Defensive stocks are companies that are less affected by general fluctuations in the general economy. Investors tend to use these when they feel a recession is imminent. Examples of defensive stocks are Coke, Pepsi, Weis Markets, and Warner Lambert.
- *Interest sensitive stocks* are stocks of companies that are largely affected by changes in interest rates; they generally pay higher than average dividends.

BONDS

692. What is a bond?

Bonds are the most common lending investment traded on a securities market. When a bond is issued, it has a specific maturity date at which you will be repaid your principal. Bonds fluctuate in value, primarily based on interest rate changes. If you have a bond worth 7 percent and the interest rates rise to 11 percent, your bond decreases in value—no one would want to buy your bond at par when they could get one at a higher interest rate.

693. What are the different types of bonds?

There are many different kinds of bonds:

- U.S. Treasury notes and bonds
- U.S. savings bonds
- U.S. government agency issues
- Municipal bonds
- Corporate bonds
- Mortgage-backed securities and CMOs
- Convertible bonds
- Certificates of deposit
- Bond mutual funds

694. What is the safest investment?

A three-month Treasury bill—an obligation of the U.S. Treasury—is considered to be a risk-free investment. This statement is based on the security of the underlying investment, not taking into consideration inflation or real return after taxes.

695. How can I figure out which bonds to buy?

It depends on the type of investor you are. If you're conservative, you probably feel comfortable with passbook savings accounts and government securities. Other investors like risk. In general, the more risk you're willing to put up with, the greater investment returns you may have. All funds have some risk, but you can control some of the risk by the types of mutual funds that you choose.

696. What are the two types of municipal bonds?

1. General Obligation (GOs) bonds are backed by the government; the bonds are repaid when the government collects taxes. Thus, a school district bond is a direct obligation of the district. If they don't have enough money to pay on the bonds, they raise new funds by raising taxes.
2. Revenue bonds are issued to finance a specific project, such as a turnpike or sewer or water project. These bonds are not backed by the full faith of the issuer, but are repaid from money generated from the project that was financed. By nature, these bonds are riskier than GOs and thus command higher interest rates for similar maturities.

697. Is interest from a municipal bond taxable?

No. Interest received on municipal bonds is not taxed by the federal government although there are taxable municipal bonds. A Pennsylvania resident won't pay taxes on a Pennsylvania municipal bond, but Pennsylvania would tax that resident for interest earned on a Vermont municipal bond. You need to discuss your state's tax situation with your accountant. Because muni interest is generally not taxable, the interest on these bonds is lower than on taxable investments.

698. I recently received my year-end statement for my municipal bond fund and it reported capital gains. How can there be capital gains in a muni fund and is this taxable to me?

Capital gains are taxable. Even though the interest on a municipal bond fund is income tax free, you have to pay tax on any capital gains within the fund. Capital gains occur when the internal municipal bonds within the account are sold by the fund manager at a gain.

699. Are most bonds short- or long-term investments?

Most municipal bonds available to the general investing public tend to be longer term because the institutional investors (banks, mutual fund managers, and so on) gobble up the short-term bonds. Be aware that if your bond is for longer than five or seven years, it may be more risky and volatile.

700. Are bonds easy to manage?

Yes, you buy and hold bonds for their interest; they don't require constant attention and will provide a source of dependable income.

701. Are there riskier bonds?

Yes. Riskier bonds are called high-yield bonds (also known as junk bonds). You can put money into a junk bond in the way you would invest in a speculative stock. These bonds are lower in quality and have a possibility of default. You get more interest payment because you are taking a greater risk that you won't have your principal repaid at maturity. If the bond issuer can't repay the bond, it's called a default. Often you do get a portion of your investment back or the bonds are reissued at a lower interest rate. Either way it can take years to get your money back. In times of economic recession, 10 percent of the junk bonds held go into default. Understand the higher risk of this investment when you purchase such a security.

702. How are bonds rated?

They're rated by credit-rating agencies for their safety (usually on a scale beginning with AAA as the highest rating). Safest bonds are Treasuries, high-grade corporate bonds—the most likely to pay you back. Next are general bonds (A or BBB)—just a little less safe. Junk bonds are BB or lower.

703. What is a corporate bond?

These are bonds issued by companies to raise capital to run the business. There is a legal document, called an indenture, that states the repayment schedule. In case of a bankruptcy, corporate bond holders receive their money before stockholders do. If you have corporate bonds, you must pay state and federal taxes on the interest earned.

704. What is a debenture?

Debentures are bonds that are unsecured; bondholders do not have any right to any assets of the company in the case of default or bankruptcy. The bondholders are general creditors of the company.

705. What are U.S. government agency bonds?

Various governmental agencies issue debt as a way to finance a variety of activities and projects. Some agencies are directly backed by the United States while others have implied backing by the government. Because these bonds are not as liquid as a Treasury obligation, they have a slightly higher yield than T-bills as well as a slightly higher degree of risk.

Agency bonds include:

1. Federal Home Loan Bank
2. Farm Credit Assistance Corporation
3. Federal Land Bank
4. Resolution Funding Corporation
5. Federal Farm Credit Banks
6. Fannie Maes
7. Tennessee Valley Authority

706. What is a Treasury Direct account?

In this account, an investor sets up an account with a regional Federal Reserve office and buys Treasury obligations directly from the Federal Reserve. The only fee for having the account or investing in the Treasury obligations is the annual fee of $25 on accounts over $100,000. No certificates are produced for these securities. The account must be set up with a direct deposit format with your banking institution.

707. When my certificate of deposit matured, I purchased a bond from my bank and it's now worth less than I paid for it. How can this happen?

The value of bonds changes on a daily basis as do stocks; however, generally the volatility is not as great as in stocks. You purchase bonds for income and security. However, think of the value of bonds as a seesaw. If interest rates drop, the value of your bond increases; this is called a *premium bond*. If you have an 8 percent bond and current rates are 6 percent, obviously your bond is more valuable than the 6 percent bond. If interest rates increase, the value of your bond drops; this is called a *discounted bond*. If you hold a 6 percent bond and current rates are 8 percent, your bond will be worth less than its face value. Who would want to give you $1,000 for your bond when they can go elsewhere and get 8 percent?

708. I'm not worried about investing in a long-term bond. The bond has a call provision. I'm protected, right?

You're not protected, the bond issuer is. You are protected for a number of years since most bonds can't be called for a period of time. However, after that, the issuers will call in the bonds if interest rates drop—at a time when you don't want the money back. For example, current interest rates are 4.5 percent on municipal bonds. You own a 6.85 percent municipal bond with a call date of 12/15/98. The municipality can call in that bond, giving you your money back. Where will you invest the money to get the same yield? You can't. If current interest rates are at 8 percent on munis, the municipality isn't going to call in the bonds because they can't invest the money cheaper than your bonds. Thus, the call provision is for the protection of the issuer, not you.

709. What are the different call features on a bond?

Every bond has a call feature, which specifies if it is callable or noncallable. Noncallable means that the issuer can't retire the bond. "Freely at any time," is one type of call provision while a "deferred call" feature prohibits the issuer from retiring the bond before a certain period of time has passed.

Treasuries are noncallable, while investors are hard pressed to find corporate bonds and munis that are issued without call provisions.

710. If my bond can be called prior to maturity, how do I know if it's a good investment?

When you purchase a bond, you ask the broker what the yield to maturity will be on the bond. This is an estimate of the total return on a bond given the stated interest rate, the price you are paying, and the length of time until it matures. Yield to maturity assumes you will hold the bond to maturity and is the single most important tool to use in evaluating individual bonds for purchase or sale after credit. Yield to call assumes the bond will be called in on the call date; it also gives you a total return figure to use as the calculated total return if the bond is called in. *Always* ask for the yield to call if a bond has a call feature. Then, when you have both yields, compare them and use the more conservative number to decide if it is an investment in which you are interested.

711. What does triple tax-free mean?

Triple tax-free means exempt from federal, state, and local income tax liability. A Pennsylvania resident must invest in a Pennsylvania municipal bond/fund, which holds only Pennsylvania bonds to receive a triple tax exemption.

712. Are EE bonds and HH bonds a good investment?

EE and HH bonds are very complicated. They do not have guaranteed interest rates any longer. It used to be that you bought an EE bond at half the face amount and within a period of years, you could redeem it for its full face value. That doesn't happen any more. Today, EE bonds earn a variable rate which is 85 percent of the yield of the five-year Treasury notes for the six months before each May and November. The current rate on EE bonds purchased is 5.59 percent. HH bonds purchased today yield 4 percent. A good thing about HH bonds, besides not having to pay state income tax on the interest, is that they are a way to defer the accrued interest of EE bonds. The good thing about EE bonds is that the accrued interest can be deferred until the bonds are redeemed. This income is not taxed for your state income tax. It's a nice gift for children and a way to accumulate funds.

MUTUAL FUNDS

713. What is a mutual fund?

A mutual fund is a company that pools the money of many investors and invests it in stocks, bonds, or other securities. This is called diversification and helps reduce risk by spreading investments around. Each investor owns shares, which represent a part of these holdings.

714. Could I lose all my money in a mutual fund?

Theoretically you could, but it's very unlikely that you would lose *all* your money since the fund is diversified. Because you are invested in many different securities, they would all have to fall for you to lose your money. Most financial advisers do suggest that you invest in more than one fund so that if one of your funds is down it won't affect all your money.

715. I was sent a prospectus when I purchased my mutual fund. What is it?

A prospectus is a document describing in detail the key aspects of the fund, its management and financial position, the securities held in the fund, the operation of the fund, its objectives, the fee structure, and its historical performance. Once received, it is presumed you have read it and understand what you have purchased.

716. What is a no-load fund?

No-load funds are mutual funds that don't charge you a commission.

717. What is a front-end load?

A front-end load is a sales charge paid up front when you buy shares. According to the law, a front-end load can't be more than 8.5 percent of your investment. If you put $10,000 into a mutual fund with a 4.75 percent front-end load, the investment adviser and the fund receives $475 and you are actually only investing $9,525. You need to earn the load back before you have even made any money on your investment.

718. Is it similar to a back-end load?

Yes. This is also known as a deferred load. When you withdraw from the fund, you pay a sales charge called the back-end load. A back-end load usually starts out at about 5 percent for the first year and gets smaller each year afterwards until it reaches zero.

719. I don't see a fee within my mutual fund. Is there one?

The management fees are as important a consideration as the sales commissions (loads). Management fees are charges taken directly from the fund by the firm managing the assets. These fees can range from a low of .2 percent to over 2 percent. The total return a fund advertises is the amount after the fee has been subtracted. Fees are an important consideration when choosing a mutual fund.

720. Is the management fee the same as a 12(b)-1 fee?

Mutual funds that charge 12(b)-1 fees (and all funds do not have this charge) are passing their marketing expenses on to you. The analogy I use is that it's like shipping and handling when you purchase from a catalog. These fees can be as high as 1 percent. It is imperative that when investing, you look at the total fee scenario for the fund.

721. My broker told me this mutual fund is just like a no-load fund. Is that true?

Probably not. There may not be a front-end load, but check the fee table in the prospectus to see what other fees you may have to fork over.

722. Who manages a mutual fund?

They are managed by portfolio managers and a research team whose job it is to screen for investments for those that best meet the objectives of the fund. The portfolio team visits companies, analyzes reports, and spends all its time in research.

723. How shall I pick a good mutual fund?

You don't want to make your choice in mutual funds by seeing how well it performed the year before because many of them don't continue to perform well. In one recent study of funds making the five Top 10 lists in five years, only five made the list more than once.

724. Can I exchange my shares in a mutual fund for shares of another fund managed by the same person?

Possibly. Many funds allow you to do this.

725. My brother recommended I invest with a family of funds. What does he mean?

A family of funds is a group of mutual funds invested within a company, such as Vanguard, Fidelity, T. Rowe Price, Dean Witter, and so on. If you invest in a family of funds, you can switch from one fund to another by telephone or letter. A family of funds is very important when an investor has paid a sales commission to buy the mutual funds because the umbrella means you can change from one fund to another without incurring additional fees. An investor should think seriously about any load investment that is not in a family of funds.

726. How do I buy and sell shares in my mutual fund?

You can buy some mutual funds by contacting the companies directly. Others are sold primarily through brokers, banks, insurance agents, and financial planners. All mutual funds will buy back your shares on any business day and must send you payment within seven days. Before you make your decision, you should read all parts of the mutual fund prospectus, which will discuss the risks, investment goals, and policies of the fund.

727. Can I get into mutual funds if I don't have a lot of money to invest?

Yes. Many of the no-load mutual funds waive the $1,000 minimum if you agree to invest $50 a month (that's just $11.54 a week). If you do this and your investments earn about 12 percent a year, you'll have more than $10,000 in ten years.

728. What kinds of funds are there to invest?

There are a variety of investments. Here are a few, beginning with the most conservative:

- *Blue-chip funds:* If you invest in mutual funds that buy blue-chip companies when they are depressed temporarily, you can make money. Try the no-load Neuberger & Berman Focus (800) 877-9700 at a $50 monthly minimum.

- *Mutual funds that invest in midsize firms:* These companies have passed through the risky initial start-up phase, but haven't quite made it to blue-chip status. These so-called mid-cap stocks are usually less risky than smaller companies, but they have more potential than blue chip. Over the past ten years, they've gained about 15.7 percent each year. For a good mutual fund that invests primarily in this category, try T. Rowe Price Mid-Cap Growth (800) 638-5660 at a $50 minimum monthly. In the past three years, it has earned a 25.7 percent return.

- *Small company stocks:* Firms with less than $500 million in annual sales can consistently deliver a solid 12 percent return, which makes them good for a long-term savings plan. Try Founders Discovery (800) 525-2440 at a monthly $50 minimum.

- *Emerging market funds:* Today's emerging markets in Latin America and Asia can offer a good profit potential, but there is much more risk than for a blue-chip stock. There may be incredible swings in price, but there are opportunities as well. Try T. Rowe Price Emerging Markets Stock Fund at (800) 638-5660 for a $50 monthly minimum.

- *Gold funds:* Mutual funds that invest in gold-mining shares could deliver big profits; funds that invest in gold mining around the world are safer than those which concentrate on one country alone. Try Scudder Gold at (800) 225-2470 with a $1,000 minimum.

- *Technology funds:* If you're unfamiliar with computers or you just think that technology stands a good chance of maintaining its strong performance, you might enjoy the mutual funds which focus on new technology. There are risks but also good opportunity. Try Invesco Strategic Technology (800) 525-8085 at a $50 monthly minimum.

729. I'd like to start my child off saving wisely, but government bonds are boring. Is there a more exciting way to teach her about investing?

As a matter of fact, there is. Stein Roe in Chicago (800-403-KIDS) has a Young Investor Fund with a portfolio including stocks kids know, such as Disney, Mattel, McDonald's, and Coca-cola. USAA in San Antonio (800-382-8722) has a similar First Start Growth Fund. Both will send your kids fun, colorful information brochures that explain investing and mutual funds. The smallest investment you can make in Stein Roe is $100 if you arrange for $50 deposits to be deducted automatically from your bank account. You don't need *any* minimum upfront at USAA if you invest at least $20 a month. Other firms that offer automatic investment programs for minimums of $50 include Invesco funds in Denver (800) 525-8085; T. Rowe Price funds in Baltimore (800) 638-5660; American Century funds in Kansas City (800) 345-2021; and Strong funds in Milwaukee (800) 638-1030.

730. What about buying stocks myself for my child?

If you have a brokerage account, you could buy shares in a company your child likes and teach her how to follow the stock prices in the paper. This is particularly good if you let the child pick her own stock. If you do this, you'll need to get the forms for the Uniform Transfers to Minors Act from your broker since your child can't hold the stock directly.

Children can't legally make investment decisions. If the child owned the stock outright and it became necessary to sell, the child would need a court-appointed guardian to issue the order. With UTMA (in some states, it's called the Uniform Gifts to Minors Act), stock is instead held in custody by an adult (usually the parents) who can buy or sell as necessary. When the child reaches age eighteen or twenty-one (depending on the state), she can take over. This is necessary because minors are unable to own property.

731. What is a Statement of Additional Information?

All mutual funds must prepare this statement (called part B of the prospectus) and they must send it to you if you ask. It explains a fund's operations in more detail than the prospectus.

732. Can I get other information about the mutual fund?

Yes. You can read the annual and semiannual reports to shareholders which the fund will send you if you ask. You also can research the funds at most libraries. Check out fund investment books, investor magazines, and newspapers. The fund companies also can provide you with more information.

733. How do I know which stocks or bonds to invest in, in my mutual fund?

When you buy a mutual fund, you don't need to know. That's up to the portfolio manager, whose job it is to figure out which investments the fund should hold based on its objectives. The prospectus and semi-annual reports do provide a listing of holdings every six months.

734. Where can I find out how my mutual fund is doing?

Look in the business section of the newspaper. Once you locate the sponsoring company's name, you will need to look for a specific mutual fund. Look for the column marked NAV (net asset value per share). This will tell you the value of one share in a fund. When you buy shares, you pay the current NAV per share. When you sell, the fund will pay you NAV less any sales load. A fund's NAV goes up and down every day, depending on the value of its holdings. If you spent $1,000 in a mutual fund with a NAV of $10, you will own 100 shares of the fund. If the NAV drops a dollar, you will still own 100 shares but your investment is now worth only $900. On the other hand, if the NAV rises, your investment is worth more.

735. Are there other ways to make money in a mutual fund besides selling the shares when they increase in value?

Yes, you can earn money from your mutual funds in three ways. First, you can get income in the form of dividends and interest on the securities it owns. Next, the price of the securities a fund owns may increase and when a mutual fund sells a security that has increased in price, the fund has a capital gain. At the end of the year, most funds distribute these capital gains to investors. Finally, if a fund holds onto its securities that have increased in value, when you sell your shares, you make a profit.

736. Do I have a choice of taking the dividend or reinvesting it?

Yes. The fund can send you a payment for the dividends or distributions or you can reinvest them in the fund to buy more shares.

737. Do I have to pay taxes on distributions and dividends?

Yes, in the year you receive them. You also owe taxes on capital gains you made when you sold your shares.

738. What about if I have invested in a tax-exempt mutual fund?

If you invest in a tax-exempt fund such as a municipal bond fund, some or all of your dividends will be exempt from federal (and sometimes local and state) tax. Still, you will owe taxes on any capital gains.

739. What are the main categories of mutual funds?

Money market funds, bond funds, and stock funds. Of course, there are a bunch of different types of funds within each category.

740. What is a money market fund?

A money market fund has lower risk than other mutual funds since they are limited by law to high-quality, short-term investments. Money market funds aim at a stable $1 per share NAV. While investors can't usually lose money in money market funds, it is possible.

741. What's the difference between a money market fund and a money market deposit account in a bank?

A money market fund is a type of mutual fund that is not guaranteed. It comes with a prospectus. A money market deposit account is a bank deposit that is usually guaranteed by the federal government.

742. What is a bond fund?

Also known as fixed income funds, bond funds have higher risks than money market funds but try to pay higher yields. Unlike money market funds, bond funds aren't limited to high-quality, short-term investments. Bond funds can vary a great deal in risks and rewards due to the different types of bonds.

743. What is a stock mutual fund?

Also known as equity funds, these funds generally involve more risk than money market or bond funds, but they also can offer high returns. A stock fund's value (NAV) can fluctuate over the short term, but historically stocks have performed better over the long term than other types of investments.

744. Are all stock funds the same?

No. Growth funds, for example, focus on stocks that might not pay a regular dividend, but have the potential for large capital gains. Others specialize in a particular industry segment, such as a technology stock.

745. Are there any computer services that track performance of mutual funds?

Morningstar, Value Line, Micropal, and *CDA/Weisenberger* monitor mutual fund prices and performance.

746. What should I look for when reviewing *Morningstar*? My neighbor said to only invest in five star mutual funds.

With over 7,000 mutual funds available, there are now more mutual funds available than individual stocks for an investor to choose from. Use *Morningstar* to review the three-year historical performance of the fund versus the index for that fund, all fees charged in the fund, comparison of this fund to other similar funds, analysis of the fund, beta, and so on. *Morningstar* provides so much more information than just the stars.

747. What is a growth fund?

A growth fund is a mutual fund comprised of growth stocks. Growth stocks usually have sales, earnings, and market share growing at rates that are higher than the average company or the general economy. These companies typically don't pay large dividends because the companies generally reinvest earnings back into the company. These companies are expected to grow and appreciate more rapidly than ordinary companies.

748. What is a derivative?

Some funds may face special risks if they invest in derivatives, which are financial instruments whose performance is driven by the performance of an underlying asset. Their value can fluctuate wildly by even small market movements. A fund's prospectus will explain how it uses derivatives, which may not necessarily increase risk and can actually lower it.

749. What is a balanced fund?

A mutual fund that earns both current income and capital gains. The objective of the fund is both growth and current income. The theory behind the balanced funds is that when stocks don't do well, bonds will, and when bonds don't perform well, stocks will.

750. How did I lose money if my mutual fund is invested in only U.S. Treasury Notes?

The value of the notes within the mutual fund is based on current interest rates. Thus, if you purchased the fund when interest rates were lower, the value of your fund will decrease as interest rates increase because the bonds become discounted. The opposite is true, too; if you purchased a fund when interest rates were higher and rates drop, the bonds within the fund become more valuable. Thus, when investing in a U.S. Treasury Note Fund you are eliminating credit risk, you are not eliminating interest rate risk.

751. Is it possible to find out whether someone is receiving a commission?

Common sense tells you someone is receiving a commission when you make an investment. An investor may not pay a commission (as in newly issued bonds); however, the broker is being paid for his sale. Often times, the commission on a stock trade is included in the sale so the buyer and seller haven't a clue as to the charges for the transactions.

752. What is the difference between a growth and an aggressive growth fund?

- Aggressive growth stocks are typically stocks of smaller, younger companies. The reason an investor purchases such a fund is because historically they have been rewarded with a greater growth because there is a greater risk in newer companies. Companies, particularly in times of economic hardship, do go bankrupt.

753. Is international investing a good idea?

International investing adds diversification to your portfolio. There is no direct correlation between the United States markets and other global mar-

kets. Thus, adding foreign securities is similar to adding securities from different sectors of the U.S. market. The reason the markets are not all linked
together is because each country has its own economic system with its various cycles. Normally, international funds are defined as funds that can only
invest in stocks outside the United States. Global funds are able to invest
internationally as well as within the United States stock market.

754. Is it riskier to purchase a sector fund?

When you invest in a sector fund, you buy a segment of a particular market. Thus, a gold fund is invested in gold stocks; a health care fund is invested in that type of investment. There are innumerable sector funds. If a
particular portion of the economy does well or if you own a sector fund
(such as bank stocks) and this area has a great year, your fund should have
a fantastic return for the year. The risk is that sector funds are diversified by
companies, but not types of stocks.

755. Are there added risks to investing internationally?

There are tremendous additional risks to investing in international markets.
Obviously, the problem of fluctuating foreign currency is one of the major
risks in international investing, but there are also many problems unique to
dealing with international companies, the location, unstable governments,
and so on. Foreign companies have substantially different accounting standards (there is no unified international accounting standard) so it is often
difficult to compile accurate information on a foreign company. There is
also a risk of nationalization of foreign companies (not limited to South
American countries—nationalization has occurred in France). Then there is
the risk of political coups and the International Monetary Fund bailouts (in
South Korea) that created terrible losses in stock values.

756. What is a Net Asset Value (NAV)?

The NAV is the price at which you purchase one share of a particular fund
and the price you get when you sell your shares.

757. What is the difference between an open-end
and a closed-end fund?

An open-end mutual fund is permitted to issue an unlimited number of
shares (units) to investors. The fund continues to grow in size as long as in-

vestors continue to place funds with the fund. Open-end funds can close themselves to new investors. Vanguard's Windsor Fund is an example of an open-end fund that is no longer taking new money. Open-end funds are sold at Net Asset Value (NAV), which is the fair market value of the securities within the fund less any outstanding liabilities divided by the number of shares in the fund. Once a closed-end investment company is funded, no other funds are permitted to be invested in the fund unless reopened by vote of the shareholders. Shares are traded on stock exchanges similar to actual stocks. Often the value of the units trades are at a premium or discount to the net asset value depending on the supply and demand for the fund.

758. What is a value fund?

A value fund is a certain investment style. A value investor looks for individual stocks of companies that are quality companies; however, for some reason, the current stock price has dropped to attractive levels to purchase the stocks. A value fund uses this investment style.

759. Once I invest in a fund, how do I keep track of how it is doing?

Morningstar, newspapers, and the quarterly report of the fund should keep you abreast of how your fund is performing. Your monthly statement will show you month end value. Comparing that to your original cost tells you how much you have made, while the reports explain total return for the quarter and year to date. The quarterly reports show a listing of the investments within the fund, statements from the fund managers of their opinion of the market, and so on.

760. What is meant by the fund manager? Is it important if there is a new manager?

The fund manager is the professional investment team who handles the management of the investments within a mutual fund. The manager's style, philosophy, and historical performance, within the parameters of the specific fund, make the mutual fund what it is. When you are reviewing historic performance, it is important to note how long a fund manager has been with the fund. New managers shouldn't receive credit for their predecessor's performance.

761. The *Morningstar* has a section called sector weightings. What is that used for?

The sector weightings portion of the *Morningstar* report or a fund report show the investor by percentages how the funds within the account are actually invested. For example, a person who can't tolerate high risk wouldn't want technology.

OTHER INVESTMENTS

762. Art and collectibles are often called investments. Is this a good idea?

Collectibles are fun and should be invested with that in mind. You can lose investment opportunity dollars by indulging in collectibles. Collectibles need storage and usually additional insurance coverage, which increases the annual expense. Collectibles aren't usually liquid and there may not be many people to whom you can sell your collection. Many times the increase in value on the collectible is due to inflation over the years—unless you happen to discover the next Claude Monet oil underneath the floorboards in your grandmother's attic.

If investment is your goal, you'd be better off in the stockmarket; if you love to collect, here's how to go about it:

1. Buy what you love.
2. Specialize—read everything you can, follow shops and shows, and go online.
3. Learn about the trends. If you can figure out a trend ahead of time and start collecting, you've got a head start on everyone else. However, making money this way is still mostly luck.
4. Avoid speculation. When items start bringing huge prices, you should be selling, not buying.
5. Buy quality goods. It's better to have five really fine pieces than twenty-five pieces of junk because the top-grade collectibles will retain their value.
6. Avoid manufactured collectibles. This includes anything marketed as a limited edition or collectible.

7. Look for the unusual and you'll have more fun—you might make some money eventually.
8. Search out bargains. It's not likely you'll find an unknown piece of art in a yard sale carton, but it's still possible.
9. Guard against fraud. Reproductions and forgeries abound. Beware.
10. Quit collecting when it stops being fun.

763. How can I go about trying to sell my collection?

When the value of something you have collected skyrockets, it may be time to sell. Look for collectors who advertise in specialized publications, via the Internet, or with a local dealer. Remember if you sell to an auction house or dealer, you'll have to pay them a percentage of the selling price. You want to avoid selling something to a dealer that you just bought from a dealer because this means you've bought retail and are selling wholesale. You'll most likely lose money.

764. I'd like to get into gold investments. Is this a good investment?

Unless you buy gold and silver based only on the current price of gold, you need to know the intrinsic value of the gold coins you are purchasing. I recommend silver coins for the investor who doesn't want to place a large amount of funds into a $320 per ounce asset. Silver is around $10 per ounce. In major economic disasters, you can always use gold to survive, while stocks and bonds are only paper. Another form of investing in gold is to invest in gold stocks. Many times the performance of gold stocks is based on the valuation of gold. Because an investor still has to consider the underlying company's performance, I recommend a gold mutual fund for diversification.

765. My broker told me about a limited partnership that pays 10 percent interest. Should I buy this?

Frequently, investors don't understand the underlying investment. The partnerships are often not liquid, internal fees are extensive, and the partnerships are not valued on investor's monthly statements so you haven't a clue what they are worth. You are forced to value the partnership by the annual statement and that's an unrealistic request of the common investor. The partners have numerous additional forms for inclusion with their individual tax returns.

766. I understand that REITs have performed very well. What are they?

Real Estate Investment Trusts (REITs) involve a company that invests money obtained from the shareholders in mortgages and real estate. They are a way for smaller investors to invest in real estate. They are considered to be long-term investments. Before investing in a REIT, carefully assess the investment objectives and expected rate of return based on the current price.

767. What is an option?

An option is an agreement that provides an investor with an opportunity to purchase another security or property at a specified price over a stated period of time. Everyone understands the option to purchase a piece of real estate, i.e., a lot for $30,000 between now and year end. The comparison is similar with securities.

768. What are commodities and futures? Can I make money on them?

Commodities and futures are risky investments. Basically, it's gambling. You may win when the market moves in the right direction at the right time, but in the long run you'll lose. Most investors understand increases in the stock market and although you may not have the best return, you can have a good return. Commodity trading is different and very risky. For every winner in a transaction, there is a loser.

769. My 401(k) has a Guaranteed Investment Contract (GIC). Is this a good idea?

GICs have historically been securities sold by insurance companies primarily to pension funds. The rate of return is guaranteed for a fixed period of time. The GIC return is guaranteed by the insurance company and can be a major liability for the insurance company if interest rates decline drastically. GICs are similar to Certificates of Deposit. Having a GIC within a 401(k) or defined contribution plan where the investor can allocate funds is a good way to control the volatility of interest rates.

MAKING CHOICES

770. Can you give me an idea of investments that are less risky?

- Treasury bonds and money market funds
- CDs and short-term bond funds
- Well-established mutual funds, stocks, or high rated bonds
- Investments that emphasize long-term growth

771. What are some of the ways I can tolerate the risk of the market?

There are several ways to make it through financial ups and downs:

- Remember that it takes risk to earn a bigger return on your investments. In the long term, taking some risk should increase your reward.
- Take risks you can live with and buy stocks and mutual funds that have a stable history.
- Keep the bulk of your money in investments that don't require constant monitoring.
- Discuss concerns and changes in investment strategy with your financial adviser.

772. What about the political climates of the countries in the mutual fund I own?

A period of instability in an emerging market can drive down the value of investments in that market. The returns of investing internationally can be significant, but the risks are higher as well.

773. How does a recession affect the value of my stocks?

There are four phases of the business cycle: expansion, peak, recession, and trough. During a recession—a period of economic slowdown—investments of all kinds can lose value since employment, production, prices, availability of money, interest rates, and profits are declining.

774. How does the interest rate affect inflation?

When interest rates increase, inflation increases. In periods of increasing interest rates, the price of your existing fixed-income investments (bonds) decline since they're paying less interest than the new bonds being issued. Higher interest rates usually mean that the values of stocks decline for several reasons:

1. More investors purchase the higher yielding bonds for the security so stocks drop in value.
2. Companies have more difficulty increasing or keeping earnings the same because the price of borrowing is greater since interest rates are higher.

775. What is the Rule of 72?

It's a way of calculating how long it will take you to double your money at the current interest rates. For example, if a CD pays 10 percent interest, your money will double in 7.2 years (72 divided by 10). It gives you an idea of how well you're doing on your investments.

776. I'm afraid of losing money in the stock market. Isn't it risky?

There is a risk in investing; however, over the past seventy years, equity investments on average have increased in value in most years. During that period, there has been no fifteen- or twenty-year period when stocks haven't made money. The secret is to find a good adviser, have a grasp of the basics of investments, and stay abreast of financial matters by reading.

777. What percentage of my portfolio should be in high-risk versus low-risk investments?

The percentage is up to your risk tolerance, your investment objectives, your wealth, how close you are to retirement, and what the funds are for. There is no easy answer nor any particular percentage to all investors.

778. How do I minimize risk while investing in the stock market?

You should diversify your portfolio; that means include a variety of investments. You diversify by owning a variety of mutual funds, collectibles, real estate, stock, bonds, money market funds, and cash. You should attempt to diversify within each of these areas by purchasing a number of various types of assets to help reduce the risk.

779. How much do I invest in growth and in income to meet my investment needs?

The allocation between stocks and bonds (growth versus income) depends on your ability to handle risk due to your personality, wealth, and age. A general rule of thumb is to subtract your age from 100 and invest that amount in stocks. A fifty-year-old woman would therefore have 50 percent of her portfolio in bonds and 50 percent in stocks, while a thirty-year-old should have 70 percent in stocks and 30 percent in bonds. An eighty-year-old would have 20 percent of her portfolio in stocks and 80 percent in bonds.

However, like so much of the investment world, the rules change if you can't sleep at night due to the riskiness of your portfolio. You may be very comfortable and your assets may be producing too much income at age eighty-five so you move a bigger portion of your assets in stocks.

780. I'm sixty-seven years old and have a good pension and Social Security. I feel comfortable with a 50 percent/50 percent allocation of stocks and bonds. Where do I go from here?

Buy a variety of taxable or tax-free individual bonds, depending on your tax bracket, to make up the 50 percent bond of your portfolio. Then, you need to diversify the stock portion between a variety of companies or mutual funds to reduce risk.

781. How do you determine whether or not a portfolio is balanced?

A portfolio is balanced when the investments earn income and have capital growth. Usually about 45 percent of the portfolio is in income, and 55 percent in stocks. You determine when a portfolio is balanced by listing all the assets within the portfolio at market value and income yield. Then, review the portfolio for growth potential investments. Prepare the percentage of fixed income to growth assets and see how close you are to 45/55.

782. How do I diversify?

It isn't by buying stocks that you heard about at a cocktail party. Don't buy impulsively when a stock sounds intriguing. Increasing the sheer number of your investments doesn't guarantee diversity. Carefully plan the types of stocks and investments you want—how many oil stocks, technical stocks, and blue-chip stocks. Then review the companies available and do your re-search. Just as there's no ideal investment, there's no ideal formula for di-versifying your investments. Some assets grow in value; others produce in-come. Some protect principal; others outstrip inflation. Some do well during economic expansions; others do well in recessions. Some invest-ments are in U.S. companies; others are international.

783. Will the asset allocation create a difference in the long-term performance of my portfolio?

Obviously. The more stocks you have, the greater your risk, and histori-cally, the higher the growth potential. Over the last twenty years if you compare the same amount of money invested, a portfolio with 60 percent stocks, 30 percent bonds, and 10 percent cash grew to $550,000. A portfolio of 30 percent stocks, 60 percent bonds, and 10 percent cash grew to $400,000, while a 10 percent stock, 30 percent bond, and 60 percent cash portfolio only grew to $275,000. There is a phenomenal difference in value and quite a difference in risk.

STOCKS/BONDS

STOCKS

Brokerage _____   **Account #** _____

Broker _____   Type of account _____

Address _____

_____

E-mail address _____

Mobile phone/beeper _____   Work phone (   ) _____

Certificate location _____

Location of statements _____

Brokerage _____   **Account #** _____

Broker _____   Type of account _____

Address _____

_____

E-mail address _____

Mobile phone/beeper _____   Work phone (   ) _____

Certificate location _____

Location of statements _____

CHAPTER 10

REAL ESTATE INVESTMENTS

For most people, buying a home is the largest single investment they ever make. Of course, a home is more than an investment, but you should never lose sight of that aspect of homeownership. Selling a home is the kind of large financial transaction that the average person doesn't make every day. You should have a basic understanding of both these situations, which this chapter provides.

What about investing in real estate other than your home? There are proven techniques and strategies that can make real estate investment a profitable venture. This chapter also answers key questions concerning investment property.

BUYING A HOME

784. When buying real estate, what's the most important item to remember?

Location, location, location. You need to love your home. It should have 90–95 percent of the things you are looking for in it. The average person takes between fifteen to forty-five days to find a house after looking at ten to twenty-five properties. By then you know what's available in your price range. You should know details about zoning, schools, and the types of people buying nearby houses (that is, families with young children compared to retirees) and so on.

785. Is it better to own a home instead of renting?

Americans have always been under the impression that it is better to own than rent. For most people, buying a home is the single largest investment they will ever make. One reason to buy a home is that you usually get more living space per dollar than you do with renting. However, before you make the decision to buy it's imperative to review your situation and know what the total transaction will cost you. Know the trend of market values in the area you live. Are interest rates steady? What will it cost to sell your home? How long do you think you will live there? How long has it taken for homes in the area to sell in your price range? Know the cost of mortgage payments versus paying rent.

786. What should I look for in a real estate agent?

A person with experience, whom you can trust and have confidence in, who is honest and has the integrity you need. When you are ready to look for a home, interview three prospective realtors who were recommended to you. Ask for references.

787. Is it better to work with a realtor in a big firm or someone in a small office?

With large firms, you can get lost in the shuffle; however, larger firms have agents who specialize and this may be of help to you. A smaller firm should give you the personal attention you want so you know where you are at all stages of your transaction because the realtor is easily accessible.

The type of realtor for you really depends on the agent and his or her expertise, not the size of the office.

788. What is a buyer's broker?

Normally, a real estate broker always represents the seller and has the seller's best interests at heart. That means *your* interests, as buyer, are secondary. A buyer's broker, on the other hand, works for *you*. A broker is hired at your expense or receives a portion of the seller's commission at settlement. If you buy a home, your buyer's broker will get paid.

789. My realtor showed me a house that he listed. Whom does he really represent?

If you have a buyer's brokerage agreement with your realtor, he can't represent the sellers, too. A realtor can represent both the buyer and the seller—it's called a limited dual agency agreement—but it must be disclosed up front. Obviously, the realtor can represent just the seller. You should always ask the realtor for whom they work and keep this in mind when looking at properties.

790. When I'm thinking about making an offer on a piece of real estate, should I have the property reviewed by an inspector?

Yes. In today's world, the word in real estate is disclosure. You can only gather more information from the inspection and the information might be important in your deciding to acquire the house. An inspector helps make you aware of what you are purchasing and aids you in being as thorough as possible.

791. What should the inspector include in her report?

The report should include a whole-house inspection. The inspector will verify that all systems and appliances are working, review the furnace efficiency, and give a report on the present condition of the roof and presence of termites and other pests. If necessary, she can report on ground water contamination.

792. What is the price of an inspector and who pays for it, the seller or the buyer?

Although everything is negotiable, most inspections are paid for by the buyer. In central Pennsylvania the general cost of a standard inspection is $175–225.

793. What do lenders look at when deciding whether or not to grant a mortgage?

The 3 Cs: character, capacity, and collateral. Your character is your credit history, your capacity is your total household income, and your home is your collateral. The number one factor your lender looks at is job stability.

794. Is it better to obtain a mortgage with a local company or doesn't it really matter?

You don't want to pay more for a local mortgage than you would pay elsewhere; however, there are benefits to a local mortgage lender. The most important reason is that you can hand-deliver your tax and insurance payments and mortgage payments when they are due and have payments credited that day. When you are mailing to a post office box in Texas or California, you have no control over when they credit the payment. This can subject you to late fees. Also, it's nice to be able to call locally if there are problems with your loan.

795. What is a mortgage broker?

A mortgage broker is a person whose job is to match you with a lender. If your initial mortgage application is denied, meet with a mortgage broker to see if he or she can match you up with a lender.

796. What's the best way to compare mortgage rates among lenders in town without trying to call up fifteen lenders? Should I shop around?

Absolutely. Mortgages, like all products, vary in cost. Mortgage rates of area lenders are usually in the real estate section of local papers or you can review rates on the Internet on the web.

797. What about shopping around for other fees—is there that much difference?

Yes. In addition to the mortgage rate, comparison shopping for application fees, points, and so on is also important. The best mortgage rate is not always the best place to go; it may have higher fees in other areas.

798. My builder has stated he can negotiate with his bank for a quicker approval rate on a mortgage. Is this common or is he getting some sort of kickback for the referral?

I'm not an advocate of involving your builder in every transaction with your house; however, if your builder has a relationship with a lender, why not use the information and connection if it is to your advantage? The builder's referral is probably not financially motivated; the referral is to expedite the mortgage with people he feels comfortable with, who are competent, and who know his homes and their value. The sooner you settle, the sooner the builder receives his money.

799. My bank has offered me a chance to prequalify for a mortgage. Is this a good idea?

Prequalification tells you exactly what you can and can't afford in a home. It limits you to look for a house in your price range and quickens the mortgage approval period since you have previously given the bank your financial information. Prequalification can produce a stronger contract with better terms for you since the sellers know you are serious buyers who can afford their home.

800. If I prequalify for a set mortgage amount and then find a house for more, does that mean the bank won't grant the mortgage?

If you have prequalified for a set mortgage amount, unless you have additional information to add (additional income or you have paid off some debt) for the lender, the lender will not grant you a higher mortgage to purchase the home. You will need to make up the difference in price by having a larger down payment.

801. I've heard that in order to qualify for a mortgage, my payments can't be more than a certain percentage of my income. Is this correct? If so, what are the percentages?

Your monthly payments shouldn't be more than 28 percent of your total household income. The payments include the principal, interest, home-owner's insurance payment, and real estate taxes. Thus, if you escrow, the 28 percent figure would be your maximum mortgage amount permitted.

802. What about my other debts? How do they figure into the equation?

The lenders also look at the percentage of 36 percent. You shouldn't be paying more than 36 percent of your total income in mortgage and all other debts. This would include your car payments, college loans, and mortgage combined.

803. How much of a down payment must I have?

You need to have at least 5 percent of the value of the property as a down payment to qualify for a mortgage. There is a special program that permits a 3 percent down payment for individuals with a total household income that is no greater than $42,000.

804. What's the best way to invest for a down payment on our first house?

You want security as well as income for a down payment for your first house. I recommend one of the innumerable money market funds, which presently are yielding about 5 percent. As you invest more money into the account, the account grows safely. Although funds may grow better in a stock fund or other investment, the security of the funds is not guaranteed. You need to be sure the money will be there for you when you find your first house.

805. I have a lot of money saved up in my IRA. Now I want to buy a house. Can I use my IRA as collateral for a mortgage?

No. The government won't allow anyone to borrow against an IRA. The feds take a dim view of anybody cashing these in (there are strict penalties) or using them for anything other than retirement benefits. Some people have gotten into trouble this way by stashing extra cash into an IRA with the assumption that they can always tap into it in an emergency. IRAs are ***not*** good holding places for money you think you might need in a year or two. There are new rules for first time home buyers. You may withdraw up to $10,000 towards the purchase of a home. See Question 535.

806. What about my other investments, such as my CDs?

You can use them as collateral for a loan. This would include stocks, bonds, certificates of deposit, and securities.

807. How much will the banks loan me against these?

Most banks will loan you up to 80 percent of the value of these investments. If you had a $100,000 CD, for example, the bank would usually loan you $80,000 with the CD as collateral.

808. Okay, I won't tap into my IRA for a loan to buy a house. What about my 401(k) plan at work?

Sorry. In most cases, you can't borrow against a 401(k) plan either, for the same reason; the plan has been set up to provide you with retirement benefits. However, a few businesses ***will*** allow you to borrow against these plans. You need to sit down with your company's employee benefits expert and find out what your company's policy is.

809. Does it matter where the down payment comes from? Can I receive the down payment as a gift?

The lender only cares that you come to settlement with the money to pay the down payment and closing costs. The down payment can come as a gift. If you borrow for the down payment, this information will be used as part of the 36 percent debt-to-income ratio.

810. My uncle was going to lend me money towards the down payment for our first house. However, the issue of imputed interest arose. What is imputed interest and how does it work?

The law requires that a minimum interest rate be charged on loan transactions unless a specific exception covers the transaction. Where minimum interest is not charged, the law imputes interest as if the parties agreed to an interest rate at the time of the loan. Therefore, even though your uncle doesn't charge you interest, interest is assumed to have been charged. Thus, your uncle is really giving you the interest as a gift each year. If your uncle lent you $200,000 with imputed interest of 7 percent, he is really giving you $14,000 per year. There are exceptions to the imputed interest rules; however, if the loan is less than $100,000 and the borrower has investment income (interest and dividends) of less than $1,000 a year, the imputed interest rules don't apply.

811. We have a very small down payment. Should I get insurance to protect the payments?

If your down payment is less than 20 percent of the appraised value of the property, your lender will require you to buy principal mortgage insurance. This insurance protects the lender from default. You pay for it with your monthly mortgage payment.

812. What types of information should I have available when I meet with the mortgage officer?

To speed up the mortgage process, you should bring along to the first appointment the following:

1. Last year's W-2s
2. Documents showing two years of residence and employment history (this would include canceled checks for mortgage or rent payments)
3. Proof of your gross monthly income (by bringing a current paycheck)
4. Your employer's address and telephone number
5. Any financial statements for your personal assets and any if you are self-employed
6. Your last three tax returns
7. List of all assets you own, including loans and deposit account numbers (bring along the last monthly statement available on each account)
8. Copy of your deed, if refinancing
9. For a construction loan, bring along a fixed price contract, specifications, plans, and agreement of sale.

813. What is my banker obligated to tell me when I get a mortgage?

The lender is required to tell you the annual percentage rate for the loan, how much interest you will be paying if you hold the loan the entire term, your monthly mortgage payment, and your monthly payment if insurance and escrow are included.

814. What is title insurance? Do I need it?

Title insurance guarantees that the title to your property is clear and that the new owner will not have any problems. It's required by your lender. In Pennsylvania, the rates are regulated and the charges are approximately $6 per every $1,000 in loan amount.

815. Should I shop around on title insurance or do all companies offer the same deal?

Ask your realtor as well as the mortgage company to provide you with three names of title companies they know and like. Today most settlements occur at the title company. Lenders and realtors know who is competent and efficient. Ask how title insurance is priced and comparison shop for the ancillary fees the title company charges, such as a deed preparation fee or a tax certificate. Call and ask for a price list. You probably won't need an attorney if the title company prepares the deed and handles settlement.

816. My lender talked about a three-point fee to obtain a mortgage. What are points?

The term points is used to describe certain charges you pay to obtain a home mortgage. Points may also be called loan origination fees, maximum loan charges, loan discount, or discount points. One point is 1 percent of the amount borrowed, two points is 2 percent of the amount borrowed, and so on. Three points on a $100,000 loan is $3,000. This amount must be paid at settlement or added to the amount of your loan.

817. I was given the choice of paying the points up front or putting the points into the mortgage. Which is better?

There are several questions here. You can pay your points or you can borrow them if you are refinancing. Thus, on a $100,000 mortgage you would either pay the $3,000 at settlement or borrow $103,000. However, if you can't pay the points and you can't borrow more and still qualify for the mortgage, you can get a mortgage with a higher interest rate. The points are paid over the life of the loan by your paying a higher interest rate.

818. How much will we need in cash to close the deal?

This sum has increased over the years as the fees increase with mortgages. However, creative alternatives to closing the deal have developed. Often the seller will pay points or pay both transfer taxes and so on. When you make an offer on the house, the realtor is obligated to give you a good faith estimate of the money you will need at settlement.

819. What is the percentage of total closing costs to the mortgage?

If you acquire a mortgage in which you paid three points initiation fee, the percentage of expenses is 6–7 percent of the total loan. Keep this in mind when you refinance as well as when you decide to buy and sell properties.

820. I have never defaulted on any loan but a few of my credit card payments have been a month late. Will the bank hold that against me?

No. Impeccable credit is the exception to the rule in today's world. If your credit is somewhat tainted, the lender may seek more collateral or charge a higher rate.

821. I'm single. Is it harder to get a mortgage?

No. A mortgage is acquired on total household income and debts. The parameters for a single person are the same as for a couple. If you qualify within the guidelines, you will receive a mortgage.

822. I'm living with my boyfriend. Will we have a hard time getting a mortgage together to buy a house?

Again, receiving a mortgage will be no different for an unmarried couple than for a married couple. Siblings purchase houses together, friends do—it's a financial transaction in which total household income and debt are the guidelines. Know that both your names will be on the mortgage note and you both are responsible for repayment, if one of you leaves the relationship.

823. What is the difference between a fixed rate and an adjustable rate mortgage?

A fixed rate mortgage means that after you agree to an interest rate, it won't change throughout the life of the loan. The mortgage is set up with scheduled payments, and the payments remain constant until the loan is repaid. Adjustable rate mortgages (ARMs) are loans in which the lender can adjust the interest rate. Some loans even have a maximum that they may increase to. The original loan should be carefully reviewed. If you decide to borrow with an adjustable rate mortgage, understand what you are agreeing to and what your monthly payments can be in the worse case scenario. You need to be aware that the interest rate on most ARMs can vary a great deal over the lifetime of the loan; an increase in several percentage points can raise your payments by hundreds of dollars per month.

824. What are some of the different types of ARMs?

Like all things financial, ARMs are varied in their differences. A 7/1 ARM has an initial rate that is locked in for seven years, then the rate can change every year after that. Another type of ARM is a 3/3. Initial rate is locked in for three years, then rate can be adjusted every three years, 2 percent at a time with a 6 percent increase cap per the life of the loan. There are also 3/1 and 1/1 ARMs. For a minimal fee ($250), some ARMs can be converted into a fixed rate mortgage. Review all the various rates and options, then compare payments, total amount of interest to be paid on the loans, review how long you will be in your home, and then decide which type of mortgage is best for you.

825. Are the qualifications different for an adjustable rate mortgage?

Lenders all have their guidelines for their institutions; however, most lenders qualify adjustable rate mortgages as if they are standard rate mortgages. Some qualify you for only a 2 percent increase in interest rates assuming your income will increase over the period of the loan. Be careful so that you will be able to afford your home, if interest rates skyrocket.

826. Why would someone take an ARM over a standard mortgage?

ARMs usually don't have points; the initial interest rate is often significantly lower than standard rates so if you are only going to be in your home for a short time, the ARM might be the sensible way to go. Review the offerings along with your objectives.

827. Is it better to have a fifteen-, twenty- or thirty-year mortgage?

Common sense tells you that if you borrow $100,000 for fifteen years (180 monthly payments at $555.55 per month principal repayment amount), your monthly payment will be greater than if you borrow $100,000 for thirty years (360 monthly payments at $277.78 per month principal repayment amount). Thus, first time homeowners often can only afford a home with a longer term loan. However, the longer the mortgage, the greater the amount of interest that you are paying. Borrowers should compare the amount of interest that they are paying with the different mortgage terms. There is a phenomenal interest repayment amount increase the longer the mortgage period. If a thirty-year mortgage is the only way a family can afford a home, then you need to go the thirty years. However, if you can afford to go fifteen years, I highly recommend it.

828. When I went to settlement, I was told there was a good chance that my mortgage would be sold within a year. What does that mean to me?

Mortgages are bought and sold as investments. Lenders don't want them in their portfolios so the original lender often processes the mortgage and then sells them. When you apply for a mortgage, you should ask if the local lender will continue to process the loan after it is sold. If they don't, go elsewhere. If they do, it shouldn't matter who holds the loan.

829. Can you give me an idea of how interest rates affect my mortgage?

If you are acquiring a thirty-year fixed rate $125,000 mortgage, the payment is $749 at 6 percent, $917 on an 8 percent loan, $1,097 on a 10 percent loan, and $1,285 on a 12 percent loan. Taken over the number of years, the extra interest on the higher rates is exorbitant.

830. What does 1 percent difference in interest rates mean to me?

Common sense tells you that the higher the interest rate on your mortgage, the more you will be paying in total cost for your home. It's just unbelievable the difference you do pay. Look at the differences:

Interest Rate	Term	Monthly Payment	Total Interest
6.5%	15 Years	$871.11	$ 56,799.80
6.5%	30 years	632.07	127,545.60
7.5%	15 years	927.01	66,861.80
7.5%	30 years	699.21	151,715.60
10.00%	15 years	1,074.61	93,429.80
10.00%	30 years	877.57	215,925.20

831. Should I consider a biweekly mortgage payment?

Absolutely. Instead of paying twelve large installments each year, you are paying twenty-six smaller payments (not twenty-four). Biweekly payments are deducted automatically from your checking or savings account. With this system, a thirty-year mortgage is repaid in a little less than twenty-three years and a fifteen-year mortgage is repaid in eleven years. Obviously, there is a significant savings in the total interest you will pay for the life of the loan. You are usually limited to taking out a mortgage with a bank or savings and loan with a biweekly payment plan. If you don't have the option of biweekly payments, you can get the same benefit if you are making one extra principal payment a year on your mortgage.

832. Will I save anything in the long run if I pay extra on my mortgage payment every month?

Yes, you'll save quite a bit. If you add just $25 a month to a thirty-year fixed-rate 8 percent mortgage, you will save $23,337 in interest over the life of the loan. If you can pay an extra $100 a month, you'll save $62,456.

833. Does it make sense to pay off my mortgage?

It depends on your situation and how the real estate market is growing in your area. Several years ago the value of a home increased faster than the growth in the stock market. and certainly faster than earnings on a savings account. At the time, it made economical sense to borrow as much as possible and get as much house as you could afford. With real estate as a whole at a standstill in value increases, an individual must look at the total picture to know what is best. You're saving money each month by making a mortgage payment—you're building equity in your home. If you pay off your mortgage, the funds will need to be invested elsewhere to continue building your total net worth.

834. What should I do if I have been turned down for a mortgage?

You have two choices. The first is to find out the reason the loan was denied. If you don't qualify for the mortgage because the property is too expensive for your income, then you should look for a less expensive home. If you have credit problems, talk with the lender and find out what they need for you to qualify—pay off some of your debt, making set payments for a year or so to provide some credit history, and so forth. The second choice (which I don't advocate) is to go to a B or C lender. You will pay a higher interest rate (if the current rate for a mortgage is 6.9 percent, they will charge you around 8 percent) but this type of market specializes in persons with a history of credit problems. Some of these lenders will permit you to convert into an A credit mortgage after a period of time.

835. Interest rates have dropped significantly. When does it make sense to refinance my mortgage?

When interest rates drop 1.5 percent below the rate you're paying, you should refinance your mortgage. Some mortgage officers say you should consider refinancing when rates drop as little as 1 percent, depending on whether interest rates are heading back up, your cash flow needs, conditions of the borrower, and how long you will be in your home to recoup the refinancing charges. All these factors are important when you review if it is economically sound to refinance. Review the fees involved and the savings in interest. Your lender can give you the figures to compare.

836. Am I required to have insurance the entire time I have my mortgage?

Principal Mortgage Insurance (PMI) is required if your loan is for more than 80 percent of the value of the property. The Homeowner's Protection Act of 1998 cancels your PMI when your equity equals 22% of the purchase price (or appraisal at closing), whichever is lower. The lender usually is not making money from PMI insurance—the insurance is subcontracted.

837. Is a home equity loan a good idea?

Home equity loans are often more cumbersome to acquire (you need to have your house appraised, pay closing costs, and so on) than a regular bank loan. The good news: The interest can be deducted on your income tax (like a mortgage), if you itemize your deductions. If you are thinking about a home equity loan, compare the costs of at least four banks, considering not just the interest rate but also points, closing costs, other fees, and the index for any variable rate change.

838. How about a home equity line of credit?

I recommend a home equity line of credit for emergency funds. Usually the line of credit comes with checks so all you do is write a check for the funds needed. You then receive a statement at the end of the month from the bank with the amount of principal and interest due. Home equity lines of credit almost always have much lower interest rates than credit cards as well. The bad part of a line of credit is that the credit must be repaid when the home is sold. This can be a problem if you bought a big-ticket item (like a car) through the credit line. You also need to realize that if you default on your line of credit, you could lose your house.

839. How do I calculate the equity in my home?

You take the value of your home, either estimated or appraised, subtract the remaining balance of your mortgage, plus subtract any other debts on the house, and the answer is your equity. Depending on the lender, they usually permit you to borrow up to an 80 percent total (mortgage and equity loan) lending amount for the line of credit.

840. It seems to me that I'm paying an awful lot for my property taxes. My house is assessed at a much higher rate than my neighbor's. Am I stuck with their assessment?

No, you're not and neither are the other 60 percent of Americans whose homes are overassessed, according to the National Taxpayers Union. Yet most of us law-abiding citizens just accept our assessments at face value, assuming we can't fight City Hall. Well, you can. Get a copy of your assessment at your local assessor's office or the local library. Check it for accuracy. Is the lot size, square footage, and number of rooms correct? If there

---

HOME EQUITY ESTIMATOR

Use this simple worksheet to calculate the equity in your home.

Value of your home (estimate)	$ _____
Subtract remaining balance of any mortgage on your home	$ _____
Estimated equity	$ _____

The amount of the loan for which you qualify is based on the value of your home, your credit standing, financial status, and annual income.

---

are any errors or the local real estate values have fallen and the assessments haven't, you can challenge the assessment. You don't even have to hire a lawyer. The American Homeowners Association (888-470-2242) can send you a Homeowners Property Tax Reduction Kit ($19.95) to help you challenge your assessment.

841. Am I required to put my real estate taxes and homeowner's insurance in escrow?

Most lenders require you to put money into escrow to cover taxes and insurance if you owe more than 80 percent of the value of your home. Once you reach that point in your mortgage, you can decide if you want to put your real estates taxes into an escrow account or pay the taxes yourself. Not all lenders require the escrow accounts. If you don't want to put money into an escrow account, find a lender who doesn't require it.

842. If I put money into escrow originally, am I required to continue escrow throughout the period of the loan?

No, unless required by your financial institution. Many homeowners escrow when they originally acquire their mortgages and then stop escrowing at a time when their incomes increase enough to have breathing room to pay the tax payments on their own.

843. My mortgage payment just changed again. What creates this need to change the payments?

Unless you have an adjustable rate mortgage, your mortgage does not change. The adjustment in your monthly payment is caused by the increase needed to maintain your escrow account balances. You should receive information about the increase and then calculations with the notice increase.

844. At settlement I had to reimburse the seller for real estate taxes and then pay extra for my taxes. Why is that required?

From what you described, you are putting your tax payments into an escrow account along with your monthly mortgage payment. Real estate taxes are paid on different cycles so you must catch up for the payments since last year's taxes were due. Real estate taxes are paid ahead so you are required to reimburse the seller the taxes that they paid. Then, since you are escrowing funds, you need to set aside the funds in the escrow account as if you paid the escrow amount each month since the last tax payment was paid.

845. The realtor told me that I can deduct my mortgage interest on my taxes. Is this true?

Yes. You can deduct mortgage interest on a primary residence as well as the interest on one vacation home if you itemize. Your standard deduction is currently $6,000 for a couple filing jointly so you need to have paid more than $6,000 a year in itemized deductions to make the itemization worthwhile. If you can itemize, you are saving taxes on a portion of the interest that you paid on your mortgage. If you are in a 15 percent bracket and paid $4,800 in mortgage interest this year, you saved $720 in taxes if you were able to itemize your deductions. In the 28 percent bracket, the figure increases to $1,344. There are income limits to this deduction. Although it's a pleasure to know you are saving taxes in April with the deductions, borrow what is economically feasible to your lifestyle and peace of mind, not for the deduction. If you save twenty-eight cents on the dollar, you still must pay the seventy-two cents of the mortgage.

846. Who pays for the transfer taxes when I buy a house?

Everything is negotiable. If a seller is desperate and the house has been on the market for awhile, he will be more willing to pay some of your expenses to make the deal. Normally:

- The buyer and seller split the real estate transfer costs.
- The seller pays the realtor.
- The buyer pays the points.
- The buyer pays for inspections.
- The seller needs to fix anything that is broken.

SELLING A HOME

847. What is the best time of year to sell my house?

Usually spring is the best time to sell your home; however, each geographic area is unique. In spring, people are out enjoying the weather and they often start thinking of moving on. Many homes are bought by people who weren't particularly thinking about moving—they just saw a sign while walking or riding. People with children like to move in the summer. The holidays aren't usually a good time since they tend to be hectic enough without the thought of moving.

848. Is this always true?

No. The best time to sell can often be a local phenomenon. College towns have unique timetables as does real estate near medical facilities, when the next group of professionals move in to begin their contracts (often, July 1).

849. I plan to sell my house next spring. What do I do to prepare my home for listing?

Interestingly, most realtors say that the final decision to buy a particular property is most heavily influenced by the wife. That's why many builders have designed homes with this in mind; you should think about what might attract a woman to your house. Large fix-up expenses shouldn't be necessary unless the house doesn't sell and you'll only know that after the house has been on the market for awhile. Too many homeowners over-improve their properties. Remember that the value of your house is usually limited by what's typical for your neighborhood. Here's what you should concentrate on:

- Repaint indoors with light, neutral colors.
- Clean your carpets, don't replace them—your taste might be different from the buyers.

- Clean everything well.
- Clean out the attic and basement so they don't look cluttered.
- Remove furniture to alleviate clutter and make the rooms look larger.
- Make certain the landscaping of your home is in good order. Cut back old shrubs to let light into the house. The exterior of the house is the first impression—you want it to be a good one.
- Repaint the front door.

850. What fix-ups should I avoid when getting ready to sell?

The biggest losses are expensive replacement windows, swimming pools, decks, room additions, extra closets, and expensive fixtures. Never make your home the largest home in the neighborhood. You rarely get your money back on a fireplace, but an additional bath can be cost effective.

851. What improvements will help me recoup my money?

Putting money into your kitchen is usually money well spent as are the funds for central air, simple repairs, and replacements. You can usually re-coup the money you spend to fix a cracked driveway, repaint peeling exteriors and walls, and mend a leaky roof.

852. Is a home warranty policy a good idea?

The seller usually buys home warranty insurance as a marketing aid when selling their home. First-time home buyers are often frightened about taking the plunge into home ownership in case something major goes wrong in the first several years of ownership. Home warranty coverage, after a small deductible, will fix the problem for the buyer. The cost of the policy is on a menu process; the more coverage you get, the more you pay. The general cost is approximately $225 for residential coverage. The coverage isn't total and the benefits are based on a pro rata basis. Home warranty insurance helps the first-time buyer have some peace of mind.

853. Do I really need a real estate agent?

In certain types of real estate markets, a real estate agent is invaluable by getting you more money for your home than you would get on your own. Realtors know the market, have the clientele, and should know that the persons viewing your home can afford it. Realtors often help keep a deal together, walking the buyers through the process. You are paying for their expert advice.

854. What if I don't want a real estate agent?

In the litigious world we live in, if you aren't using a realtor you should work closely with a real estate attorney to guarantee you have followed all the rules as required by law.

855. What is a discount broker?

An individual or company who charges less than the standard real estate commission in your area. There are all types of programs from flat fee and/or a menu type of program where you pay for services rendered. Using a discount broker puts a great deal of the burden of selling your house on you as well as the liability and responsibility. Using a discount broker is possible, but you need to do your homework and seek competent advice.

856. Can I get my real estate agent to lower her commission?

Everything is negotiable; all you can do is ask. If she does lower the commission, wonderful. If not, you can decide if you want to go elsewhere. Many realtors can't lower their commission because they don't work on their own and their employer doesn't permit it. On the other hand, many realtors are willing to lower their commission to list a very marketable property.

857. I've seen a For Sale by Owner real estate sign on properties. How do they work?

These companies are set up to help you through the process of selling your home. They are not your agent—they serve as advisers. You pay an up-front fee (anywhere from $700 to $1,000) and get a menu of items they can handle, each with a fee.

858. This sounds like an easier way to sell my home than by going through a regular real estate agent. Is it?

You must be careful because you can pay the same or even more than you would with a full-service broker.

859. What should I do if I am thinking about selling my home on my own, then?

Investigate what services are available with this type of adviser and compare them to a full-service realtor or an attorney.

860. My real estate agent told me to leave my house when people come to look. Why did he recommend this?

It's important for prospective buyers to be able to confide in their agents about what they do or don't like about a house and this doesn't often happen when the owners are present. Potential buyers feel uncomfortable mentioning what they don't like about a home when the owners are standing right there. Realtors need to know buyers' objections so they can attempt to neutralize them and they need the information to discover the type of home the buyers want. Often potential buyers have no concept of what they are looking for in a house or their expectations are much higher than their budget.

861. Are there some things I must fix in my home before I can sell it?

If there are problems in your area, such as underground radon gas in some parts of the country, you must have them checked. Most areas require other items, such as a pest check, and certain safety regulations, such as handrails on stairways.

862. What is a reverse mortgage?

A reverse mortgage enables older homeowners to tap the equity they have in their homes. As you get older, you may have problems with increasing property taxes, health care expenses, or rising homeowner's insurance. Reverse mortgages—which have become available only in the past few years—provide an option to selling. Reverse mortgages don't work like conventional loans; instead, they let you convert your home's value into cash while you live there. The loan doesn't come due until you sell the house or die. The mortgage company charges interest on the payments. When you sell your home, the accrued interest and the mortgage amount you have received through the years are due and payable, usually from the proceeds when the home is sold. Any proceeds in excess of the amount owed to the mortgage company belong to you or your estate. Even if you take out a reverse mortgage and live in the house beyond the point where the checks stop coming from the bank, the mortgage doesn't come due until the homeowner dies or moves.

863. Who is eligible for a reverse mortgage?

You and any co-borrowers must be at least sixty-two years old and own your single family home with no present mortgage or with only minimal debt on the property.

864. Will a condominium qualify for a reverse mortgage property?

Yes. The property must meet HUD minimum property standards and if so, then a condominium property does qualify.

865. What types of payments are available under a reverse mortgage plan?

There are five choices in payments: tenure, term, modified tenure, modified term, and line of credit. The monthly payment amounts are calculated based on your age, the interest rate charged by the mortgage company, the amount borrowed, and if you want the loan for a set amount of time or for your lifetime.

- *Tenure:* Sets you up with monthly payments for as long as you occupy your home.
- *Term:* You receive monthly payments for a fixed period of time that you choose.
- *Modified tenure:* Sets aside a portion of loan proceeds as a line of credit, providing equal monthly payments as long as you occupy your home.
- *Modified term:* Sets aside a portion of loan proceeds as a line of credit as well as monthly payments for a fixed period of time.
- *Line of credit:* permits you to obtain funds as needed.

866. What happens if I borrow more than my home is worth?

HUD pays the difference to the mortgage company. You are never responsible for more than the value of your home. You cannot be forced to sell your home when you have maxed out your loan. A reverse mortgage is a wonderful way to stay in your home.

867. How do I apply for a reverse mortgage?

By contacting HUD in Washington at 800-424-8590 and asking for three mortgage companies that handle reverse mortgages in the area that you reside.

INVESTMENT PROPERTY

868. Does real estate make a good investment?

Real estate can be a good investment, but it is *not* a liquid investment. People often use emotion to purchase their home or invest too much in remodeling and/or additions. Good choices can help you make a good investment. Know your market and the reason you are investing and remember that location is crucial.

Unlike the stock market, real estate is a regional market. The Boston real estate market may be booming while Washington, D.C., is in a slump. Most of us remember a time when real estate always increased in value—it was just a matter of how fast and how much. There is no longer a guarantee to an increase in value so you must be prudent when you take the plunge to purchase.

869. Are condominiums considered a poor investment?

Certainly not—although condominiums are more of a regional investment. They are perfect for individuals who still want to own their own home, but don't want the upkeep a standard home requires. As Baby Boomers mature, condominiums should become even more popular. Condominiums tend to be more difficult to sell than a single home. There are condo restrictions (such as no dogs or children) that can make it more difficult to sell the condo, plus there are monthly maintenance fees used for snow removal, gardening, painting, roof repair, and so forth.

870. I'd love to own a place in the country to get away on weekends. Does a weekend or vacation home make a good investment?

Vacation homes *can* be a good investment: I have settled estates where people bought a home at the seashore for $35,000 and eventually sold it for $600,000. Even considering inflation and the number of years involved, this was a good investment. Look at the mortgage payment, real estate taxes, upkeep, insurance, and expenditures (new roof, painting, and so on) and then figure out if you can afford a second home. You can deduct the interest on a mortgage on a second home; this lowers your current income tax liability. If you decide you can afford it, next ask yourself if you *want* to afford it. Your vacation home will be your vacation for many years, and just like your primary residence, real estate always seems to require money for a new project or unexpected expense.

871. Should an investor consider purchasing distressed property?

Real estate is most often a long-term investment and it's not a source of ready cash; that's why purchasing distressed property is a riskier investment than purchasing a home. If it is rental property, will you be able to find renters? Distressed properties are not for the fainthearted. Do your homework with the finances, know the area you are considering buying into, and understand that unless you have a manager (who usually takes 10 percent of the rents), you will be spending a lot of time on this investment.

872. What about time-shares? Are they a good deal or are they a financial pain?

Time-shares are very interesting and imaginative products, but I don't consider them an investment. They are more of a rental agreement with a company for vacation property. There are annual fees and transfer expenses. If you can get the time-share for a reasonable price and you use it frequently to travel to many different areas, it can save you money on your trips. Comparison shop and review the situation with a time-share realtor in the area you are looking into, not through the time-share company itself. Before you buy a time-share, check around to see if you can buy a used time-share from a previous owner. You can often save thousands of dollars this way.

873. Are rental properties a good investment?

Just because a real estate investment is real estate doesn't mean it can't be a poor investment. Real estate prices tend to move up or down depending on the economy and which geographic areas are growing. The interest rate environment, your local job market, and the general economy at the present time are all considerations because to make money, rental property needs renters. You need income coming in to help pay the expenses of the property.

874. How do I figure out whether to take the plunge?

To know if real estate is a good investment, take the rental income, deduct your expenses, and see what the rate of return is before and after taxes. Remember that your funds are at risk, the investment is long term, and not liquid. It's imperative to question your expenses: Rents have stabilized at the present time, but taxes have increased as have water bills and other related expenses, so the total return on real estate at present isn't as lucrative as it once was.

875. What are some of the creative ways to purchase real estate?

You can purchase a home through a lease purchase agreement or you can have the seller pay the points and fees. One realtor told me a buyer got a house by trading a sports car for the house and taking over the debt. The seller can take back a mortgage so that you don't need to acquire a mortgage from the bank and won't need to have a down payment. When the real estate market is booming, creativity isn't as common, but when the market is stagnant there's more opportunity to be creative.

876. Can I purchase a home for $1, like advertised on television?

Usually you buy real estate for $1 when it's a buyer's market and often the property is in a distressed area. The owners want to sell and are willing to take back enough financing so they can walk away from their commitment/liability. Be very careful of what you are buying. If you then have to sell, you may not be able to sell the property without a loss either.

877. My husband and I must move a lot because of his job. How should we buy a home?

Plan your exit strategy up front. If you consider buying, it should be a standard, low-maintenance home—one that will be very marketable when or if you need to sell. You will pay for personal taste because you may have to wait for your house to sell.

878. My friend and I are thinking about buying a house together (we're both women and not married). Can we own it as a sole ownership?

No. Sole ownership is just what it says—one person owns the property and can sell, give it away, or will it away. Nonmarried persons should own property jointly. You may own your share of the property as a tenant in common. Then, at death, the property can be left by will or trust as you decide.

879. What does the term "joint tenants with rights of survivorship" mean?

Two or more people own the property equally. One person can sell her share, but usually only with the consent of the other owner(s), and only if the proceeds of the sale are shared equally with the other owner(s). If the owners are married and they divorce, the property is included in the marital property subject to division. If one owner dies, their share immediately becomes the property of the other owner(s).

880. What does the term "tenants by entirety" mean?

The property must be owned by a married couple who owns the property together. Neither can sell without the other's permission. When one spouse dies, the other becomes the sole owner. In divorce, spouses become tenants in common; either has the right to sell his or her half without the consent of the other.

881. What are tenants in common?

Two or more people who own a share (usually an equal amount) of the property. Each owner can sell his or her share independently and keep the profit. The other owner(s) have no right to inherit (although they could) and have no control over what happens to a co-owner's share. In case of divorce, property bought during a marriage could be counted as marital property subject to division. At death, the property can be left by will or trust, however the owner wishes.

REAL ESTATE

Home type _____ Zoned? _____

Address _____

_____

Title in name of _____

Deed in name of _____

Purchase date _____ Purchase price $ _____

Current value $ _____ Assessed value $ _____

Location of deeds _____

First mortgage held

Mortgage type _____ Interest % _____

Address _____

_____

Phone number _____ Fax _____

Monthly payment $ _____ Payment due date _____

Amount owed/date _____ Date due (in full) _____

Annual property insurance _____

Escrow taxes? _____ Amount $ _____

Line of credit

Bank _____ Account # _____

Date opened _____ Credit limit $ _____

Current balance _____ Interest rate % _____

Property tax

Amount owed $ _____ Mils _____

Spring payment amount $ _____

Fall payment amount $ _____

MORTGAGES/LOANS

Bank

Type of loan   #

Name(s) on loan   Length of loan

Address

E-mail address

Contact   Work phone (   )

Monthly payment $ Due date

Final payment $ Due date

Interest rate %   Location of loan papers

Bank

Type of loan   #

Name(s) on loan   Length of loan

Address

E-mail address

Contact   Work phone (   )

Monthly payment $ Due date

Final payment $ Due date

Interest rate %   Location of loan papers

Bank

Type of loan   #

Name(s) on loan   Length of loan

Address

(continued)

E-mail address
_____

Contact _____   Work phone (   )_____

Monthly payment $ _____   Due date _____

Final payment $ _____   Due date _____

Interest rate % _____   Location of loan papers _____

Bank

Type of loan _____   # _____

Name(s) on loan _____   Length of loan _____

Address
_____

_____

E-mail address
_____

Contact _____   Work phone (   )_____

Monthly payment $ _____   Due date _____

Final payment $ _____   Due date _____

Interest rate % _____   Location of loan papers _____

Bank

Type of loan _____   # _____

Name(s) on loan _____   Length of loan _____

Address
_____

_____

E-mail address
_____

Contact _____   Work phone (   )_____

Monthly payment $ _____   Due date _____

Final payment $ _____   Due date _____

Interest rate % _____   Location of loan papers _____

CHAPTER 11

ESTATE PLANNING

While you are still alive, you should develop a plan for transferring your assets to your loved ones after your death. An estate plan doesn't have to be elaborate or expensive, but not having one can make matters much more complicated and expensive for your heirs. If you haven't developed a plan and filled out the proper documents, your assets will be distributed in accordance with the laws of your state and it will cost your heirs more to settle your estate. By knowing the fundamentals of estate planning, you can ensure that your assets are distributed according to your wishes and that more of your assets are passed along to your heirs. This chapter provides the kind of information you need to get started on setting up an appropriate estate plan.

GETTING STARTED

882. What does estate planning really mean?

It's the process of preparing what is going to happen to everything you own when you die.

883. What is the first step in estate planning?

Before you begin making plans, you need to know what assets and liabilities you have. You should prepare an inventory of your assets as well as a list of all your debts. The process of estate planning begins by knowing where you are now.

884. What are the most important estate planning documents?

These are the four documents everyone should keep in their estate planning files:

1. Power of Attorney
2. Living Will
3. Will
4. Deed of Trust

WILLS

885. What is a will?

A will is a document that appoints an executor after your death to take care of:

- paying your bills and final expenses;
- gathering and valuing your assets;
- paying death and final income taxes; and
- disposing of remaining funds to your heirs.

886. Why is a will so important?

If you have dependent children, a will is crucial if you want to name a guardian for them. Do you really want the courts to decide who will care for your children if you and your spouse die before your children reach adulthood? If you die without a will, the state will appoint an administrator to supervise the distribution of your assets—costing about 5 percent of the value of your estate. The administrator also must post a bond, which costs several hundred dollars.

887. I just can't decide who will raise my kids right now. What should I do?

You should appoint a trust guardian who could decide for you if you die before you have written a will.

888. I don't have kids. Do I need a will?

Yes. If you have a will, you're the one who gets to say how your property will be distributed. If you die without a will, the state steps in and divides your property for you according to state law. In this case, odds are your favorite third cousin, a charity, or close friends will likely get nothing.

889. Do I need an attorney to prepare a simple will?

Most attorneys prepare wills using software packages. A will is made valid not because it is prepared by an attorney, but because it is witnessed by three people, and you were of sound mind and not under pressure to make a will when you signed it. Computer-generated wills have not apparently caused legal problems in those cases where they have been used. However, if you have more than $625,000 in your estate (the level at which estate taxes begin), it's a good idea to use an attorney to prepare your will.

890. My lawyer stated that he doesn't write a will until the first spouse dies.

Please have him put that in writing so your heirs can sue him. That's what I advise people when they receive this response. Unfortunately, I hear this more often than you can imagine. If a couple has assets of more than $625,000 in 1998, the estate of the second spouse to die may have to pay inheritance taxes because of adding the funds from both estates.

891. Is there another choice between hiring an attorney and doing it myself?

You could hire a paralegal to help you prepare the documents. The National Association for Independent Paralegals (707) 935-7951 can refer you to paralegals in your area.

892. Do I need to rewrite my will as soon as I get married?

Absolutely. Your new marriage can invalidate your present will. If you die after you get married and you haven't made a new will, the court, in many states, will treat your estate as if you had never made a will at all. As a result, many of your special bequests might not be carried out. The danger here is not that your new husband won't inherit—in most cases, he will—but any special requests you had included in your old will might not be honored. Many people assume their old will is good enough to tide them over until they get around to having a new will made. It's just not true.

893. Is it better to have percentages or specific amounts of money bequests in my will?

Both are appropriate. Gifts of cash to your church, housekeeper, friends, neighbors, and other charities—remembrances that aren't too significant a part of your estate—should be in cash. That way the distribution isn't too large. Percentage gifts should be for the family, your residuary heirs. Since none of us can know exactly how much our estates will be at death, giving a percentage guarantees a proportionate division of what is in your estate. You always need a clause that distributes all funds after the specific bequests.

894. With the Taxpayer Relief Act of 1997, should I redo my will?

I would have it reviewed if you have business interests in your estate that are more than half of your estate. There is now a $1.3 million death tax exemption for business property in an estate.

895. What is a self-proving will?

This is a will that can be presented for probate without witnesses coming to the Court House. The witnesses verified at the time the will was signed that they knew the person who signed the will and the person had the capacity to write a will, all before a notary public. This is a big savings in time and money when the will is probated. Unless it's not possible to write a self-proving will, that's the only type I recommend.

896. Am I taxed on money I receive from an estate?

In general, funds received from an estate are not income taxable. Tax deferred funds, IRAs, annuities, and so on, can carry income tax liability with them.

897. What is a Living Will?

A Living Will, also called an advance directive, is a document that states your wishes should you become profoundly ill, irreversibly incompetent, and need life support systems or heroic measures to keep you alive. It spells out to your doctor, the hospital, your family, and to all concerned what measures may and may not be taken so that you may be allowed to die with dignity and without unwanted intervention. There are also medical or health directives that give general direction to your family and the hospital. Many hospitals and medical facilities want you to sign their medical directive form upon entering their facility. Samples of a living will and health directive follow.

898. I love my daughter, but I'm uncomfortable with my son-in-law. How do I set up things at my death so that he doesn't get anything from my estate?

You can't stop your daughter from giving assets that are hers to her husband. The only way to prevent funds from going to your son-in-law is to place your daughter's inheritance in a trust so that she receives the income for her life with the principal if needed for care or emergencies. Then either at your son-in-law's death or your daughter's death the funds can be distributed to your grandchildren.

899. My aunt died more than a year ago and I haven't heard a word from either her attorney or the executor. Do I have a right to ask for information?

If you are receiving a specific bequest, you have the right to ask when you will receive it. Personal property shouldn't take too long since executors

LIVING WILL

DECLARATION

I, _____, being of sound mind, willfully and voluntarily make this declaration to be followed if I become incompetent. This declaration reflects my firm and settled commitment to refuse life-sustaining treatment under the circumstances indicated below.

I direct my attending physician to withhold or withdraw life-sustaining treatment that serves only to prolong the process of my dying, if I should be in a terminal condition or in a state of permanent unconsciousness.

In addition, if I am in the condition described above, I feel especially strong about the following forms of treatment:

I ( ) do ( ) do not want cardiac resuscitation.

I ( ) do ( ) do not want mechanical respiration.

I ( ) do ( ) do not want tube feeding or any other artificial or invasive form of nutrition (food) or hydration (water).

I ( ) do ( ) do not want blood or blood products.

I ( ) do ( ) do not want any form of surgery or invasive diagnostic tests.

I ( ) do ( ) do not want kidney dialysis.

I ( ) do ( ) do not want antibiotics.

I realize that if I do not specifically indicate my preference regarding any of the forms of treatment listed above, I may receive that form of treatment.

Other Instructions:

I ( ) do ( ) do not want to designate another person as my surrogate to make medical treatment decisions for me if I should be incompetent and in a terminal condition or in a state of permanent unconsciousness. Name and address of the surrogate:

Name and address of alternate surrogate (if surrogate designated above is unable to serve):

I make this declaration on the _____ day of _____, 19_____.

(continued)

Declarant's signature: _____

Declarant's address: _____

_____

The declarant knowingly and voluntarily signed this writing by signature or marked in my presence.

Witness's signature: _____

Witness's address: _____

_____

Witness's signature: _____

Witness's address: _____

_____

and attorneys like to distribute this type of property as soon as possible after death so they can eliminate insurance on the property. Money gifts are paid when and if there is money. In Pennsylvania, the estate must pay interest on a specific money bequest if you don't receive it within a year of death. You may ask about distribution if you haven't received any information after the initial contact and it's been a while. Residuary heirs (nonspecific beneficiaries) have a right to receive copies of all inventories, tax returns, and various other documents filed at the courthouse. If you haven't received anything after a year, I would ask how the estate is proceeding and ask for an informal accounting of what has transpired to date. Attorneys' offices have estate transactions on computer; you could ask to see what has happened to date.

900. How is it determined which state I probate my will in?

The place that you consider your permanent residence is where the will is probated: where your income tax address is located, where you reside for six months and a day during the year, and where your cars are registered. It is important to have a definite home so that several states don't feel you are a resident of their jurisdiction.

ADVANCE DIRECTIVE FOR HEALTH CARE DECLARATION

I [print your name] _____
being of sound mind, willfully and voluntarily make this declaration to be followed if I become incompetent. This declaration reflects my firm and settled commitment to refuse life-sustaining treatment under the circumstances indicated below.

I direct my attending physician to withhold or withdraw life-sustaining treatment that serves only to prolong the process of my dying, if I should be in a terminal condition or in a state of permanent unconsciousness.

I direct that treatment be limited to measures to keep me comfortable and to relieve pain, including any pain that might occur by withholding or withdrawing life-sustaining treatment.

In addition, if I am in the condition described above, I feel especially strong about the following forms of treatment (please check one box for each statement, but only if you have a preference at this time):

I do ___ do not ___ want cardiac resuscitation.

I do ___ do not ___ want mechanical respiration.

I do ___ do not ___ want tube feeding or any other artificial or invasive form of nutrition (food) or hydration (water).

I do ___ do not ___ want blood or blood products.

I do ___ do not ___ want any form of surgery or invasive diagnostic tests.

I do ___ do not ___ want kidney dialysis.

I do ___ do not ___ want antibiotics.

I realize that if I do not specifically indicate my preference regarding any of the forms of treatment listed above, and I do not name a surrogate to make medical treatment decisions for me, I may receive that form of treatment.

Other instructions:

I do ___ do not ___ want to designate another person as my surrogate to make medical treatment decisions for me if I should be incompetent and in a terminal condition or in a state of permanent unconsciousness. I authorize my surrogate to make decisions regarding any of the medical treatments listed above as to which I do not specifically indicate my preference, and any other form of treatment not listed in this declaration. Name and address of surrogate if applicable:

(continued)

Name and address of substitute surrogate (if surrogate designated above is unable to serve):

I do ___ do not ___ want to make an anatomical gift of all or part of my body, subject to the following limitations, if any:

_____

I made this declaration on the _____ day of _____, 19_____.

Declarant's signature: _____

Declarant's address: _____

_____

If this declaration was signed by another person on behalf of and at the direction of the declarant, please explain the circumstances.

The declarant or the person on behalf of and at the direction of the declarant knowingly and voluntarily signed this writing by signature or marked in my presence.

Witness's signature: _____

Witness's address: _____

_____

Witness's signature: _____

Witness's address: _____

_____

Please note: This declaration is based on the model form set forth in the Pennsylvania Advance Directive for Health Care Act at 20 Pa. CSA 5404(b). This form may not be best suited for every individual. If you have any questions, please consult your attorney.

901. Just how public will my will be?

Very public. Once your will is probated, anyone can go to the local probate court and ask to see the will and read it. You will see who has been appointed as executor, who is to receive specific bequests, and how property was disposed of.

902. What if the will is found to be invalid?

Then the probate court will order that creditors and taxes be paid. The remainder of the estate will be distributed in accordance with state law.

903. Can I give my personal property away by labeling the furniture in my home?

Obviously, labeling property means that the gifts were not made prior to death. You may place labels on furniture and state in your will that you want the executor to distribute everything according to the labels. However, it's better to have an actual list of your personal property attached to your will with a clause in your will distributing the property according to the list. This way you can change the list without having to rewrite a new will if you change your mind about who should get what.

904. I don't need a will since I hold everything jointly with my wife, right?

This can work especially if your estate totals less than $625,000. However, you never know what the future holds and it's imperative to have a will if you have minor children in case you both die in a common accident. More than 70 percent of the population does not have a will. It is sad to see when a wife must pay taxes and probate expenses on her own home because it was never deeded from one name to two, possibly losing her home because of stepchildren inheriting half the property. People inherit property, win the lottery, and die without changing beneficiaries in life insurance policies; you never know if a will will be necessary. Why take the chance?

905. Now that I've written a will, what is the best thing to help my executor?

Place all your important documents in a safety-deposit box with a listing at home. Tell a family member or your executor where your lock box key is located. Providing information for your executor is the best thing you can do.

906. How often should I rewrite my will?

You should review your will when family circumstances warrant, when there are major changes in tax law (as in 1997), or if you have a major change in your business, such as a new partner. For example, I was shocked to find that my in-laws' will predated my daughter's birth. Their attorney named the grandchildren by name and a grandchild born after the will was written was automatically disinherited.

907. I want to leave all my money to my oldest son and let him divide the money among his brothers and sisters. Is that a problem?

Money should never be left to one family member with the instruction that it be divided after death. Once your son inherits the money, it is no longer part of your estate. It's an important point because if he tries to divide your money among all his siblings the day after he inherits it, the court considers the money to be a gift to the other siblings, not an inheritance. Your son can legally give each of your kids only $10,000 a year; if he gives away more than that, it becomes subject to a gift tax. What this means is that if you leave $500,000 to be divided up among your five children, your son could not give each child $100,000 upon your death without incurring the gift tax. He would have to spread the payments out over ten years. If you want your money to be divided equally among your children, you need to say so in your will.

908. How much can I leave my children without them having to pay federal estate tax when I die?

As of 1998, you can pass on $625,000 before it is liable for federal estate taxes. Gradually it increases to $1,000,000 in 2006.

909. How can I transfer property for my wife's benefit (it's a second marriage for us both) and still guarantee that it goes to my children at her death?

There is a marital deduction trust that gives your wife income, but controls the principal so that your children ultimately receive the funds. It is called a QTIP (qualified terminable interest trust). The trust must provide income (at least annually) to your wife during her lifetime, but directs the principal to your children after her death. This QTIP trust is taxed in your wife's estate. It's a wonderful estate planning tool so that you can provide income to her, yet guarantee the funds go to your children.

910. I want to control the funds held in trust for my wife so that I know it will go to my four children; however, I want her to be able to divide the funds among our children as she sees fit. Is this possible?

You might think about a power of appointment. There are general powers of appointment and there are specific powers of appointment. The specific power of appointment would give your wife the ability to change the distribution amounts, but not who gets the money. If she does nothing, each of your four children will inherit 25 percent each. If she exercises her power, she could give one child nothing and the others each a third or one child everything. This type of trust can guarantee that a child with a problem, be it substance abuse, marital problems, and so on, won't inherit funds.

911. What happens if there is real estate left in a will, but not enough cash to pay all the expenses and taxes?

If there isn't enough money to pay expenses and taxes, but the estate is large enough to have assets, there are two choices—either liquidate the property to produce cash to pay all the bills or allow the heirs the chance to buy assets from the estate. Making sure there is enough cash to take care of expenses is an important part of estate planning.

912. Explain why I should have a simultaneous death clause in my will.

If you do not have simultaneous death clauses in your wills, or a clause that requires your spouse live a specified number of days after you die, there could be a problem if you and your spouse die in a common accident and you can't tell who died first. You will lose one of the unified credit amounts. This happens because all the wife's property passes to the husband while all the husband's property passes to the wife. If you can't tell who dies first, the law presumes the husband dies first.

PROBATE

913. What is probate and can I avoid it?

Even if you have an ironclad will, some or all of your assets must be shuffled through a court process known as probate—the legal process for implementing the directions given in a will and the formal process of proving the authenticity of the will.

Assets that don't need to be probated include:

- assets owned in joint tenancy; and
- assets inside retirement accounts, such as IRAs and 401(k)s.

914. Isn't it important that I bypass probate so I don't have any death taxes?

Bypassing probate does not bypass taxation. Inheritance tax is the tax associated with the transfer of assets in your state. The federal estate tax is a tax on the right to transfer property.

915. Must I have an attorney to probate my will?

No. However, you have to be very careful to file all the right papers at the right time. The courthouse staff can guide you part way through the process as can your accountant. If you hit a problem, if there is any real estate involved, or you want someone to review your work, find an attorney who will charge you on an hourly basis. Good legal counsel is worth the money.

916. Is it ever advantageous to go through probate?

Probate provides clean title to heirs, increases the chance that everybody has notice of all proceedings, and provides for an orderly administration of a person's assets.

917. What are the disadvantages?

Probate adds to the expense of the transfer of your assets. The biggest problem is that it is public and the information is available to anyone who wants to know. Anyone can go to the courthouse and read your will so they know who your heirs are, read the inventory of assets so they know how much property is being transferred, and review the accounting to know exactly what bills, expenses, and transactions occurred.

918. At what point during probate can you challenge a will?

You can challenge a will during probate by filing an objection with the court within a specified period of time (check your state laws). Challenges to wills can take up a lot of time and money; think hard about this before you file.

EXECUTORS

919. Who should be my executor?

An executor is the person responsible for settling your estate. You may choose anyone who hasn't been convicted of a felony. You may select your spouse, adult child, relative, or friend—especially if the estate isn't too big. Being an executor can be a time-consuming process, especially if the estate is large or there are any problems. The executor is responsible for gathering and valuing the assets, paying all bills and taxes—even on property that is transferred outside the will. Executors are often second-guessed by the heirs, particularly if the heirs are siblings. Your executor is legally obligated to act in your interests and to follow your wishes contained in your will.

920. Can I appoint my attorney to be my executor?

Yes. Some people name their accountant or attorney as executor, but there can be some problems with this. What if you die on April 3—that's busy tax season for an accountant. What if your attorney is busy with an important case? You want someone who has the time to work for you.

921. Should I ask the person I want to have as executor if he will accept?

It's a good idea. Being an executor is a lot of work. You have to track down lots of details and you may even need to help defend the terms of the will against squabbling heirs.

922. I've been named as an executor, but I don't want to serve. Can I get out of it?

Yes. You need to file a document with the court called a declination or re-nunciation that declines your designation as executor. The contingent executor named in the will takes over at this point.

923. What if there is no contingent executor?

Then the court will appoint one.

924. Can I have all my children serve as co-executors?

You can, but do you really want to? Settling an estate by committee can be a nightmare. The executor doesn't need to be a son or the eldest child. The executor should be a person who is responsible, who will follow your in-structions, who is nearby (if possible), and who will administer the estate according to law. The person doesn't even need to be family—it can be someone you trust.

925. What are my duties as executor?

They are many, but you may hire an attorney to help you. The attorney's fees are chargeable to the estate as expenses of administration. For your own protection, you should keep copies of all records for at least two years. Your duties include:

- Finding the will
- Hiring a lawyer (if necessary)
- Applying to appear before probate court
- Notifying beneficiaries named in the will
- Arranging for publication of notice to creditors and mailing a copy to each creditor
- Sending notice of the person's death to the post office, utilities, banks, credit card companies, and so on

- Inventorying assets and having them appraised
- Collecting debts owed to the estate
- Identifying any unpaid salary, insurance, and employee benefits
- Filing for life insurance benefits
- Filing for city, state, and federal income tax returns
- Filing state and federal estate tax returns
- Paying claims against the estate
- Distributing assets and getting receipts from beneficiaries
- Filing papers to finalize the estate

SURVIVOR'S TO-DO LIST

Immediately	**Completed**	**Date**
Notify friends and relatives		
Enter safety-deposit box (if spouse) for documents		
Make funeral arrangements		
Send obituary notices		
Make list of all expressions of sympathy		
Arrange gathering after service		
Obtain 20 copies of death certificate		
Open checking account in your name		

First Month		
Establish estate bank account in deceased's name		
File for insurance benefits		
Notify all other insurance companies		
Notify all credit card companies		
Review auto insurance policy		

(continued)

Apply for pension benefits and Social Security

Meet with attorney to begin probate

Notify financial adviser

Notify Keogh and IRA accounts

Notify stockbroker and banker

Second Month

Revise your will

File estate and inheritance tax returns

Make sure attorney files will

Transfer all real estate titles

Transfer all car titles and insurance policies

Change telephone and utilities to your name

Notify creditors

926. Should my executor get paid?

Most states have set a maximum amount an executor can earn as compensation. Because the payment is compensation, it's subject to income tax, but not self-employment tax (unless you are in the estate settlement business). If you are an heir **and** an executor, it's not a good idea to take the fee unless the amount of money you'd pay in death taxes is higher than your personal income tax bracket. If you are the executor but not an heir and you've done the work and taken the responsibility, you should take the fee. Sometimes executors have not taken the total fee permitted, but worked on an hourly basis instead. An executor is usually entitled to be reimbursed from the estate for expenses incurred in settling. For example, if you live in Maine and you must settle an estate in California, the estate would pay for your commute.

927. If my attorney is also my executor, does she get two fees?

Yes. Although in some states, the law prevents the attorney/executor from collecting both fees. That's why you should name an independent party as executor.

928. Why does it take so long to settle an estate?

Being executor is more than gathering the assets and paying the funds. The assets need to be valued, tax returns must be filed, and creditors must be given notice. If a federal estate tax return is filed, it can't be filed until after the six-month alternate valuation date passes. There is nothing worse than distributing funds to heirs and then having to tell them that you need the money back. That's why I like to wait to distribute property until the final income tax return is filed. If advance distributions were not done properly, heirs must give you back the funds, but they may have invested them or worse—spent them. The executor is then responsible.

929. If I don't like my mother's attorney, must I use him to settle her estate?

No. The attorney for the estate represents you as executor. There is no obligation to use the attorney who wrote your mother's will, although he should have an excellent understanding of her desires and her will. If you seek counsel, it's imperative to use a capable, proficient, experienced attorney who will guide you through the process.

POWER OF ATTORNEY

930. What is a Power of Attorney?

A Power of Attorney (POA) is a legally recognized transfer of authority to another person. If you grant POA to your son, this would authorize him to step in and do all the things that you have given him the power to do. That power, however, ends at your death. The powers that you grant to someone else can be broad or very specific. It's important to grant a Power of Attorney so that someone you choose can handle your affairs in case you become incompetent or incapacitated. Otherwise, the court would appoint

GENERAL POWER OF ATTORNEY

KNOW ALL MEN BY THESE PRESENTS that I, _____,

of _____ (county) _____ (state)

by these presents do constitute, make, and appoint _____

_____ and/or _____,

either jointly or severally, my true and lawful attorney for me and in my stead:

1. to sign checks or other instruments of deposit, withdrawal, or instruction on my checking account or other banking account or bank deposit standing in my name;

2. to collect, demand, sue for, recover, and receive all such sums of money, debts, rents, goods, wares, accounts, and other demands whatsoever which are or shall be due, owing, payable, and belonging to me or detained from me in any manner whatsoever;

3. to execute and affirm or swear to all returns for the purposes of federal, state, or local taxation and all other papers in connection with my tax liability including claims for refunds of taxes;

4. to sell and assign all stock and bonds belonging to me and to have access to any safety-deposit box rented to or belonging to me;

5. to sell any real estate standing in my name and to make, execute, acknowledge, and deliver a deed for said real estate to the purchaser or purchasers and to satisfy mortgages;

6. to make gifts;

7. to create a trust for my benefit;

8. to make additions to an existing trust for my benefit;

9. to claim an elective share of the estate of my deceased spouse;

10. to disclaim an interest in property;

11. to renounce fiduciary positions;

12. to withdraw and receive the income or corpus of a trust;

13. to authorize my admission to a medical, nursing, residential, or similar facility and to enter into agreement for my care;

14. to authorize medical and surgical procedures;

15. and generally to do and perform all matters and things, transact all business, make and execute and acknowledge all contracts, orders, writings, mortgages, bonds, U.S. Savings Bonds, assurances and instruments which may be requisite or proper to effectuate any matter or thing appertaining or belonging to me with the same powers, and to all intents and purposes with the same validity as I could, if personally present;

16. and to appoint one or more attorneys in fact under them for the purposes aforesaid, to make and constitute and again at pleasure to revoke such

powers of attorney; hereby ratifying and confirming whatsoever my said attorney shall and may do by virtue hereof; and hereby revoking any previous Power of Attorney signed by me. Notwithstanding the foregoing, this Power of Attorney shall apply not only to titles, documents, or assets standing in my name alone, but shall also apply to titles, documents, or assets standing in my name along with the name of another or others, such as joint tenancy, tenancy by the entirety, or tenancy in common, or tenancy in partnership.

This Power of Attorney shall not be affected by my disability or incompetency.

This Power of Attorney supersedes and replaces any prior Power of Attorney.

IN WITNESS WHEREOF, I have hereunto set my hand and seal this _____

(date)

day of _____

(month, year)

_____ (SEAL)

WITNESSES

_____ residing at _____

_____ residing at _____

On this ___ day of _____ 19__, before me, the undersigned officer, personally appeared _____, known to me (or satisfactorily proven) to be the person whose name is subscribed to the within instrument and acknowledged that he or she executed the same for the purposes herein contained.

IN WITNESS WHEREOF, I hereunto set my hand and official seal.

_____

Notary Public

a guardian, who might not be someone you would have selected. If you're married and you become incapacitated, your spouse won't be able to make those decisions for you without a Power of Attorney.

931. What is a personal Power of Attorney?

A personal POA gives your agent the right to make decisions about medical care, entering a nursing home, non-financial decisions, and so on.

932. What is a financial Power of Attorney?

A financial Power of Attorney gives your agent the power to handle your financial decisions. For example, if you had a stroke, your husband couldn't access your personal checking account to pay your bills without a financial POA.

933. What is a medical POA?

A medical Power of Attorney grants authority to someone you trust to make decisions with a physician about your medical care options.

934. What is a standard POA?

A standard POA gives your agent the right to make decisions in all areas of your life. You and your spouse each need a standard POA for the other.

935. My father says he doesn't need a will since he appointed me his Power of Attorney. Is this correct?

This is a common misconception. A Power of Attorney ends at the moment of death. Then the power ceases and your dad's assets will become part of a probate estate. An executor must receive authorization from the local courts to act in that capacity. The will is filed at the courthouse and authorization via Letter Testamentary and short certificates is given.

936. What is the difference between a regular Power of Attorney and a durable Power of Attorney?

A nondurable Power of Attorney ceases when you really need it most. Most nondurable Power of Attorneys are used for limited transactions, such as real estate settlements while you are out of town, bill payment while you are abroad, and so on. A durable Power of Attorney, on the other hand, is permanent and permits your appointed agent to take appropriate legal actions on your behalf when you become incapacitated, without a court proceeding. Unless you have a durable Power of Attorney, if you become disabled you will need to have a guardian appointed to pay your bills and take care of other legal matters. A guardianship proceeding is dreadfully hard on a family, not to mention the cost and time involved. You must be competent when you sign the Power of Attorney.

937. Do I need a Power of Attorney if my son has the bank's Power of Attorney form for my checking account?

The bank's Power of Attorney covers only that bank account. If the form is general enough it might cover a group of listed accounts; however, it doesn't cover all your other needs. You definitely need a general Power of Attorney form.

938. I had an aunt who lost everything to her agent acting as Power of Attorney. I'm worried about that.

You can restrict your Power of Attorney (POA)—such as the power to fund a trust, power only over various accounts, and so on. If you question the integrity of the person whom you are appointing, for goodness sake, don't name her—name a local financial institution or someone who is in the business of handling a person's financial affairs and is bonded.

939. What are some of the Power of Attorney provisions that you feel are important?

Don't overlook two very important provisions: You want the person who holds your Power of Attorney to be able to do everything you can, and also begin the gifting process as well as fund a standby trust. If you haven't gifted so far because of the fear of not having enough money, you want your Power of Attorney to be able to begin gifting if you become disabled. That doesn't mean the person with POA has to give away your property, but it just gives the person the ability to do so if she feels it is a good estate planning tool. The provision to gift is important. Also, you want your Power of Attorney to be able to fund your standby trust, if necessary. If you never funded a trust and you become disabled, it is important that your agent be able to fund the trust to have a good portion of your assets bypass probate.

GIFTS

940. My husband talks about gift splitting. What exactly is that?

Each one of us can give $10,000 per year as a gift without paying taxes on it. This exclusion amount can be increased to $20,000 if the gift is split with your husband. If you gift split, you'll need to file Form 709 (a gift tax return), although you won't have to pay any taxes. I recommend that rather than splitting a gift, each spouse gift $10,000 to the individual from a joint checking account so a return need not be filed. To qualify for the gift splitting rule, the spouses must be U.S. citizens who are legally married at the time the gift is made. Neither spouse can marry someone else during the calendar year the gift is made.

941. Can a gift be a partial gift?

You can give part of an interest if you sell the rest. For example, you could sell $1,500 worth of stock for $1,000 to your niece. You would be giving a $500 gift in this situation. I have had clients sell a $500,000 farm to a family member for $200,000. That means there was a gift of $300,000, which needs to be reported on a federal gift tax return (Form 709).

942. If I add my son's name to my bank account, is this a gift?

If you have contributed 100 percent of the money in a joint bank account, there is no gift made until your son withdraws the money with no duty to account to you. Thus, putting your son's name on a joint account is not necessarily a gift.

943. Are there ways to transfer an interest that is not considered a gift?

Yes. One of the most interesting estate planning tools is the use of a disclaimer. I've used disclaimers for people who don't wish to inherit the property they were given, if they have enough assets and don't want to add the property to their estates. Disclaimers must be in writing, made before the disclaimant accepts any benefits of the property, received by the executor within nine months of death, and be irrevocable. You can't direct where the property goes. The other non-gift transfers are qualified tuition payments (payments to an educational institution directly for an individual's training) and qualified medical payments (payments for medical care).

944. Can I hold a mortgage for my daughter and then give her a portion of the mortgage each year?

Yes and that's a nice way to let her own her home now without paying the expenses of a regular mortgage (points, fees, and so on). Often, private mortgage rates are lower than standard rates, although you want to be careful of imputed interest. There are two ways to handle this. Pay your daughter her annual gift tax exclusion of $10,000 and have her repay you the funds, paying down the mortgage. Or forgive a portion of the note. Forgiving a portion of the mortgage takes some paperwork; however, you don't need to come up with the $10,000 in cash.

945. I understand if I gift property, it's pulled back into my estate if I die within three years of the gift.

This is one of the largest misunderstood concepts in estate planning. There is a three-year rule; however, it is only for life insurance policies. If you transfer or gift ownership of life insurance policies *within three years of death,* the death proceeds are pulled back into one's estate. All other property can be gifted up until the time of death. This annual gifting is a wonderful process to lower one's estate tax liability.

TRUSTS

946. What is a living trust?

A living trust is a legal document into which one transfers assets. The trustee controls the assets. The owner can revoke the trust if she wishes. The advantage of a living trust is that when you die, the assets pass directly to your beneficiaries without going through probate. This is desirable because probate can be a long, costly hassle for your beneficiaries (and the lawyers may get between 5 to 7 percent of the value of the assets). Moreover, your assets become a matter of public record when the will is probated; the trust assets do not. Remember that living trusts keep assets out of probate, but they don't lessen your tax burden.

947. Who benefits the most from setting up a living trust?

Someone who is over age sixty, not married, and has assets above $100,000 that must be probated.

948. Do I need an attorney to prepare a valid living trust?

No. You can use software or hire a paralegal. However, if you have a large estate (more than $600,000) and you don't have the time or expertise to worry with estate planning, a lawyer could be a good investment. It's not cheap, however. Attorney fees to set up a living trust may range up to $2,000.

949. What is an unfunded trust?

You can set up a trust within the terms of your will and it is only funded if and when the will is probated. At that time, assets are transferred to the trust from the estate.

950. Aren't trusts only for rich people?

Absolutely not. Trusts are for people who need them. They are for special needs children, children who spend too much or can't say "no" to friends, tax savings, and to protect your children in the event of a second marriage. There are many reasons for a trust and being wealthy is only one of them.

951. Why use a trust?

Trusts are set up for the following reasons:

1. To bypass probate
2. Tax savings
3. Spendthrift provisions
4. To manage property if you become incapacitated
5. To provide for multiple beneficiaries

952. Why it is important for my husband and I to have trusts to benefit each other when we don't have that much money?

Define "that much money." Paying $1 more in death taxes than you have to is hard for me to comprehend. Total the value of all your property including the face value of your life insurance if you would die tomorrow. Life insurance and retirement benefits can really bulk up an estate quickly. If, at your death, all your funds pass to your spouse, these funds along with your wife's assets can quickly reach the unified credit amount. This can create a situation where taxes will be owed at the second death because of the loss of one unified credit amount, when it shouldn't be necessary with the proper planning. If planned properly, a couple can transfer $1,250,000 to the next generation ($2 million by the year 2006) without taxation. If only the unlimited marital deduction plan is used, only $625,000 can pass to the next generation without death tax planning. The taxes due would be approximately $246,000. An expensive error.

953. Rather than setting up a trust for my spouse, can I pass the property directly to my children?

Of course, although I'm not certain I would ever feel comfortable enough to recommend that you give (via will or outright) property to your children rather than your wife by using a unified credit trust. Passing property directly to children is frequently done, especially when families are older, because the spouse doesn't need the income and it only increases her annual income and continues to increase her estate. It's a plan that both spouses should understand and agree with during the planning process.

954. I want to provide for my son when I die, but he is always spending more than he makes and he has credit problems. How can I help him?

You are a perfect candidate for a trust. A trust can be set up, either before your death or at death, which will hold funds for your son. He can receive income for his lifetime, yet creditors can't attach the funds held in trust to pay his other debts or bills. This is known as a spendthrift trust. Your son's creditors can't have the trust attached to pay his other bills.

955. Can I set up a trust to help my disabled child?

Special needs trusts are wonderful and they are imperative if you have a special needs child. The provisions can be as broad or as limiting as you wish. Frequently, attorneys and their clients work to set up a trust that will provide funds for a special child without limiting their ability to receive government funding. If you are interested in a special needs trust, call the director of your local Association for Retarded Citizens (ARC) office and ask for a list of attorneys they recommend in your area who specialize in special needs trusts.

956. Should I name my spouse as co-trustee?

Unless there is some reason not to, I always recommend that a spouse be appointed co-trustee. This way, they feel like a part of the process. Their livelihood depends on the trust so they should be part of the process.

957. I want my spouse to have as much money from my trust as possible without having the property taxed at her death. Is that possible?

There are guidelines and court rulings that limit how much control a beneficiary has over a trust until the property becomes taxed in their estate. One of the restrictions is that a beneficiary may have the right to all the income, but not control the principal. The greatest flexibility for your spouse is that she get 100 percent of the income each year from the trust and have the ability to withdraw 5 percent or $5,000 payout of principal each year without question.

958. Can I schedule periodic payouts over the child's lifetime?

The great thing about trusts is that they can be set up to be paid out at any time in any way. I have seen children receive funds at age seventy-five. I have seen trust documents that pay out so much a year over a twenty-year period or that match the income the beneficiary earned at an outside job.

959. Under the provisions of my will, can I have funds held until my children are older, and can I permit them to receive assets to help them in life?

Yes. The trust and your trustee in many ways are there to serve your children as you would if you were alive. Would you help your children acquire their first home and provide for their education? You certainly want your trust to do that in your place, especially when your children are going to get the money anyway at age thirty-five. When you prepare a trust with your attorney, discuss the provisions for withdrawal of principal, for what uses, and when. Your will is what you desire for your children.

960. What if the trustee isn't doing the job as anticipated?

Every document should allow the beneficiaries to change the trustee for cause—this means that if the trustee isn't performing as expected, if the investments aren't satisfactory, taxes aren't paid, and information isn't provided, then the beneficiaries should have the ability to remove the trustee in favor of a newly-appointed one. You can restrict the trustee from one corporate trustee to another corporate trustee, from one family member to another, or whatever. I always recommend the ability to change because the world changes so quickly.

OTHER MATTERS

961. Should I prepay my funeral?

Unless the funds are delegated to a burial reserve fund independent of any corporation, it's not a good idea to pay for your funeral ahead of time. However, it *is* a good idea to make funeral plans with the funeral director of your choice and let your family know what you want. This guarantees you get the funeral that you desire—not one planned with guilt or emotion. You will probably be more financially sensible with your funeral than your children would be. If there is to be a service, let your children know who you would like for pallbearers and what hymns and scripture you want.

962. If I want to be cremated, how can I arrange it so I can save money?

You can be cremated through the American Crematory Society to save money. However, funeral directors can be very helpful with the details, such as the number of death certificates you will need, newspaper announcements, and so on. Ask your funeral director what his fees are and then comparison shop.

963. My husband died four years ago and I live in an apartment. I hold all my certificates of deposit jointly with my children, one each with a different child's name. Is this satisfactory?

This can be a disaster. What if you enter a nursing home and one CD is cashed in to help pay expenses? Your estate just became inequitable. If one of your children goes through a divorce or bankruptcy, the court could attach your property. If you want to avoid probate, use a trust.

964. If I own property in Pennsylvania and New Jersey, how is my estate settled?

Real estate works differently than bank accounts. If a Pennsylvania resident dies having a bank account in Florida, the executor probates the will in

FUNERAL ARRANGEMENTS

Name

Cemetery   Lot #

Location of cemetery deed

Burial insurance   Policy #

Company

Address

Phone number   Fax

Have you made funeral arrangements?   Prepaid?

Funeral home

Contact

Address   Phone number

PEOPLE TO CONTACT AT DEATH

Name   Relationship

Address

Phone number   Fax

Name   Relationship

Address

Phone number   Fax

Name	Relationship
Address	
Phone number	Fax
Name	Relationship
Address	
Phone number	Fax

Pennsylvania and then sends the Florida bank a short certificate—a court paper authorizing the bank to send the proceeds to Pennsylvania. It doesn't work this way for real estate, however. If real estate is located in another state, ancillary administration must occur—probating the will in another state. It increases the expense of the estate.

965. I don't want my children fighting over personal property so I'm going to have everything sold at death. Won't this make everything easier?

A public or private auction can allow family to dispose of property without a hassle. The problem with a public sale is that family members might not get the personal property they want because someone outside the family is outbidding them. I recommend certain property be specifically mentioned, such as jewelry to granddaughters, watches to sons, and then a private auction among the children and heirs. The remainder can then be sold. Trust your executor to control the situation if the parties disagree.

966. I recently received property from my father's estate. I want to put my wife's name on the property. Is this possible?

There are very important estate planning and marital considerations here. If you want to put your spouse's name on the property, however, you can do

FUNERAL ARRANGEMENTS—OTHER INSTRUCTIONS

Funeral or cremation? _____

Closed or open casket? _____

Church or graveside service? _____

Spiritual advisor name _____

Church/Synagogue _____

Address _____

_____

Phone number (home) _____ (office) _____

Pallbearers _____

_____

_____

_____

_____

_____

Special music/other arrangements _____

_____

_____

_____

_____

_____

_____

_____

_____

_____

it without incurring any additional taxes because an individual can give an unlimited amount of funds to a spouse who is a U.S. citizen.

967. It seems as if it will be impossible to give my business to my son, who is in the business with me, and still have enough in my estate to equalize assets for my other three children. What should I do?

The son who has been working with you may have had a smaller salary over the years than his siblings who worked elsewhere. He may have sacrificed to stay in the area and help his father. This would mean he inherits the business, but nothing else. Or the father and maybe even the son should purchase enough life insurance within an irrevocable life insurance trust for the siblings who aren't in the business to get an equal share. It's a good idea to meet with your financial advisers so there aren't problems down the road with inequality.

968. I'm afraid my family won't be able to pay the estate taxes on our small business when I die. What can we do?

If your business is worth more than $1 million, you may want to consider cash value life insurance. If you don't think they will be able to pay the estate taxes and you don't want your beneficiaries to have to sell the business, the insurance can be used to pay the estate taxes at your death.

969. What are the advantages of giving away money during my lifetime?

Cash and bonds are wonderful property to gift during one's lifetime. You can give away $10,000 each year to as many people as you wish without having to pay taxes on that money. This can really lower the value of your taxable estate and lower the death tax liability. An important reason one gives away property above the $10,000 per person limit is to give away property that is appreciating at a substantial rate (i.e., shares of Microsoft stock over the last ten years).You can give away a good portion of a business through annual gifting, as you can a farm or other large pieces of real estate through family limited partnerships.

970. If I give my home to my children, but I live there until I die (thereby retaining some benefit) will this create a problem?

This is considered an incompleted gift—retaining any benefit on gifted property will pull the property back into your estate at death where it will be taxed. Find other property to give, if possible, rather than retaining an interest, thus tainting the gift.

971. My insurance agent recommends a new life insurance policy rather than risk the three-year rule on transfer of an existing policy. Should I follow his advice?

Obviously a new policy is cleaner and if you want to purchase a new policy to achieve your insurance goals, a new policy is fine. However, you should be buying a new policy for that reason, not because of the three-year rule. The transfer of an existing policy is possible and should occur as soon as possible to begin the clock running.

972. If I don't have an estate when I die, will I still have an estate tax return due?

Yes, if your estate is over the $625,000 limit. You can have all your funds in a trust, joint property, and nonprobate assets and your executor will still need to file a federal estate tax return within nine months of your death. A major problem with federal estate tax liability is that often assets are transferred to heirs without the liquidity to pay the death taxes. An important consideration in your planning process is to know your tax liability and figure out how it is going to be paid.

973. You've talked about IRD income. Please give me several examples of it.

Income in Respect of a Decedent (IRD) occurs with royalties, deferred compensation payments, pension benefits, and IRA accounts. IRD income is income earned by the decedent that was not received by the decedent before death. IRD income is subject to both income and death taxes.

974. A local charity recommended I make them the beneficiary of my IRA at death rather than leaving them money. Why?

IRD occurs when one inherits a tax-deferred product. The value of the property is in the estate and it creates a possible death tax liability. Because the income has been tax deferred, it doesn't go away—you still have to pay income tax in addition to the death tax. Thus, whoever inherits the IRA will be burdened with the income tax liability. If the beneficiary of the IRA is a charity, however, the income liability passes to a tax-exempt organization— thus, your heirs will not be responsible for the income tax on the deferral.

975. My husband just died. How should I have his pension paid out?

Call the human resources department of your husband's employer. If he was receiving a pension payment, your payment should begin almost immediately, but transferred into your name. Providing the company with your Social Security number, current address, and so on should expedite the transfer of benefits to you. If your husband wasn't retired and hadn't begun to take a payout, make an appointment and discuss your options with the company. Then discuss the alternatives with your financial adviser—if you have the choice of a lump-sum benefit or taking a monthly payment. If your only alternative is a monthly check, find out when the payments begin and plan accordingly.

976. Should I sell my house to my children for a dollar?

This is a question I get all the time. If you give the house to the children (that's what you are doing when you sell it below market value), you are giving your basis in the property to them. Thus, if or when the house is sold, your children will have to pay capital gains on the house because they don't have the primary residence exclusion. (See question 208.) I'm an advocate of giving—just remember the reasons for giving property since your cost basis follows the property.

977. My insurance agent recommended my children own my life insurance policies. Why would I do that?

If your children own your life insurance policy, the entire policy is out of your estate and thus not taxable. There shouldn't be any problems with your children as owners if they pay the annual premiums on the policy.

This is one estate planning tool for ownership; the second is an Irrevocable Life Insurance Trust (ILIT).

978. What is a family limited partnership?

Family limited partnerships are used to transfer minority shares of property to family members, usually at a discounted value. Family limited partnerships are a great tool for transferring an asset over $10,000 to numerous family members, such as real estate or a business. Many people assume that the family limited partnerships are for the wealthy. I have seen them used as a method of giving a home to a child on her marriage. The house is bought by the parents inside a partnership and gradually gifted to the daughter through shares of the partnership each year until the house belongs to the daughter free and clear.

979. How should I register my safety-deposit box so there isn't a problem at death?

If a safety-deposit box is registered with husband and wife, when one dies the other (or their Power of Attorney) can enter the box to locate a will, gather important papers, and so on. However, if there is a third party's name on the box, the death of anyone seals the box until the assets in the box are inventoried for death tax purposes. Therefore, have a child be a deputy, not an owner.

980. How much can you inherit before you have to pay federal taxes?

At present, the first $625,000 of a person's estate is not subject to federal estate tax. If a person's estate does not have more than $625,000 (in 1998), you don't need to do any federal estate tax planning. The $625,000 exclusion rises to $1 million in 2006. If a person's estate is above this, estate tax planning is important. Your financial planner should focus on deferring the tax, paying for the tax in a tax-efficient way, obtaining a low value for the assets subject to tax, or deferring the actual payment schedule.

981. What is the amount of estate tax due if only the marital deduction is used rather than the unified credit and the marital deduction?

If a family has $1.25 million in property—$625,000 in the husband's name and $625,000 in the wife's name—and the first spouse to die leaves everything to the survivor, there are no federal taxes. At that time, all the property passes to the spouse free of tax. However, when the second spouse dies, the death tax due will be $246,250.

982. How is that death tax avoided?

You would plan so that the first spouse's assets would be placed into a unified credit trust. The survivor would receive income for life and principal if needed; then only the survivor's assets are taxed at the second spouse's death. *No* taxes would be due.

983. Why doesn't everyone do that then?

Besides not planning or not planning correctly, it isn't always easy to get enough assets in a spouse's name alone and be able to fund them into the unified credit trust. So many of a family's assets in today's world are retirement benefits: 401(k)s, IRAs, profit sharing plans, and so on. If you have them fund a trust, the IRD income (the tax deferral) is taxed all at one time. If the IRA's beneficiary is the spouse she can rollover the funds into her own IRA. Another problem is having the house in one spouse's name. Surviving spouses don't like to have their home held in a trust, owned by the trustee. A good way to fund a unified credit trust is with life insurance proceeds.

984. Can I pay the taxes due in installments?

The estate taxes are due within nine months of death unless the decedent had a business interest.

985. You mentioned about a new exemption for business owners. How does that work?

The Taxpayer Relief Act of 1997 gives a business owner whose business is more than half of his adjusted gross estate a $1.3 million exemption from estate tax liability. It sounds wonderful, but this exemption is not in addition to the $625,000 exemption. The maximum total exemption (both unified and business interest) is $1,300,000. Thus, by 2006, the business interest will be only $300,000 more than the $1,000,000 unified credit amount. The reason executors and decedent's families want to qualify for the exemption is that if you qualify, you can pay the death taxes over a fifteen-year period at 2 percent interest. The down side is that your estate is open for that period of time and your executor is responsible for paying the tax.

986. Do you have guidelines for naming a guardian for your children?

Naming a guardian if my husband and I die before our youngest child reaches age twenty-one has been the most difficult decision for me in the entire estate planning process. Naming your parents is not recommended because you need youth and energy to raise children. You must discuss the guardianship relationship with the people you would like to have to make sure they agree to serve in that capacity. They may not feel up to the task. Here are some guidelines:

- Someone who will love your children as their own
- Someone who has the values and the ideals similar to yours
- A couple with a stable marriage
- Someone who understands teenagers and who will have the energy to go to sporting events and stay up waiting for them to come home from dates

987. Should my children's guardian also be the one to handle their finances?

No. I don't recommend that the person actually taking care of your children also handle their finances. There may be a conflict of interest and at the least, it is very difficult for the person taking care of your child to say no if the child demands access to their money.

988. What is the difference between being appointed guardian of the person and guardian of the estate?

Guardian of the person is the individual or individuals appointed who will have physical custody of your children if you die before they reach adulthood. These guardians have control of the child and act as a parent. A guardian of the estate handles the money on behalf of the child. If there is any significant sum of money involved at all in the estate, I recommend that the guardian of the person not be the guardian of the estate.

989. What is a survivorship insurance policy?

A survivorship, also known as a second-to-die policy, is an insurance policy on the lives of a married couple. The policy pays a death benefit when the second spouse dies although an interesting planning technique is to have a rider on the life of the husband (who usually dies first) to provide funds to continue paying the policy. The purpose of the policy is to provide money either to pay estate tax or to replace taxes paid. Second-to-die policies are interesting because the premiums on this type of policy are cheaper than paying premiums for an equal sum of insurance for both lives.

990. What is a family trust?

The family trust (also known as the unified credit trust, the B trust, bypass trust, and so on) is funded with the total amount of money available that passes tax free at the person's death. Thus, if you died this year when you can leave $625,000 without incurring federal tax, that's the amount that would be used to fund this trust. If the year is 2006, the amount in this trust could equal $1,000,000. Funds from this trust pass death tax free to the next generation at the surviving spouse's death no matter how great the growth of the funds.

991. At what ages should my children receive money if my husband and I die before they reach age eighteen?

I find it interesting that we think our children are less able to handle money than we were at their age. However, I have seen funds dissipated because of immaturity, poor judgment, and friends—all the reasons people overspend money. This occurs more often when children are young so I recommend distribution in thirds at ages twenty-five, thirty, and thirty-five. If the document is written properly, the funds are there for emergencies, first homes, education, yet distribution isn't finalized until age thirty-five.

992. My appointed trustee has died. Do I need to rewrite my will?

If your trustee is named within your will, you will need to have a codicil (an amendment) prepared to make a change. If the trust document stands alone, you will only need an amendment to replace the trustee.

993. There is a provision in my mother's will that says I can take property in kind. What does that mean?

The phrase "distribution in kind" means that the property can be transferred to you as is instead of having to have the property sold and you receive the cash.

994. What is a power of appointment?

The right given to a person to dispose of property that he doesn't own. If your husband gives you a general power of appointment over his marital trust, then you could name a second husband, his children, your church, or anyone to receive the property.

995. I'm a recent widow. What should my investment goals be?

Your investment goal should be security for the present with planning for the future. First, you need to gather a picture of your current financial situation, your debts, your assets, what income you have coming in, how your current income is lowered, and how you will survive from this point forward. There are many varied ways to address your situation, but no investment decisions should be made immediately. Your investments should be short-term until you have an accurate, total picture of your situation. Then you can begin to set your investment objectives.

996. As a widow, what investments should I avoid?

This is hard to answer since widows can be in various financial situations when their husbands die. Avoid making long-term investments at first. I would avoid limited partnerships, options, commodities, and other high-risk investments. Always remember that you will also need to have funds set aside for possible emergencies.

997. My aunt died two years ago leaving everything to her brother and now he has died. Are death taxes owed on the entire amount again?

There is a full credit for the prior tax paid if the two people die within two years. If the deaths occur more than two years apart, the credit is prorated until there is no credit after ten years. The credit works as follows:

Time Period	Allowable Credit
2–4 years	80%
4–6 years	60%
6–8 years	40%
8–10 years	20%
More than 10 years	0%

998. Can I give my entire estate to charity?

Yes, after debts and expenses, there is no percentage limitation on the amount of funds a person can give to charity; you can give your entire estate to charity.

999. How can I provide an income for my sister yet have the funds go to charity at her death?

You receive a charitable deduction from death taxes for property that goes to a qualified charity. A great way to receive a charitable death tax deduction and still provide income for a family member is to set up a charitable remainder trust in your will or trust. A Charitable Remainder Trust (CRT) provides an income to your sister for her life and the funds go to charity at her death. Death taxes are computed on a discounted basis, which depends on the age your sister is at death. CRTs are wonderful ways to provide for family yet your estate pays smaller death taxes.

1000. Can I let my sister live in my house until her death and then pass it on to my nephew?

Yes, you can. You are giving your sister what is called a life estate. She has the right to live in the house during her lifetime and when she no longer can live there or dies, the property passes to whom you wish. Life estates are difficult to administer because real estate is expensive to maintain. Usually the owner of the real estate also leaves money in trust to maintain the real estate during the life tenant's lifetime. The major problem of having a life estate is that the life tenant does not feel the house is hers and doesn't take care of it the way she might if she owned it. The property could begin to deteriorate. Often the real estate values fall because of the lack of care.

Another problem is that the decedent didn't leave or have enough funds available to set up funds to help pay for the care of the property. The person who will get the house someday must help pay for maintenance. The life tenant is only responsible for general maintenance and upkeep, paying utilities, and so on. New roofs, siding, or exterior painting shouldn't be paid for by the life tenant. The nice part of a life estate is that someone will have the enjoyment of rent-free living in your home until her death and then the house will go to whom you wish.

1001. What is a sprinkling trust?

A sprinkling trust enables the trustee to use her discretion to direct income for the benefit of the beneficiaries as appropriate. For example, if money is held in trust for a family with four children, the income would normally be distributed equally to the four. However, let's say two of the children are very wealthy and don't need the funds. You can give your trustee the power to sprinkle the income to only the children who need income. Sprinkling is a nice tool although I have seen family feuds erupt over the sprinkling—very few people feel they have too much income. The sprinkling provision needs to be explained to all involved and the decedent must understand the position he or she is possibly putting his or her trustee(s) into with this situation.

GLOSSARY

Adjusted gross income (AGI) — A method used to calculate income tax that is computed by subtracting the allowable deductions from gross income.

Aggressive growth fund — A mutual fund that has a primary investment objective of seeking capital gains.

Amortization — Reducing the principal of a loan by making regular payments.

Annuity — A contract between an insurance company and an individual in which the company agrees to provide an income for a specific period in exchange for money.

Asset allocation — The process of determining what proportions of your investment portfolio should be invested in a particular type of investment, based upon your financial objectives and your risk tolerance.

Balanced mutual fund — A mutual fund whose primary objective is to buy a combination of stocks and bonds. This tends to be less volatile than stocks-only funds.

Bear market — A sharply declining market.

Beneficiary — The person who is named to receive the proceeds from an investment vehicle. A beneficiary can be an individual, a company, or an organization.

Beta — A measure of risk based on calculations of a fund's fluctuation. A beta less than one is less volatile than the market. A beta above one is more volatile than the market.

Blue chip — A solid-performing common stock with a sterling reputation based on consistent long-term earnings despite market fluctuations; twenty-five years or more of paying quarterly cash dividends and leadership in solid industry with an expectation for continued success.

Bond — An instrument on which the issuer promises to pay the investor a specified amount of interest and to repay the principal at maturity.

Bull market — A stock market that is rising sharply.

Capital gain — The difference between the cost of an asset and its higher selling price. Tax on this gain is usually due when the asset is sold.

Certificate of deposit (CD) — An investment available from a bank that pays a fixed rate of return for a specified period of time.

Common stock — Shares of ownership in a corporation.

Compound interest — Interest figured on the principal and the interest that has built up during the preceding period. Compound interest may be figured daily, monthly, quarterly, semiannually, or annually.

Consumer Price Index — A measure of the relative cost of living for a family of four compared with a base year.

Defined benefit plan — A qualified retirement that specifies the benefit you will receive at retirement, usually expressed as a percentage of preretirement compensation.

Defined contribution plan — A qualified retirement plan that specifies the annual contributions to the plan, usually expressed as a percentage of your salary. Contributions can be made by the employer, you, or both.

Diversification — Dividing funds among different companies or investment categories to cut down on risk.

Dividend — The proportion of net earnings paid to stockholders by a corporation. Dividends are usually fixed in preferred stock; dividends from common stock vary as the company's performance shifts.

Earned income — Salary, wages, and self-employment income. Unearned income includes money you get from investments.

Equity — The value of your ownership in property or securities. Your equity in your home is the difference between the current market value of the home and the money you still owe the bank on the mortgage.

Financial adviser — A professional who helps people arrange and coordinate their financial affairs.

Fixed assets — Assets that produce fixed income, such as investment certificates, fixed annuities, certificates of deposit, and most bonds.

401(k) plan — A retirement plan into which you can contribute a portion of your current salary (usually before taxes). Contributions can grow tax-deferred until they are withdrawn upon retirement.

Government obligations — Treasury bills, notes, bonds, savings bonds, and retirement plan bonds that are all fully backed by the U.S. government.

Government securities — Bonds, bills, or notes sold by the federal government to raise money.

Gross income — Income that includes all potentially taxable income, including wages, salary, dividends, interest, retirement plan distributions, and so on. Gross income is the starting point in determining tax liability.

Growth fund — A mutual fund that invests in common stocks that grow faster than normal. Growth funds are long-term investments.

Individual Retirement Account (IRA) — A retirement savings plan in which you can contribute up to $2,000 that can grow tax-deferred until withdrawn at retirement age. Contributions may or may not be tax deductible depending on income level and participation in other retirement plans.

Inflation — An increase in the price of goods and services over time, representing the decreased buying power.

Interest — The cost of borrowing money.

Investment — Process of purchasing securities or property for which stability of value and level of expected return are somewhat predictable.

Liquidity — Your ability to convert your assets into cash without significant loss.

Money market fund — A mutual fund that specializes in short-term securities (such as Treasury bills). Money market funds are very safe and offer slightly more interest than a traditional bank savings account.

Money market securities — Short-term debt (usually for ninety days or less).

Municipal bond — Obligations of states, cities, towns, school districts, and public authorities; interest paid on munis are usually tax-exempt.

Municipal bond fund — A mutual fund that invests in municipal bonds; you receive dividends that are usually exempt from federal income tax.

Municipal securities — Bonds that are issued by state or local governments.

Mutual funds — An investment that pools money and invests in portfolio of stocks, bonds, options, or money market securities. Mutual funds are diversified and professionally managed.

Portfolio — Total assets held by an investor.

Preferred stock — A class of stock with a claim on the company's earnings before payment is made on the common stock, if the company declares a dividend.

Price/earnings ratio (P/E ratio) — A measure of a stock's performance by taking its market price and dividing it by its current or estimated future earnings.

Qualified retirement plan — A plan that is sponsored by an employer and that is designed to meet retirement benefits.

Risk — Chance that the value or return on an investment will differ from its expected value. Chance that something undesirable will happen.

Speculation — The process of buying investments in which the future value and level of expected earnings are highly uncertain.

Tax-deferred — Tax treatment of certain assets so that income tax is due only when the funds are withdrawn or mature. Tax-deferred assets include those in an IRA, 401(k) plan, 403(b) plan, tax-deferred annuity, tax-deferred life insurance, and others.

Total return — The current income plus capital gain from an investment.

Treasury bond — A U.S. government long-term security with a maturity above ten years.

Treasury stock — Stock issued by a company and later reacquired.

Trust — A form of property ownership in which the legal title to the property is held by someone (trustee) for the benefit of someone else (beneficiary).

Trustee — A person or corporation appointed to administer or execute the trust for the beneficiaries.

Yield — Also known as return, this is the dividends or interest paid by a company expressed as a percentage of the current price.

Appendix A

Internet Web Sites

The sites contained in this appendix are not endorsed by the authors. Responsibility for their content rests solely with the authors of the sites.

American Express

This handy financial site walks you through seven financial planning subjects, including the cost of procrastination.
http://www.americanexpress.com/401k

American Stock Exchange

http://www.amex.com

College Financial Aid Information

An overview of all the financial aid information in cyberspace with links to numerous resources including student aid publications, organizations, scholarship databases, and contact information for financial aid offices.
http://www.finaid.org

Divorce Online

The American Divorce Information Network's site for those considering divorce includes articles discussing taxes and divorce/remarriage, common tax questions relating to divorce, and so on.
http://www.divorcenet.com

Family Money

http://www.familymoney.com

FinanCenter

A collection of interactive worksheets designed to help with financial decisions about homes, cars, credit cards, and more.
http://www.financenter.com

Financial Data Finder (Ohio State University)

This web site is a good place to locate financial and economic data on the web and elsewhere.
http://www.cob.ohio-state.edu:80/dept/fin/overview.htm

Internet Finance Resources

A web site that constantly screens and finds new financial information on the Internet.
http://www.lib.Isu.edu/bus/finance.html

Investorama

A web site with plenty of financial information with links to the field of finance.
http://www.investorama.com

Jane Bryant Quinn column

A compendium of past finance columns as appeared in the *Washington Post,* arranged by topic.
http://www.washingtonpost.com/wp-sv/
business/longterm/quinn/columns/030697.htm

John Hancock

A comprehensive site that walks you through financial subjects, taking into account financial drains like college expenses while you're trying to save.
http://www.jhancock.com

National Association of Investors Corporation

Elaborate site that includes stock evaluation help, links to Standard & Poor's company reports, and other data. Many sites give updated stock quotes and allow online trading during the day.
http://www.beter-investing.org

Morningstar, Inc.

A wealth of mutual fund data and market news.
http://www.morningstar.net

NASD Regulation

Find out if your broker is playing by the rules.
http://www.nasdr.com

North American Securities Administrators

If you have a problem with your broker, go here.
http://www.nasaa.org

S&P Equity Investor Service

News headlines and stock picks from Standard & Poors.
http://www.stockinfo.standardpoor.com

Securities and Exchange Commission

All kinds of good financial web sites and documents.
http://www.sec.gov

The Syndicate

Another great site with lots of links to the financial world on the Internet.
http://www.moneypages.com/syndicate

USA Today Money

A comprehensive grouping of financial news and data.
http://www.usatoday.com/money/mfront.htm

Wall Street Research Net

http://www.wsrn.com/

Yahoo! Finance

Lots of information on financial news, data, and stock quotes.
http://www.quote.yahoo.com

Appendix B

Internet Financial Search Engines

Stock Wiz

A new search engine exclusively for investment information.
http://www.stockwiz.com

streetEYE

Index and search engine that provides access to all resources of interest to
investors.
http://www.efrontier.com/

Yahoo! Finance and Investment Index

http://www.yahoo.com/Business/Finance and Investment

Appendix C

Financial and Investment Companies Online

American Express Financial Advisors

http://www.americanexpress.com

Budget Master, LLC

http://www.budgetmaster.com

Dreyfus Service Corporation

http://www.dreyfus.com

The Guardian

http://www.theguardian.com

INVESCO Funds Groups, Inc.

http://www.invesco.com

Janus

http://www.janus.com

The Montgomery Funds

http://www.xperts.montgomery.com

Neuberger & Berman

http://www.nbfunds.com

Prudential Investments

http://www.prudential.com

Charles Schwab & Co., Inc.

http://www.schwab.com

Stein Roe Mutual Funds

http://www.steinroe.com

Strong Funds

http://www.strong-funds.com

T. Rowe Price

http://www.troweprice.com

Transamerica Premier Funds

http://www.transamerica.com

The Vanguard Group

http://www.vanguard.com

Veritas/Ameritas Life

http://www.ameritas.com/veritas

Appendix D

Internet Financial Forums

Financial Planning Forum

Register at this site and then follow to the forum.
http://www.fponline.com

Green Jungle

http://www.greenjungle.com/pub

Silicon Investor

Discussion forum featuring small-cap companies.
http://www.techstocks.com

Appendix E

Financial Publications on the Web

Barron's

http://www.barons.com

Business Week Online

http://www.businessweek.com

The Economist

http://www.economist.com

The New York Times

http://www.nytimes.com

Reuters News and Quotes

http://www.reuter's.com/news

Wall Street Journal

http://www.wsj.com

INDEX

automobile insurance. *See* car insurance
automobiles. *See* cars

B

baccalaureate bonds, 227
banking
    ATM fees, 18
    certificate of deposit (CD), 17
    checking accounts
        obtaining credit and, 45
        selecting type of, 15–16
    FDIC insurance, 17–18
    fees, 18
    money market deposit accounts, 16
        using, 16–17
    savings accounts, 16
        closing, 16
        as investment for college, 228
        liquidity and, 23
        passbook savings *vs* statement
            savings, 16
        separation/divorce and, 145
    tracking accounts, *19–22*
    virtual, 17
bank machine cards. *See* ATM cards
bankruptcy
    alternatives to, 49
    Chapter 13 reorganization, 51
    exempted property, 52
    filing for, 50
    hiring attorney for, 53
    length of process, 53
    listing debts/creditors for, 51–52, 54
    paying wages and, 52
    property liens and, 54
    reaffirming loans after, 54
    repeated filings for, 53
    timing of filing for, 53
    types of, 50
banks
    bankers acting as brokers, 184
    customer service representatives (CARS),
        183
    financial advisers with, 183
    personal bankers, 183
    private bankers, 183–184
    selecting, 15
    trust officers, 183–184
benefits. *See also* dental insurance; health
        insurance; pensions; Social
        Security
    disability, 83
    taxable *vs* nontaxable, 83, 90
bereavement leave, 141
beta, 250
Bloomberg News web site, 355
blue chip funds, 262
blue chip stocks, 252
bond funds, 265
bonds
    baccalaureate, 227
    call provisions on, 257–258
    corporate, 256
    debentures, 256
    defined, 253
    discounted, 257
    EE, 88–89
        for education expenses, 225–226
        as investments, 258
    HH, 258
    investing in within IRAs, 206
    municipal, 254
        capital gains on, 255
    premium, 257
    ratings, 255–256
    riskier, 255
    selecting, 254
    short-term *vs* long-term investments, 255
    vs stocks, 245
    Treasury Direct account, 256–257
    triple tax-free, 258
    types of, 253
    US government agency, 256
    worksheet for, *277*
    yield to maturity *vs* yield to call, 258
    zero coupon bonds, 224–225, 227
brokerage houses. *See* stockbrokers/
        brokerage houses
broker agents, 190
budgets
    preparing, 5